POLAND

Marxist Regimes Series

Series editor: Bogdan Szajkowski, Department of Sociology, University College, Cardiff

Afghanistan Bhabani Sen Gupta
Angola Keith Somerville
Bulgaria Robert J. McIntyre
Cape Verde Colm Foy
China Marc Blecher
Cuba Max Azicri
Ethiopia Peter Schwab
German Democratic Republic Mike Dennis
Ghana Donald I. Ray
Grenada Tony Thorndike
Guinea-Bissau Rosemary E. Galli and Jocelyn Jones
Guyana Colin Baber and Henry B. Jeffrey
Hungary Hans-Georg Heinrich
Kampuchea Michael Vickery
Laos Martin Stuart-Fox
Madagascar Maureen Covell
Marxist Local Governments in Western Europe and Japan ed. Bogdan Szajkowski
Marxist State Governments in India T. J. Nossiter
Mongolia Alan J. K. Sanders
Nicaragua David Close
Poland George Kolankiewicz and Paul G. Lewis
P.D.R. Yemen Tareq and Jacqueline Ismael
Romania Michael Shafir
Soviet Union Ronald J. Hill
Surinam Henk E. Chin and Hans Buddingh'
Vietnam Melanie Beresford
Yugoslavia Bruce McFarlane

Further Titles

Albania
Benin and The Congo
Czechoslovakia
Democratic People's Republic of Korea
Mozambique
Zimbabwe
Adaptations of Communism
Comparative Analysis
Cumulative Index

POLAND

Politics, Economics and Society

George Kolankiewicz and
Paul G. Lewis

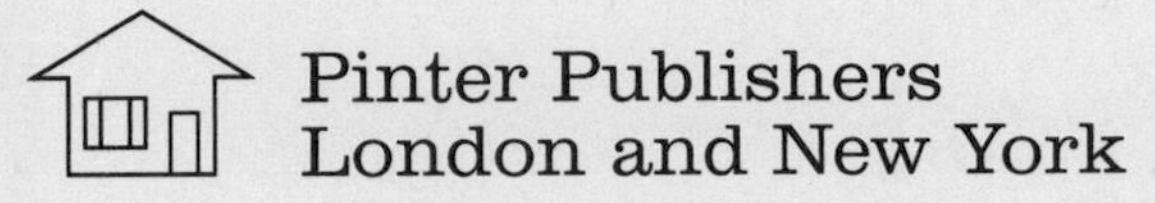

Pinter Publishers
London and New York

First published in Great Britain in 1988 by
Pinter Publishers Limited
25 Floral Street, London WC2E 9DS

British Library Cataloguing in Publication Data

A CIP catalogue record for this book is available from the British Library.

Library of Congress Cataloging-in-Publication Data

Kolankiewicz, George.
Poland: politics, economics, and society.
(Marxist regimes series)
Bibliography: p.
Includes index.
1. Poland—Politics and government—1980- .
2. Poland—Economic conditions—1981- . 3. Poland—Social conditions—1980- . I. Lewis, Paul G., 1945- . II. Title. III. Series.
DK4442.K635 1988 943.8′05 88-5858
ISBN 0-86187-436-6
ISBN 0-86187-437-4 (pbk.)

Typeset by Joshua Associates Limited, Oxford
Printed in Great Britain by SRP Ltd, Exeter

Editor's Preface

Poland, geographically located at the cross-roads of the European continent, has during the past two decades been at the cross-roads of its economic, social and political development. With a thousand years of history punctuated by constant struggles for national survival against encroachment from its neighbours, the character of contemporary Poland has in the main been formed by its ethnical homogeneity, the long association with a democratic tradition and the influence of the powerful Roman Catholic Church. The mass movement of Solidarity that surfaced in the summer of 1980 quintessentially embodied these dimensions in Polish society, which, if the country is to find its way from the cross-roads, must play a predominant role in the future shape of its economic, social and political structures.

This timely, comprehensive and penetrating study provides the reader with an in-depth analysis of the background and current state of complexities of the Polish situation. It is, of course, an important contribution to the overall analysis of Marxist regimes. The study of Marxist regimes has commonly been equated with the study of communist political systems. There were several historical and methodological reasons for this. For many years it was not difficult to distinguish the eight regimes in Eastern Europe and four in Asia which resoundingly claimed adherence to the tenets of Marxism and more particularly to their Soviet interpretation—Marxism-Leninism. These regimes, variously called 'People's Republic', 'People's Democratic Republic', or 'Democratic Republic', claimed to have derived their inspiration from the Soviet Union, to which, indeed, in the overwhelming number of cases they owed their establishment.

To many scholars and analysts these regimes represented a multiplication of and geographical extension of the 'Soviet model' and consequently of the Soviet sphere of influence. Although there were clearly substantial similarities between the Soviet Union and the people's democracies, especially in the initial phases of their development, these were often overstressed at the expense of noticing the differences between these political systems.

It took a few years for scholars to realize that generalizing the particular, i.e., applying the Soviet experience to other states ruled by elites which claimed to be guided by 'scientific socialism', was not good enough. The relative simplicity of the assumption of a cohesive communist bloc was questioned after the expulsion of Yugoslavia from the Communist Information

Bureau in 1948 and in particular after the workers' riots in Poznań in 1956 and the Hungarian revolution of the same year. By the mid-1960s, the totalitarian model of communist politics, which until then had been very much in force, began to crumble. As some of these regimes articulated demands for a distinctive path of socialist development, many specialists studying these systems began to notice that the cohesiveness of the communist bloc was less apparent than had been claimed before.

Also by the mid-1960s, in the newly independent African states 'democratic' multi-party states were turning into one-party states or military dictatorships, thus questioning the inherent superiority of liberal democracy, capitalism and the values that went with it. Scholars now began to ponder on the simple contrast between multi-party democracy and a one-party totalitarian rule that had satisfied an earlier generation.

More importantly, however, by the beginning of that decade Cuba had a revolution without Soviet help, a revolution which subsequently became to many political elites in the Third World not only an inspiration but a clear military, political and ideological example to follow. Apart from its romantic appeal, to many nationalist movements the Cuban revolution also demonstrated a novel way of conducting and winning a nationalist, anti-imperialist war and accepting Marxism as the state ideology without a vanguard communist party. The Cuban precedent was subsequently followed in one respect or another by scores of Third World regimes, which used the adoption of 'scientific socialism' tied to the tradition of Marxist thought as a form of mobilization, legitimation or association with the prestigious symbols and powerful high-status regimes such as the Soviet Union, China, Cuba and Vietnam.

Despite all these changes the study of Marxist regimes remains in its infancy and continues to be hampered by constant and not always pertinent comparison with the Soviet Union, thus somewhat blurring the important underlying common theme—the 'scientific theory' of the laws of development of human society and human history. This doctrine is claimed by the leadership of these regimes to consist of the discovery of objective causal relationships; it is used to analyse the contradictions which arise between goals and actuality in the pursuit of a common destiny. Thus the political elites of these countries have been and continue to be influenced in both their ideology and their political practice by Marxism more than any other current of social thought and political practice.

The growth in the number and global significance, as well as the ideological, political and economic impact, of Marxist regimes has presented scholars and students with an increasing challenge. In meeting this challenge, social scientists on both sides of the political divide have put forward a dazzling profusion of terms, models, programmes and varieties of interpretation. It is against the background of this profusion that the present comprehensive series on Marxist regimes is offered.

This collection of monographs is envisaged as a series of multi-disciplinary textbooks on the governments, politics, economics and society of these countries. Each of the monographs was prepared by a specialist on the country concerned. Thus, over fifty scholars from all over the world have contributed monographs which were based on first-hand knowledge. The geographical diversity of the authors, combined with the fact that as a group they represent many disciplines of social science, gives their individual analyses and the series as a whole an additional dimension.

Each of the scholars who contributed to this series was asked to analyse such topics as the political culture, the governmental structure, the ruling party, other mass organizations, party-state relations, the policy process, the economy, domestic and foreign relations together with any features peculiar to the country under discussion.

This series does not aim at assigning authenticity or authority to any single one of the political systems included in it. It shows that, depending on a variety of historical, cultural, ethnic and political factors, the pursuit of goals derived from the tenets of Marxism has produced different political forms at different times and in different places. It also illustrates the rich diversity among these societies, where attempts to achieve a synthesis between goals derived from Marxism on the one hand, and national realities on the other, have often meant distinctive approaches and solutions to the problems of social, political and economic development.

University College *Bogdan Szajkowski*
Cardiff

Contents

List of Illustrations and Tables

Map

Figures

Tables

Preface

This book reflects the mood of contemporary Poland. As it goes to press, the workers of the Lenin Steel works in Nowa Huta are still on strike, 1 May official marches have seen violent confrontations between crowds and the police and Wałęsa has urged a demonstration in support of the workers holding out against the most dramatic price rises since 1982. This book focuses upon the context of real crisis, political stalemate, the growing frustration and attendant social consequences characteristic of post-martial law Poland. The removal of Solidarity from the scene left a void which the Polish leadership has been unable to fill. Much of what follows was written in an attempt to penetrate the opaqueness of reform rhetoric which was the hallmark of the Jaruzelski normalization strategy. Apparent concessions on the part of the regime always appeared to be too little too late and the mood of the country still seems to be one of profound mistrust. Through the gamut of councils, committees, elections and amnesties we have sought to pick out the underlying political processes, key institutions and points of social cleavage. For its part the so-called Second Stage of economic reform appears to be more advanced in letter than in either spirit or practice, and one can sympathize with those who have grave doubts as to the existence of the political will to push through far-reaching market reforms. On top of this, the economic results for 1987 have witnessed a severe downturn in economic growth and the good weather of the last five years has deserted Poland, presaging further misery on the agricultural front.

Poland will continue to surprise everyone, both inside and outside the country, and this book does not even attempt to forecast what the future holds in store. It will be watched by its neighbours and those nations farther afield who recognize that it is pushing the limits of 'real socialism' well beyond the boundaries marked out by Soviet *glasnost* and *perestroika*. We hope that we have done some of the groundwork essential to understanding events in Poland as they once again capture the attention of the world.

We would like to thank all those who have been patient with us as we sought to keep track of the unfolding scenario of post-Solidarity Poland. In particular the series editor, Bogdan Szajkowski, and the managing editor for Pinter Publishers, Heather Bliss, displayed forbearance over and beyond the limits expected of publishers. For his part, George Kolankiewicz would like to thank all those who shared his year with him at the Woodrow Wilson

International Centre for Scholars in Washington, DC, and indeed the institution itself, for providing the means of which this is a part product. Jadwiga Staniszkis, in her own inimitable intellectual style, provided stimulation and companionship at the Centre, whilst Janine Valentine did much useful scholarly legwork. Typing (in his pre-PCW days) was excellently administered by Carol Allington at Essex University. Needless to say, Chantal Lewis and Danuta Kolankiewicz alone know what their input into this book has been and acknowledgement seems somehow superfluous.

George Kolankiewicz
Paul G. Lewis
May 1988

Basic Data

Official name	Polish People's Republic (Polska Rzeczpospolita Ludowa)
Population	37,572,000 (31 December 1986)
Population density	120 per sq. km.
Population growth (% p.a.)	0.7 (1986)
Urban population (%)	60.6 (1986)
Total labour force	17,237,000 (1986)
Life expectancy	Female 75.1 yrs; Male 66.8 yrs (1986)
Infant mortality	17.3 per 1,000 live births (1986)
Capital	Warsaw (Warszawa); population 1,664,700 (1986)
Land area	31,268,000 hectares (312,683 km. sq.) of which 60.4% agricultural, 28.3% woodland, 2.6% water, 1.6% unutilized.
Administrative division	813 towns, 2,122 settlements (*gminy*) 49 voivodships (Województwa)
Foreign relations	Diplomatic relations with 130 states and 58 embassies situated in Warsaw
Political structure	
Constitution	Adopted in 1952 with subsequent amendments
Highest legislative body	Sejm (parliament); 460 deputies (93 women)
Highest executive body	Council of ministers
Prime Minister	Zbigniew Messner
Chairman of the Council of State	Wojciech Jaruzelski
Ruling party	Polish United Workers' Party (Polska Zjednoczona Partia Robotnicza (PZPR))
First Secretary	Wojciech Jaruzelski
Party membership	2,149,000 members and candidates; 27.2% women (31 December 1987)
Other political parties	United Peasant Party (Zjednoczone Stronnictwo Ludowe ZSL) 498,200 members; Democratic Party (Stronnictwo Demokratyczne SD) 117,100 members;

	Union of Polish Socialist Youth (Związek Socjalistycznej Młodzieży Polskiej ZSMP) 1,504,300 members

Economy

Per capita GNP	(1985) US$2,120
Gross national product (% 1985)	Industry 40.9, agriculture 13.4, non-material production 14.0
Gross national product distributed	Consumption 71.9%; Capital formation 28.1%
Defense expenditure as % of state budget	9.09
Monetary unit	Złoty 380 per US$ (1 February 1988) 170 per ruble

Growth indicators (% p.a.)

	1971–75	1976–80	1981–85	1986	1987
National income (produced)	9.8	1.2	−0.8	4.9	2.0
Industry (socialized sector)	10.5	4.6	−0.1	4.4	3.3
Agriculture (gross product)	5.7	−1.5	2.1	5.0	3.0

Trade and balance of payments (1987)

Exports	10,939 million rubles; US$7,056 million
Imports	10,945 million rubles; US$5,816 million
Main exports	Electromechanical products, 25% for shipbuilding exports; coal, sulphur, clothing, food and building construction services and materials
Main imports	Oil, iron ore, transport means, cotton, machinery
Destination of exports	Socialist bloc 58.2%, EEC 20.2%, developing countries 10.9%
Main trading partners	Soviet Union, West Germany, East Germany, Czechoslovakia and the United States
Foreign debt	US$39.2 billion (December 1987) of which 60% to Club of Paris and 25% commercial banks; 6.6 billion transferable rubles of which 6 billion to the Soviet Union

Main natural resources	Coal, sulphur, timber, minerals; increasing food self-sufficiency
Main crops	Wheat, rye, barley, oats, potatoes, sugar beet
Land tenure (% of arable land)	State farms 18.5; collective farms and agricultural circles 3.9; individual landholdings 72.0; other (e.g. State Land Fund etc) 5.6 (31 December 1986)
Armed Forces	Army 207,000, Navy 22,000, Air Force 88,000. Regulars 130,000, conscripts 187,000
Education	1986/7
Nurseries	5.4 places per 100 children ½–3 years old
Kindergarten	37.4 places per 100 children 3–6 years old
Zero year pre-school	47.5 places per 100 6 year olds
Compulsory 8-year education	4,923,000
Secondary schooling	Vocational (2–3 year duration) 782,800 Vocational (4–5 year duration) 679,000 Liceum (4 year duration) 352,000
Higher education	344,500
Health 1986–7	
Medical doctors per 10,000 population	20.1
Nurses per 10,000 population	49.6
Population per hospital bed	176
Main religion	Roman Catholic; 25 other churches and religious unions are also recognized
Transport	Rail 24,300 km. of which 9,500 km. is electrified; road 154,000 km. (1985) with 4,785,700 vehicles

Population Forecasting

The following data are projections produced by Poptran, University College Cardiff Population Centre, from United Nations Assessment Data published in 1980, and are reproduced here to provide some basis of comparison with other countries covered by the Marxist Regimes Series.

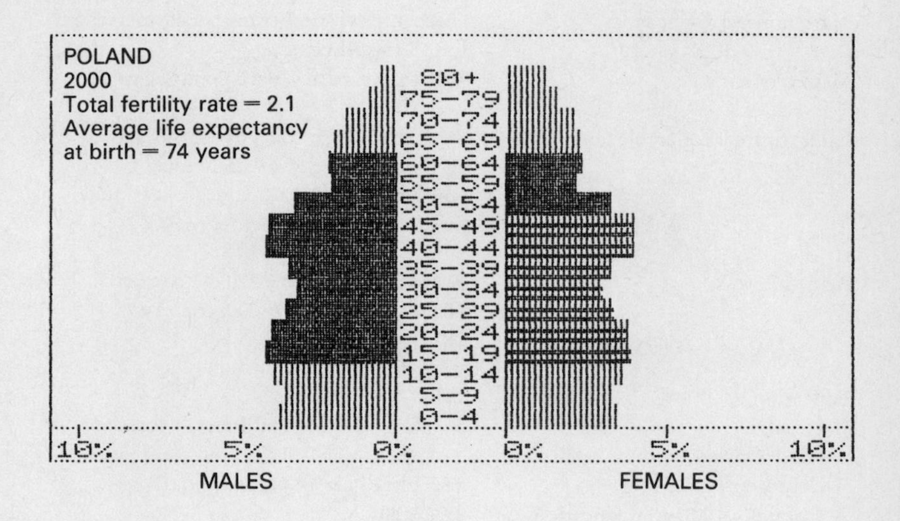

Projected Data for Poland 2000

Total population ('000)	41,216
Males ('000)	20,302
Females ('000)	20,914
Total fertility rate	2.11
Life expectancy (male)	70.0 years
Life expectancy (female)	76.7 years
Crude birth rate	14.6
Crude death rate	9.2
Annual growth rate	0.54%
Under 15s	21.47%
Over 65s	12.07%
Women aged 15–49	25.33%
Doubling time	129 years
Population density	132 per sq. km.
Urban population	67.7%

Poland: provincial boundaries and capitals

Glossary and List of Abbreviations

attestacja	job certification
CC	Central Committee—of the PZPR
CKKR	Centralna Komisja Kontrolno-Rewizyjna (Central Control and Auditing Commission of the PZPR)
CMEA	Council for Mutual Economic Assistance or COMECON
CRZZ	Centralna Rada Związków Zawodowych (Central Trade Union Council
Duma	Russian Parliament
FJN	Front Jedności Narodowej (National Unity Front)
ILO	International Labour Organization
IMF	International Monetary Fund
KOK	Komitet Obrony Kraju (National Defence Committee)
KOR	Komitet Obrony Robotniczej (Workers' Defence Committee)
KPN	Konfederacja Polski Niepodległej (Confederation of Independent Poland)
KSR	Konferencja Samorządu Robotniczego (Conference of Workers' Self-Management)
KSS	Komitet Samoobrony Społecznej (Committee for Social Self-Defence)
KPP	Komunistyczna Partia Polski (Polish Communist Party)
KW	Komitet Wojewódzki PZPR (PZPR Provincial Committee)
matura	school-leaving certificate
MFN	Most Favoured Nation
MKS	Międzyzakładowy Komitet Strajkowy (Inter-factory Strike Committee)
MPA	Main Political Administration (of the armed services)
NIK	Najwyższa Izba Kontroli (Supreme Control Chamber)
nomenklatura	system of centrally controlled appointments
NSZZ	Niezależny Samorządny Związek Zawodowy Solidarność (Independent Self-Governing Trade Union Solidarity)
odnowa	(political) renewal
OKK	Obywatelskie Konwenty Konsultacyjne (Citizens' Consultative Conventions)

OKON Obywatelski Komitet Ocalenia Narodowego (Citizens' Committee for National Salvation)
OOP Oddziałowa Organizacja Partyjna (Shopfloor Party Organization)
OPZZ Ogólnopolskie Porozumienie Związków Zawodowych (National Trade Union Accord)
PEWEX Przedsiębiorstwo Exportu Wewnętrznego (Internal Export Enterprise)
PFZ Państwowy Fundusz Ziemi (State Land Fund)
PGR Państwowe Gospodarstwo Rolnicze (State Farm)
PKWN Polski Komitet Wyzwolenia Narodowego (Polish Committee for National Salvation)
POP Podstawowa Organizacja Partyjna (Basic Party Organization of the PZPR)
PPR Polska Partia Robotnicza (Polish Workers' Party)
PPS Polska Partia Socjalistyczna (Polish Socialist Party)
PRL Polska Rzeczpospolita Ludowa (Polish Peoples' Republic)
PRON Patriotyczny Ruch Odrodzenia Narodowego (Patriotic Movement for National Rebirth)
PZPR Polska Zjednoczona Partia Robotnicza (Polish United Workers' Party)
Rada Konsultacyjna Consultative Council
Rada Ministrów Council of Ministers
Rada Państwa Council of State
RN Rada Narodowa (People's Council)
ROPCiO Ruch Obrony Praw Cywilnych i Obywatelskich (Movement for the Defence of Human and Civil Rights)
ROPP Rejonowe Ośrodki Pracy Partyjnej (Regional Centres of Party Work)
RR Rada Robotnicza (Workers' Council)
Sejm Diet (Parliament)
SD Stronnictwo Demokratyczne (Democratic Party)
Stan Wojenny State of War (military rule)
Szlachta Polish nobility (gentry)
technikum technical school
TKK Tymczasowa Komisja Koordinacyjna (Provisional Coordinating Commission)
TPPR Towarzystwo Przyjaźni Polsko-Radzieckiej (Polish-Soviet Friendship Society)
USSR Union of Soviet Socialist Republics

WOG	Wielka Organizacja Gospodarcza (Large Economic Organization)
wojewoda	provincial governor
województwo	province
WRON	Wojskowa Rada Ocalenia Narodowego (Military Council for National Salvation)
WRZZ	Wojewódzka Rada Związków Zawodowych (Provincial Trade Union Council)
WTO	Warsaw Treaty Organization, or Warsaw Pact
zjednoczenie	association (of enterprises)
Znak	The Sign (Catholic parliamentary group)
zrzeszenie	trust (voluntary grouping of enterprises)
ZSL	Zjednoczone Stronnictwo Ludowe (United Peasant Party)
ZHP	Związek Harcerstwa Polskiego (Polish Scouting Union)
ZSMP	Związek Socjalistycznej Młodzieży Polskiej (Union of Polish Socialist Youth)
Zveno	(Russian) autonomous work-team (link)

1 History and Traditions

Poland's history has been long, rich and diverse; it remains a living force in contemporary Polish politics. This is to a large extent true of the other Eastern European countries, particularly those with Soviet-imposed political regimes. The problems experienced by Poland in its recent history, however, have encouraged the tendency to review, and sometimes draw lessons from, the major themes of Polish nationhood. Poland's post-World War II experience has been more chequered than that of most other countries within the Soviet sphere of influence and it has been subject to a higher degree of political contrast and instability. Stalinism in Poland showed a greater degree of restraint than in other countries and was followed by a brief spell of communist liberalism during the months following Władysław Gomułka's return as party leader. But Gomułka's return had been preceded, and facilitated, by the Poznań revolt of June 1956 in which fifty-three people were acknowledged to have been killed by security forces. Similarly, the closing phase of Gomułka's rule was marked by the strikes on the northern coast, which rapidly built up to a confrontation in which forty-five were officially admitted to have been killed and many more wounded. These black events were again followed by a period of relative liberalism and of rapid growth in living standards presided over by Edward Gierek. His rule, also, soon changed character as abuse of office and officially tolerated corruption spread, intensifying as the Polish economy fell into a state of collapse.

The sixteen-month period of the free trade union Solidarity's open existence—in general historical terms a brief spell, but in the experience of communist systems a dangerously long aberration—was succeeded in late 1981 by Eastern Europe's first taste of military dictatorship within the post-World War II political order. Since the installation, in June 1945, of a regime dominated by those claiming adherence to Marxist principles, Poland has provided the stage for a wide variety of forms of communist rule, for a sequence of unexpected leadership changes and conflicts, and for alternating periods of political hope and resignation. Much of this diversity in modern Polish experience may be associated with, and even attributed to, the strength and structure of Polish historical traditions. The paradoxical outcome of the application of Marxist-Leninist principles to Polish society is in large measure a result of its historical heritage and reflects the continuing strength of national traditions.

Origins

Polish political history extends back some thousand years, and its formal beginnings are conventionally dated back to AD 966 when Mieszko I was converted to Christianity. The centre of this original Polish state was located at Gniezno, not far from Poznań. The history of the territorial entity known as Poland has in this sense been a circular one over these thousand years: having founded a state in the west of present-day Poland (which became known to the Holy Roman Emperor because of its conflicts with neighbouring tribes over the control of the River Oder), the Polish monarchs concentrated their attention on the east and it was in this direction that most of Poland's energies and capacity for expansion were channelled. Its borders came to touch on the Black Sea and extended for some time deep into contemporary Russia, well beyond Smolensk. But from the seventeenth century it met with growing pressure from the east, and particularly broad areas of Poland were absorbed by Russia during the sequence of partitions which had wiped Poland out as a territorial state by the beginning of the nineteenth century. On its re-emergence as a modern state in 1918 Poland was far smaller than its now distant ancestor and it found itself under growing pressure from both western and eastern neighbours as they recovered from the state of exhaustion they found themselves in at the end of the world war. Following World War II the position of the Soviet Union was consolidated and was considerably stronger; while losing yet more eastern territory, the Polish border again came to rest against the Oder.

The history of Poland has therefore been strongly influenced by its position in central Europe, the 'Heart of Europe' as one recent account puts it (Davies, 1984), and by the fortunes of its eastern and western neighbours, both of which have developed strong state systems in the modern period. This, of course, reflects also the geographical situation of Poland. Its maritime border to the north (the Baltic Sea) and the mountains to the south (Sudety and Carpathians) have created more permanent frontiers—although antagonism with the Czechs (in the south) and, particularly, with the Swedes (to the north) was not lacking and has also left its historical mark. But Poland's fate has been determined more by its position on the east–west axis and its location on the North European Plain. The very name of the country and the nation appears to derive from a reference to the people of the field or the flat ground (Pounds, 1964, p. 9). But the geographical openness of the country and its vulnerability were by no means solely a source of weakness. The accessibility of the Polish lands and the part they were able to play on several trade routes (for example, that from Prague through Cracow to the Black Sea, and from southern centres to the Baltic) contributed greatly to the swift development of the Polish state at the beginning of the second millennium. It is easy to see the fate of Poland as a tragic one because of its geographical location. But this is too simple a view and one that takes little account of other factors in Poland's historical development.

The consolidation of the Polish state under Mieszko did not lay the foundations of any lasting political stability. Although the Piast dynasty he founded lasted for some four hundred years, its lands and political power fragmented and were divided amongst the princes who were his descendants. While several attempts to reconsolidate power were made, some having a degree of temporary success, Poland weakened against its neighbours. Germans pressed from the west and settled farmland along the northern coast in Pomerania. Czechs succeeded in expanding the Bohemian kingdom from the south and south-west, and took over Silesia. Other peoples and tribes also proved difficult to deal with. The Prussians, a Baltic tribe whose lands were later controlled by Germans, threatened to the north and north-east and German settlers and warriors, the Teutonic knights, were invited in to deal with them. Such a combination of expansionist neighbours, the rather ineffectual structure of the Polish kingdom and certain unfortunate tactical decisions, provided Poland with a number of lasting problems. Nevertheless, the clannish relations that pertained amongst the Piast princes were also tenacious and enabled the Polish kingdom to survive both in the face of the German Holy Roman Empire and of the thirteenth-century Tatar invasion.

The end of the Piast dynasty was marked by the lengthy reign of one of its greatest kings, Casimir the Great (Kazimierz Wielki, 1333–70), who reformed both the currency and the legal and administrative systems, and founded one of the earliest European universities at Cracow. After his death a solution to both the dynastic and political problems was sought in a union with Lithuania through the marriage of Jadwiga of Poland to Prince Jagiełło of Lithuania, which shared a common enemy with Poland in the Teutonic knights but which was a competitor in the drive to control the lands of the Ukraine to the south-east. In the struggle to restrain and impose control over the knights, the union proved successful in the long run, although a further threat now began to develop in the east with the growing strength of the Duchy of Muscovy. The rise of Muscovite, and later Russian, power was, however, just beginning, and the two centuries of the Jagellonian dynasty named after the Lithuanian king saw Polish power at the peak of its strength. This concerned not just its territorial reach, which grew considerably with the Lithuanian union. It also involved economic growth due to the expanding grain trade, which increased the wealth of the country—or, more precisely, that of its gentry. In the late fifteenth century and during the sixteenth, the social and cultural impact of the Renaissance was extensive in Poland, and received a brilliant reflection not just in literature and the arts but also in scientific pursuits, most notably in the work of Nicholas Copernicus. In this context the Reformation also made considerable headway in Poland, and the country developed a strong reputation for social and religious tolerance, not just for non-Catholic Christians but also for Muslims and, especially, Jews.

The beginnings of more serious later problems could also be detected. The growing importance of Baltic trade and the north-west European economic area helped enrich the gentry but also encouraged them increasingly to tie the peasants to their land and enforce labour duties. Serfdom had become strongly established by the seventeenth century, a process facilitated by the gentry's growing political power. This grew from the original clan-like basis of the Polish kingdom, was further developed by the consideration paid to the gentry's interests at the time of the original union with Lithuania and in the course of its development, and was reinforced at the end of the Jagellonian dynasty when the union with Lithuania was strengthened—but at the cost of giving the gentry stronger powers and allowing them to elect the Polish monarch. This made him, in Davies's description (1984, p. 297), 'less of a limited monarch, like the kings of England or Sweden, and more of a manager under contract'. It is no great exaggeration to continue with this metaphor and to describe the Polish monarchy, in later years, as a political football.

Poland was, in fact, very well served by some of its elected kings within this institution, even if Polish national interest had not been one of the gentry's priorities. The Polish military was reformed by Stefan Batory and victorious campaigns were waged against the Russians both towards the end of the sixteenth and in the first half of the seventeenth century; later, Jan Sobieski raised the siege of Vienna and turned the tide of Turkish invasion. The military and political problems on Poland's borders were, however, growing. Sobieski's victory was obviously of great advantage to the Austrians and Hapsburgs; the Cossacks in the Ukraine were becoming increasingly restive under Polish control and resented, in particular, the threat of serfdom and the aggressive restoration of official Catholicism under the Counter-Reformation (the Jesuits were introduced into Poland in 1565)—the Eastern Ukraine had passed from Polish to Russian control well before the end of the seventeenth century; a disastrous war with Sweden began in 1655 and inaugurated the period known as the 'Deluge'; the German Prussians again began to play a major role in these conflicts, no longer as Catholic knights but as Hohenzollerns and protectors of the Brandenburg interest. Yet during this time of insecurity and the beginnings of economic decline, the tax-gathering powers of the monarch remained wholly dependent on the agreement of the gentry as a group and central political authority became increasingly insecure. The vote of one member in the Diet was sufficient to block the passage of legislation, the infamous *liberum veto*, a practice that began in 1652. From such beginnings date the Polish reputation for ungovernability—although it would be more accurate to say that this was not so much a matter of Polish temperament as a matter of historical misfortune not to have evolved an institution of common government. This misfortune was, of course, fully exploited by Poland's enemies.

Political Decline

The decline of Poland, politically, economically and militarily (and perhaps also socially and culturally) can be dated from some time in the second half of the seventeenth century. Certainly, by the turn of the century, its fortunes had clearly changed to favour those of Poland's neighbours and, in the eighteenth century, Russia had little difficulty in controlling the Sejm (the Diet) and determining the choice of the Polish monarch. Somewhat surprisingly, it was under the reign (from 1764) of Stanisław August, who had served as one of the many lovers of Catherine the Great of Russia, that the mood to take measures to stop the political and social rot arose and received encouragement from official circles. The obstacles were also enormous, not least with Catherine's intention to retain the status quo. Conflict with Russia broke out over the respective rights of members of the Catholic and Orthodox Churches, and the struggle ended with the partition treaty in 1772 by virtue of which Poland was forced to cede about a third of its territory to Russia, Austria and Prussia. This prompted Poland's rulers to more serious efforts at political reform.

At this stage, efforts at economic reorganization were made, state income was increased and the executive strengthened, measures were taken to establish a national educational system, and a final stop was put to the practice of *liberum veto*. The outcome of this process was the constitution of 3 May 1791. This lengthy process was only possible because Russia had been involved in operations against both Turkey and Sweden. Once these were completed Russia attacked Poland on the pretext of an invitation from a confederation of nobles at Targowica who protested against the abolition of their established rights. Little effective Polish resistance was offered, and a second partition of Poland took place in 1793 between Russia and Prussia. The response this time was a national uprising led by Tadeusz Kościuszko who proclaimed the end of serfdom and mobilized an army against the Russian forces. The latter, however, soon overcame the resistance and re-entered Warsaw. This time the entire remainder of the Polish state was partitioned among the three powers and the annihilation of the Polish state was completed in 1795. Warsaw lay under Prussian domination, while the boundary of the Russian portion lay very close to the Curzon line drawn in 1919—and, indeed, the border determined at the end of hostilities after World War II.

This effectively meant the abolition of Poland as a territorial entity for over 120 years, including the whole of the nineteenth century—a period which saw the spread of nationalism as a mass enthusiasm in Europe and the rise of the idea of popular participation in politics, the basis of the modern democratic state. The fact that Poland lacked a state did not of course mean that Poles were divorced from these developments. But it did lend a specific character to the set of views held by Poles on these issues and it introduced certain tensions into them. During this period, too, enormous socio-economic changes took place within Europe and the countries which held Poland in partition—although former Polish territories developed in rather different ways and at different speeds according to the situation within the different European powers. As a consequence of these and other changes, the Poland that disappeared from the map at the end of the eighteenth century was a very different one, not only in the territorial sense, from that which reappeared at the beginning of the twentieth. The agricultural, economically backward country had developed areas of industrial concentration, although farming remained the dominant sphere of activity; the Commonwealth of nobles and petty gentry became a nation of landowners accompanied by peasants, bourgeois and even workers.

Political changes and the responses of Poles to the loss of their state also played an important part in these changes. Soon after the loss of statehood some hopes were raised by the initiation by Napoleon Bonaparte of the revolutionary wars, although many Polish patriots (including Kościuszko) were sceptical of the benefits that Napoleon could bring. However, being opposed to the central European powers, Napoleon had some sympathy with the Poles and could count on support from them. In 1807 he created a Duchy of Warsaw which largely consisted of lands taken by Prussia during the partitions. Its role, though, was essentially a military one determined by Napoleon's strategy and its major function was to support a large contingent of French troops. Its ducal ruler was a Saxon king who did not in fact even live in the country. The Duchy did not survive long (not even as long as Napoleon's reputation among Poles) and expired with the defeat of the Napoleonic empire, after which it became a 'Congress Kingdom' (according to the dictates of the Congress of Vienna in 1815) subject to the Russian tsar.

Poland, in its constituent parts, now remained under the control of the same powers for virtually a century, although its political status underwent some change. Guarantees of limited constitutional autonomy were given in the Congress constitution, but these were not respected by the Russians for very long. The accession of Nicholas I and the outbreak of the Decembrist revolt, which had close connections with Polish affairs, was followed by an intensification of political repression in the Congress Kingdom. In November 1830, a Polish uprising broke out. Once this was quelled, Russian rule was strengthened and the constitution suspended. Imperial control was also reinforced in the Austrian and Prussian territories after Polish unrest in the 1840s. The last in the series of such nationalist, 'romantic' uprisings broke out in January 1863 and this time led to the abolition of the Congress Kingdom and its full integration with the Russian empire.

No further such mass outbreaks against foreign rule took place, although the nationalist feelings of Poles had clearly not diminished—and in one sense at least were increasing, as first the industrial proletariat and then the mass of the working population (predominantly peasants), were also becoming aware of their nationality. Insurrection, however, was generally held to have little prospect of success as a means of securing national autonomy and restoring the Polish state. At this time, too, the enormous changes wrought by industrialization were becoming evident, and interest turned more to the promise of social and economic development and to the possibilities held out by gradual material development. Literacy, education and social organization—all of which could be pursued (at least to some extent) within existing political frameworks—held some hope for the articulation and development of Polish national values. This was summed up in the phrase 'organic work', and was seen as an aspect of Polish 'positivism'.

Areas which had been absorbed by Prussia, which in turn became the basis for the newly established German Empire, benefited from the rapid growth of German industry—whilst the growing pressure of German nationalism brought about increased repression of Polish culture and social expression. Similar restrictions were imposed in the Russian territories. But the abolition of the Congress Kingdom had also meant the lifting of customs barriers to trade with the rest of the Russian Empire and the Polish area became one of the main areas of industrial growth within it. By 1890, although Congress

Poland accounted for only 7 per cent of its population, it was responsible for around a quarter of the empire's total production (Dziewanowski, 1977, p. 38).

The Austrian-held areas were far less favoured in terms of economic development and were characterized by relatively backward peasant agriculture, whose position was further worsened by high population growth towards the end of the nineteenth century. It was from this area that much of the migration to Western Europe and the Americas originated. Although missing the greater degree of social and economic development that occurred in the German and Russian areas, the horizons of the otherwise backward country-dwellers were widened in other ways, as emigrants often kept in touch with their home community and maintained surprisingly close links (such correspondence provided the material for an exhaustive sociological classic: Thomas & Znaniecki, 1958). The Austrian territory, notably the province of Galicia, also provided the opportunity for a greater degree of Polish political expression and granted a considerable degree of autonomy. It was in this area that broad-based peasant movements developed and gained some parliamentary representation, experience that was to prove important when Poland's political status underwent a radical change in the twentieth century.

While such diverse social, economic and (partly) political developments were clearly of great significance and often advantageous to the Polish people, it was by no means clear at the outset of the twentieth century how they bore on the issue of Polish independence. Concentration on organic work, and the dominance of 'positivism' over 'romanticism', had certainly not undermined national feeling and had helped create the material conditions for its fuller expression. But it was unclear how such social development might relate to political progress towards the restoration of the Polish state, an aspiration which had certainly not diminished. In the event, it was not Polish action of either sort that brought about this change, but a combination of other developments: the collapse of the Russian Empire in 1917 after two-and-a-half years of warfare more demanding than any previously experienced, the demise of the unstable Austro-Hungarian Empire, the defeat on the western front of the Germans, and the insistence of the victors—by no means least amongst them the Americans—on the principle of national self-determination.

Independence

The issue of nationalism and the role of national consciousness was, however, a complex one in relation to the Polish state. The awareness of belonging to a Polish nation had been a major factor permitting the Poles to survive as a group throughout the nineteenth century, when their state no longer existed. The spread of that awareness down the social scale, including the peasantry, produced a more broadly based and socially integrated national group. It was not, though, a territorially integrated group. To the east, south and west Poles lived together with Bielorussians, Ukrainians and Germans as they had for centuries, the line of division often being drawn on class or occupational grounds rather than according to the area they inhabited. Jews were also numerous, and made up a considerable proportion of the urban population. Those who were Polish in terms of native language made up barely two-thirds of the new state, or Second Republic. This was a higher proportion than in the former republic—but then national identity had not been nourished by the desire to regain statehood nor had it spread among the broader social group. The problems of integrating former Austrian, German and Russian territories in administrative and economic terms were themselves enormous; they were made more difficult by ethnic tensions and conflicts surrounding nationality.

The construction of the new state was also the basis of deeply rooted political disagreements, both in ideological terms and in relation to geographical orientation. The modern Polish state was initially (though unofficially) constituted by Józef Piłsudski, who was released from prison and took over from the German authorities to great popular acclaim in November 1918. That they should have handed over to Piłsudski was not that surprising as, having risen to political eminence from socialist circles, his orientation was essentially anti-Russian and his main strategy one of forging an alliance with a variety of Slavic groups to counteract the power of the dominant Greater Russians. Piłsudski's major antagonist was Roman Dmowski, whose stance was nationalist and clericalist and whose overall policy was one based on respect for and mistrust of German power. He had, accordingly, been inclined to seek Russian support and, following the 1905 revolution, had been a deputy to the Duma. He had ended the war as chairman of the Polish National Committee in Paris and became Poland's representative to the Peace Conference. The more important practical role in establishing the new state and deciding its borders was thus played by Piłsudski, who in 1919 was engaged in directing military operations along the undetermined border with Russia. He won considerable victories in the Ukraine and took Kiev, but then withdrew as large Soviet forces pressed forward in the conviction that they were furthering world revolution and about to join with an uprising of the working classes in the more advanced Western countries. Not very surprisingly, the Polish population showed little enthusiasm for being liberated by the invading Russian army under the revolutionary leadership of the Bolsheviks. Piłsudski succeeded in holding the Soviet army before Warsaw in August 1920 (the 'miracle on the Vistula') and eventually agreed a Polish–Soviet border further east than that proposed at the Peace Conference (the Curzon line).

The conflicting political orientations within Poland made internal solutions rather more difficult to reach. The new constitution for the republic provided for a relatively weak president and executive, as it had been influenced in its drawing up by Dmowski's Nationalists who were eager to restrict the political role that they thought Piłsudski was likely to assume. In the event Piłsudski did not run for the presidency precisely because he disagreed with its conception within the constitution. In December 1922 the newly elected president, Gabriel Narutowicz, was immediately murdered by a 'nationalist fanatic' (Leslie *et al.*, 1980, p. 155) who objected to the fact that his victory was secured by the votes of non-ethnic Poles. The price of this degree of conflict, involving sharp ideological and ethnic disagreements, and the consequence of Poland's territorial and social fragmentation was an inability to construct a party system capable of producing and implementing the policies needed to tackle Poland's diverse political and economic problems. In view of their extent, and of the complex historical origins of the modern Polish state, this could not be regarded as surprising.

The rather dispiriting state of political affairs in the new republic did not last long in this form. Making use of his considerable authority and, more practically, his support within the army, Piłsudski staged a military coup in May 1926. He did not dismantle the existing political structures but established a regime called *Sanacja* (purification, recuperation) which exercised a strong, though ill-defined form of overall political control. Some political trials and imprisonments occurred, although the form of domination exercised was mild in comparison with the other dictatorships developing throughout Europe. After Piłsudski's death in 1935, the repressive and militarist character of the regime intensified, and some semi-fascist and anti-semitic elements entered Polish public life.

By this stage, the dominant issue was becoming not Poland's internal arrangements but the prospect of the republic's survival between the two modern dictatorships that had developed in the countries of its former imperial enemies, Germany and Russia. Since the middle of the nineteenth century Germans had exerted the dominant influence in Central and Eastern Europe and the post-war weakness of Germany during the 1920s in economic and political terms was far less than is often assumed (Rothschild, 1974, p. 5). By 1933 German power was again clearly dominant and only Czechoslovakia and Poland stood out against the tendency for the Eastern European countries to become client or potential client states of Germany (Aspaturian, 1984, p. 15). The Western powers, moreover, did little to strengthen resistance to this process and appeared fully to accept the dominant, and growing, economic role of Germany in this region. Before his death, Piłsudski had been one of the first to perceive the extent of the Nazi danger, and had proposed (without success) joint preventive action to the western powers. Soviet Russia had proposed a combined anti-German agreement—but at the cost of maintaining a Soviet military presence in Poland, which carried ominous overtones of Poland's eighteenth-century experiences. Poland was therefore given little choice but to maintain an independent position between the two dictatorships as best it could.

Clear indications of Poland's fate were given by the German occupation of Austria and parts of Czechoslovakia in 1938. The green light for the invasion of Poland was given by the Soviet Union's acceptance of a pact with Germany in August 1939, which carried a secret agreement to partition Poland (duly carried out the following month) along lines little different from those arrived at in the Third Partition of 1795. The record of German action in Poland during World War II is notorious enough not to need extensive discussion. Apart from using Poland as the charnel house of European Jewry, the Nazis also regarded the Poles as a sub-species and took millions of their lives, too. Of Poland's 35 million population in 1939, 6 million died during the war, the highest proportion of deaths in any one country and twenty times the proportion suffered by the British. But the major experiences of the Poles between 1939 and 1945 were not restricted to their relations with the Germans, nor were their losses all caused by the Nazi regime. Some 2 million were deported from the Soviet zone of occupation in 1939 and 1940, and at least half of them were estimated to have died within a year of their arrest (Davies, 1986, p. 67). A particular focus of Polish resentment, the details of which were to surface later and which was to prove a major stumbling-block in Soviet-Polish relations and those within the Allied camp as a whole, was the disappearance of thousands of Polish army officers. Over 4,000 of their bodies were found by the Germans during 1943 in Katyn forest, near Smolensk. The Soviet authorities tried to blame the Nazis for their murder, but few believed this to be the case.

Given the historic competition and enmity between Poland and Russia, which showed no signs of abating in the twentieth century with the Polish–Soviet war in 1919–20, there was nothing particularly surprising about Soviet actions in Poland at the beginning of the war—although they were pursued with a thoroughness and brutality characteristic of the Stalin period. Yet with the German attack on the Soviet Union in June 1941, Poles and Russians became allies. The possibility, in this relationship, of Polish independence similar to that which had existed for a short period between the two world wars, was virtually non-existent and Poles were again forced to define their role in an unwilling, unequal and largely unwanted partnership. This situation was perpetuated and broadly stabilized in the post-war years and has come to characterize Poland's position in the modern period. Given the nature of the major powers, the part played by the Soviet Union in defeating the Nazi dictatorship and the facts of geography there was little real chance that the situation could have developed otherwise.

The tone of Soviet–Polish relations in the modern period was set by the fact that, at the time of the German invasion in 1941, Poland was distinguished by the absence of a communist party in the country. This was due neither to the anti-communist pre-war Polish regime, nor to the policy of the Nazi forces, but to the fact that the Polish Communist Party had been dissolved by Stalin in 1937–8. It was said to be infiltrated by police agents and it was evident, whatever the facts of the matter, that Stalin had little confidence in the Polish party and could see no political role for it. The Polish party had never been very large, it had operated under difficult conditions in the inter-war republic and had always found it difficult to gather much popular support because of its initial opposition to the restoration of Polish independence and the establishment of the twentieth-century state. Some ascribe greater political significance to the Polish party (KPP) than might have been evident from its size (Baryka, 1982), but its role was never a major one and Stalin clearly did not think that its elimination was a great loss.

Following the German invasion another communist party was set up in Poland in January 1942. It did not, however, bear the title 'communist' and was called the Polish Workers' Party (PPR), being intended to carry a less Soviet-orientated connotation. A major function of the new party was to participate in resistance to German forces in ways deemed appropriate to the communist authorities, who were now engaged in similar operations also in the occupied areas of the Soviet Union. But in addition to playing a role in a general anti-Nazi alliance, it soon became clear that the PPR would have more extensive political functions. Although they were formally allies relations between the Polish government in exile, based in London, and the

Soviet authorities were, for obvious reasons, not very cordial. They were never able to discuss, let alone agree on, any post-war Polish-Soviet border. The other major allies, Britain and the United States, were highly appreciative of the military value of the Soviet forces in anti-German operations and critical of Polish views which had a disruptive influence within the alliance. Britain, in any case, had never been convinced of the validity of Polish territorial claims in the east. Stalin, therefore, had every interest in encouraging domestic political forces separate from the London government who could act as an alternative to it.

The political role of the communist organization became an important one. Once the Soviet authorities recovered from the initial shock of the German invasion and made known their longer-term strategy, it became clear not just that they were loath to relinquish their 1939–41 western border but also that they were committed to ensuring that post-war Poland (whatever and, indeed, wherever it was) would be a 'friendly' nation, that it would not serve as a base for future aggression from the west, and that its foreign policy would be in line with Soviet inclinations. This conception was agreed in broad terms with the other major allies and elaborated at a series of meetings of the leaders and their ministers (in Tehran, Moscow and Yalta). As the war progressed and its end could be foreseen, the Polish government in exile found itself increasingly unable to influence the course of events. The position of the home resistance, non-communist in the great majority and generally suspicious of Soviet intentions, was also a difficult one. It was largely to strengthen the political position of the Polish national forces that the Warsaw Uprising was launched in August 1944, as the Soviet army appeared to be on the verge of driving out the German forces. In the event the Soviet army hung back, while the Germans defeated the uprising and destroyed the city. It was both a military and a political defeat, and it made continued activity on the part of the non-communist resistance seem senseless and dangerous. Those who continued operations were treated by the advancing Soviet forces virtually as enemy agents and saboteurs.

The Post-War State

Having prepared their political plans with considerable care, the Soviet authorities set up a sympathetic quasi-governmental body in the first area they liberated and which they regarded as being properly Polish (that is, to the west of the demarcation line they had established in 1939). This was the Polish Committee of National Liberation (PKWN), established in Lublin in

July 1944. It took on the role of a more formal government over time, and was recognized as the basis of one by the western powers in June 1945. By the time full-scale elections were held in January 1947, Soviet forces had been in control of much of the country for some two years. The army had been followed by security and political agencies, and extensive preparations had been carried out for the construction of communist political order—a Polish state 'friendly' to the Soviet Union, as agreed between the Great Powers. The 1947 elections therefore developed the line established by the Lublin PKWN and were used to ensure the near-final defeat of the democratic opposition.

The country in which this new order was established was considerably different from the pre-war republic. Poland's eastern border was determined according to Soviet wishes and the ethnically mixed areas that shaded into Bielorussia and the Ukraine were lost. On the other hand, Poland gained most of East Prussia and territories previously held by Germany. Areas south of the Oder and east of the Neisse river were also handed over to Poland, although Poland had no real historical claim to this area. As a result of these changes post-war Poland was some 20 per cent smaller than in 1939, although undoubted gains were the extension of Polish control over the whole of Upper Silesia with its extensive reserves of coal and other mineral resources, and the acquisition of the fertile agricultural area along the Oder. This time the border changes were also accompanied by massive population shifts—Germans were removed from their areas and Poles were transferred from what had now become Western Bielorussia and the Western Ukraine. In consequence, Poland became, for the first time, a virtually united and uniform national entity—of the post-war population of 24 million, only half a million belonged to national minorities.

This had the paradoxical effect also of making Poland a more exclusively Catholic country and enabling the Church to regard itself as representative of the Polish nation not just because of its historic status but also on the basis of popular allegiance and support. At the same time, an enormous expansion was taking place in the PPR. While the communist organization numbered some 20,000 when the PKWN was instituted in July 1944, the total was some ten times higher within a year. By this time, of course, it had become clear that the future of Poland would be determined by those not just sympathetic to the Soviet Union but prepared to work under its leadership. Communists were dominant in the practical activities now undertaken by government and social organizations. Industrial recovery and the development of a nationalized industry were under way, and a land reform and reorganization of agriculture were being implemented. While these had previously been elements of more radical programmes for social change, they had become accepted in principle by all major political groups. The occupation and development of the newly acquired Polish territories (called the 'Recovered Territories') also called for much effort. PPR leader Władysław Gomułka was the minister responsible for these areas, while other leading PPR figures were in charge of internal security and home affairs, industry and economic organization, and foreign affairs.

Although Poland by 1947 was clearly a state dominated by communist forces with intimate links with the Soviet authorities, had borders agreeable to and largely determined by the Soviet Union, and in no way could be seen as posing a strategic or economic threat to its eastern neighbour, it soon became clear that the Soviet pattern was not regarded as having been firmly enough imposed by the model power itself. The major problem was that Gomułka, though an orthodox communist and a firm supporter of Soviet hegemony within the international movement, nevertheless believed in the desirability and viability of a 'Polish road to socialism'. This meant taking account of certain Polish characteristics, notably an appropriately sensitive handling of the national issue and a gradual and initially non-collectivist approach to the problems of Polish agriculture and the Polish peasantry. This, Gomułka felt, would ultimately create a firmer basis for communism in Poland, sustain a more effective political and economic system, and enhance the authority and power of the party. Gomułka's strategy, itself unacceptable to most political forces in Poland and the majority of its population, could soon no longer be tolerated either by Stalin and the Soviet authorities.

The rapidly deteriorating relations between the Soviet Union and the western powers were accompanied by Soviet determination to strengthen the links between the Soviet Union and its Eastern European satellites, to intensify political control and enhance the role of internal security agencies, and eliminate all possible forms of political heresy and, indeed, the capacity for political disagreement. Gomułka's position came under strong attack in 1948 and he was removed from the party leadership and placed under house arrest. His place was taken by Bolesław Bierut, who oversaw the merger of the PPR with the remainder of the Polish Socialist Party (PPS) to form the Polish United Worker's Party (PZPR). This completed the process whereby Poland effectively became a one-party state on the Soviet model. A Peasant Party (ZSL) and a Democratic Party (SD) continued to exist, but they in no way qualified communist power during the Stalinist period. During the subsequent Stalinist period the collectivization of agriculture was launched, the role of the Church attacked, the development of heavy industry accelerated to the detriment of the growth of the economy as a whole, the military sector expanded to satisfy the growing demands of the Warsaw Pact alliance, and political repression intensified with the dominant role played by internal and Soviet police agencies. This situation eased with the death of Stalin in March 1953, but began to change to a significant extent only in 1956 following Khrushchev's denunciation of Stalin's crimes. It was in the subsequent period of accelerated political change, which became transformed into a crisis of party rule, that Gomułka was brought back into the party leadership.

His attempt to revive a Polish road to socialism was soon dropped in practice and Gomułka reverted to a relatively conservative form of communist rule, though with some concessions to continuing elements of Polish resistance to it (the persistence of small peasant farming, the extensive role of the Church, a somewhat more autonomous intellectual life). Polish communism thus kept some specific characteristics and developed others in the 1970s and 1980s. The Polish road to socialism has retained some meaning in that socialist development in Poland has extended and been influenced by a number of themes from Polish history, and has recapitulated traditions of the Polish nation. A major feature of communist politics in Poland has been not just the general awareness of the force of historical traditions but also the attempt of major political actors to manipulate and play on this awareness, to use it as a political resource (Walicki, 1985, p. 174). It is difficult to avoid the conclusion that the diversity of Polish history and the contrasting nature of the themes that can be detected within it have, on occasion, prompted the adoption of some of the more innovative practices of Polish communism. The parallel between Piłsudski's coup and Jaruzelski's introduction of military rule is instructive in this respect.

Numerous coincidences of Polish history have clearly encouraged such references in recent Polish political life. The establishment of the post-World War II state on the banks of the Oder obviously encouraged allusions to the original Piast kingdom and the insistence that these were Recovered Territories rather than conquered areas. It was also an implicit rejection of the subsequent Jagellonian tradition of eastward expansion and of the drive for leadership over neighbouring non-Russian Slavic groups. Recuperation of the German territories in the absence of West German ratification of Poland's western border also increased Polish dependence on the Soviet alliance and provided some rationale for the dominance of a communist government in post-war Poland. It was ironic that Gomułka's agreement with West Germany, in itself a considerable diplomatic achievement, preceded his fall from power by a matter of weeks in December 1970. The two events were largely unconnected, and the power of the anti-German argument had in any case declined with the stabilization of the international situation in post-war Europe.

Poland's relations with Russia have been a major theme in Polish history since the sixteenth century. In the post-war period, relations with the Soviet Union have been the single most important aspect of internal and external political relations. The analogy of post-war Poland with its eighteenth-century ancestor, when Russia was able to determine the choice of Poland's monarch, shape its foreign policy and, ultimately, change its borders, has necessarily been a strong one. That period has also been an important point of reference because it immediately preceded the partition of Poland and the loss of independence, the low point of Polish statehood. Different conclusions have been drawn from this example and history is, of course, put to conflicting uses. The establishment view of the Solidarity period, with its protracted conflicts and the impossibility of reaching accord on a basis for common action, was that it resembled nothing so much as the commonwealth of nobles, in which one use of the veto was able to paralyse the body politic. From this perspective the imposition of the State of War and the suspension of Solidarity broke the deadlock and opened the way to purposive action and, implicitly, prevented the perpetuation of conflict and the likelihood of Soviet intervention, which would have meant the further loss of statehood. An alternative view was that the establishment of the Military Council of National Salvation in December 1981 was the equivalent of the Targowica confederates and enabled the military commissars to act as Soviet proxies, implementing Soviet-sponsored policies.

Polish political life has been rife with such historical analogies and conscious identification with, or rejection of, specific Polish traditions. A favoured focus of attention has been the nineteenth century with its conflicting responses to the loss of Polish statehood and the contrasting approaches to the restoration of independence characteristic of the romantic and positivist outlooks (Bromke, 1967). But the lessons of history are not always clear. The restoration of Polish independence in 1918 was, after all, a consequence of the collapse of the three central European empires in which the effects of Polish romanticism and positivism hardly played a decisive part (which is not to say that they did not both play some part). Polish political life has been subject to a certain obsession with historical example whose consequences are not necessarily positive. It may be suspected that one reason for the role that a strong historical awareness plays in Polish politics is the sheer complexity of the problems which Poles have to face, the disasters and disappointments which so many Polish leaders and their policies have run into, and the difficulties of coming up with viable new solutions. In terms of contemporary Polish politics, this is closely linked with the weakness of Communist Party authority and the lack of a popular basis to communist rule in Poland. Yet policies and concrete programmes of action have had to be found and implemented. In the case of Poland in the 1980s, ruled by a quasi-military dictatorship hitherto unknown in the communist world, one suspects that the history of which Polish political actors have been so acutely aware will not be very helpful in the formulation of such policies and programmes. We shall turn to examine the nature of these challenges and political dilemmas in a later chapter. Before that, we shall consider successively the nature of contemporary Polish society, the machinery of political rule over that society, and the economic problems it has experienced in conjunction with projects for economic reform.

2 Social Structure and Social Welfare

Any contribution to the study of Poland's social structure in the 1980s has to deal with two very important new factors which have forced themselves on to the topography of social life. First, there can be little doubt that the intellectual legacy of the Solidarity period has altered our perception of Polish society as much as the accompanying social, economic and political events made an impact upon its workings. Those months revealed the workings of institutions, elaborated the dynamics of social processes and highlighted the attributes of social groups in a manner unknown in a Soviet-type society. Much of the subsequent analysis is affected by the paradigm shift this has entailed—the gestation period is far from completed and many of our formulations still retain the hallmarks of more routinized viewpoints.

Second, Poland is a society which is destined to live in an economic crisis of quite considerable proportions for the next ten years, according to best estimates. This provides a unique opportunity for studying how a socialist system of the traditional mould copes with overt poverty, growing inequality, political polarization and the prospect of a future concerned more with reattaining a previous standard of living, on a par with that obtaining in 1978, than with reaching the higher ground of developed socialism. The urgency is all the greater in that ecological deterioration, increasing mortality rates, more visible social pathologies and other tangible ills usually associated with the costs of industrialization and therefore 'progress' are now simply legacies of past dreams and promises unfulfilled.

Poland is also unique in that it retains a predominantly individual agricultural sector covering 76 per cent of arable land, and an artisan craft services sector which is largely privately run and employs nearly 1 million persons. Both these features impinge upon government policies, affect life chances and complicate our image of social structure. The political legacy of Solidarity has also made many of the indicators of inequality more symbolically loaded. Trade-union membership in the newly created government-sponsored organizations, as well as previous membership of Solidarity itself, influence attitudes in a way not comparable to other socialist societies. Managerial position and PZPR membership are still important stratification variables, but generational cleavages, sectoral employment, size of factory, and political-geographical location can now cross-cut the boundaries of white-collar/blue-collar, urban/rural and the simpler indicators of age, sex and occupation. An appraisal of the Solidarity period with its martial law aftermath is as essential to understanding the emerging patterns of social stratification as the Six Year Plan period was to comprehending the 1950s and 1960s (Holzer, 1983).

The primacy of the political over the economic and social spheres in Soviet-type societies is clearly accentuated in post-1981 Poland. It is virtually impossible to resist trying to identify the politically latent functions underlying the manifest stated purposes of any regime initiative. To that end the politicization of social structure brings with it a three-dimensional effect absent from the other communist countries.

The Historical Comparison

At the core of regime legitimacy, when all the Marxist-Leninist rhetoric was stripped away, always lay the undoubted achievements of the post-war communist leadership in the sphere of societal transformation. Looking at the make-up of the population and inter-war population changes, in 1938 over 70 per cent of the economically active population of Poland was engaged in agriculture. Rural overpopulation meant that 4.5 million peasants eked out a precarious existence. The lot of the 500,000 urban unemployed, which was exacerbated by the depression, was little better. Over 61 per cent of agricultural holdings were deemed not to be self-sufficient, similar albeit to the level in socialist Poland although before the war alternative sources of income did not exist. Less than 1 per cent of landholdings encompassed 45 per cent of arable land which did not favour intensive exploitation (Landau & Tomaszewski, 1985).

Foreign domination of share capital amounted to 40 per cent and the export of earnings from this investment was calculated to be equivalent to the total state investment budget during these years (Landau, 1985). Agrarian reform was in part stalled by the constitutional appeal to the inviolability of private property, but some redistribution with compensation was effected. Almost predictably, this served to drive the peasantry into debt rather than stimulate a rural market for industrial goods. In consequence, lack of investment and general stagnation persisted and the government-sponsored initiative of the late 1930s was a case of too little too late. Peasant emigration provided a safety valve but even this was restricted around the time of the depression.

On the credit side, Poland was one of the first countries to introduce social insurance and some limited unemployment benefits, which applied mainly to those in state employment. Officially a 46-hour week was established, something which embarrasses the present regime which has been unable to improve upon this figure except during the Solidarity interlude. Nevertheless, the socialist welfare state, building on the pre-war achievements, has dramatically changed the life chances of the average Pole. Although currently under threat, it is adequate in its comprehensiveness.

Inter-war social structure is generally given the 'official' configuration shown in Table 2.1 (Wiatr, 1979, Żarnowski, 1973). Socio-occupational differentiation (which was not highly developed and class and stratum boundaries were qualified by the ethnic mix of inter-war Poland. According to the criteria of language, Poles constituted 68.9 per cent of the population, Ukrainians 13.9 per cent, Yiddish-speaking Jews 8.7 per cent, Byelorussians 3.17 per cent, and Germans 2.7 per cent (Davis, 1982, Żarnowski, 1973).

Table 2.1 Social Structure in the Inter-war Period (percentage of population)

Ruling classes	
Landowners	0.36
Capitalists	2.00
Intermediate classes and strata	
Intelligentsia	6.00
Petty bourgeoisie	11.00
Working class	
Industrial	7.00
Other	13.00
Peasant stratum	
Owners of large holdings	2.00
Owners of medium holdings	17.00
Small or landless peasants	32.00
Peasants employed on large estates	9.00

Ethnic competition, exclusion and racism were interwoven into the complex social fabric. Anti-semitism, various forms of minority nationalisms and the overspill of German fascism heightened group conflicts which were pre-empted by the advent of World War II. Whereas Poland after 1945–6 had become an ethnically homogeneous nation-state, these antagonisms are sometimes potent memories which can be manipulated and exploited by various groups and factions within Poland's post-war ruling groups when they have sought to make political mischief. The reality of Polish anti-semitism is not a subject to be dealt with by a text such as this (Smolar, 1987).

The social transformation which accompanied the imposition of the communist regime on 22 July, 1944 can best be grasped in terms of the enormous scope for social mobility which fundamentally reshaped the lives of all Poles. In one major study as many as 77 per cent of the population sampled were found to occupy positions different to those of their fathers. Of these, 61 per cent had been upwardly mobile and 16 per cent downwardly (Pohoski, 1983). The most homogeneous, least changed strata were the peasantry and to a lesser extent manual workers, whereas the heterogeneity of social origins was most evident amongst the intelligentsia and specialized technicians, as well as the bureaucracy. It is little wonder, therefore, that the mobility imperative has become a central expectation of the population in Poland. As mobility rates decline and the mobility chances of the lower orders diminish, despite mechanisms of positive discrimination, so the regime has to 'cool out' mobility expectations. Fortunately, it appears that the declining lucrativeness of white-collar employment tied to the economic crisis and the resulting flux in the labour market, have contributed to depress somewhat the aspirations for non-manual, non-agricultural status.

Social mobility, massive geographical mobility associated with the westward shift of Poland's borders, and national 'reconstruction' occurred against the backdrop of war losses which easily compare with the much more publicized deprivations suffered by the Soviet Union. Apart from the human tragedy of 6 million lives lost and the added effects of disease and political exile, something like 38 per cent of the nation's wealth was destroyed. One in two factories was razed (73 per cent in the western territories) peasants lost the bulk of their draught animals and over 30 per cent of the housing stock was lost (Andrzejewski, 1977).

The Socialist Blueprint

The post-war aims of the new regime were the imposition of a communist system of rule and what has come to be known as enforced modernization. They were in effect enshrined in an ideology of industrialization (Morawski, 1985). Alongside the quantitative and, less successfully, qualitative growth of the new proletariat aimed at providing the much needed political base of support for the regime, there were to emerge socialist towns countering the existing bourgeois centres such as Warsaw and Cracow. Full employment, mass migration from the countryside and the subsequent collectivization attempts which were to come after the agrarian reforms were to be the major instruments underlying the industrialization drive. The adoption of the Soviet model, despite the strong support within the new elite for a 'Polish road to socialism', provided the conditions not only for Poland's subsequent development but also its almost continuous crises (Fallenbuchl, 1986).

There are four processes which provide the basic contours to present day Polish society. First, the agrarian reform of 6 September 1944, politically complex as it was in its making (Turlejska, 1987), provided for the dismemberment of the large estates without compensation, the take-over of German-owned property and the emergence of a highly fragmented structure of private landholding. Whilst western Poland and the so-called Recovered Territories witnessed different solutions to the reform, retaining larger state holdings or individual units of a greater area, the outcome was a mixed structure of landholdings which successive leaderships have attempted to rationalize. Private landholding, in the main highly fragmented, backed by a powerful Catholic Church and to a great extent by the rest of the population, (with its defining principles of individual farming—now entered into the Constitution—) combined with a situation where it is the only successful sector of the economy experiencing relative market equilibrium, although still with subsidized food prices and meat rationing, all these factors create a Gordian knot which no leadership has been able either to unravel or to cut.

Second, the nationalization of industry, mines, banks and transport (although not of land or housing) saw the demise of foreign capital (until the 1980s, that is) and of the minute capitalist class (with compensation). Individual capitalists and private sector entrepreneurship remains. Thus the residual crafts/artisan sector and those services organized privately rather than collectively generate over 7 per cent of the national income and employ nearly 1 million persons. Signalling variously hot and cold toward these supposed survivals, recent regime initiatives encouraging the inflow of foreign and not just émigré capital seem to ensure the continuance and indeed growth of vestigial capitalism.

Third, accompanying the shift of population from rural to urban and from agriculture to industry, was the burgeoning of a new working class and a white-collar state apparatus. Easy access to work for the new recruits from the countryside had negative as well as positive effects. Allowed to coalesce and develop spontaneously, poor labour discipline, low productivity and various social pathologies became part and parcel of the image of the Polish working class. Likewise in the white-collar sector and among the specialist intelligentsia the bureaucratic impulse already present within the logic of a centrally planned and administered economy was further strengthened by the mass influx of incumbents whose stereotypical perception of officialdom and the exercise of authority drew upon the worst features of inter-war Poland. The positive attributes of the creative intelligentsia and the best elements of professionalism, such as artistic integrity and codes of ethics, were not allowed to survive. Added to this the gross under-urbanization and infrastructural shortfall only exacerbated the problems mentioned above and set the scene for subsequent social problems whose echo is now being heard. In particular, the growth of the 'worker-peasant' category (Kolankiewicz, 1980), those who were originally compelled to bridge the rural-urban divide at considerable personal cost in order to provide labour without the costs of urban development, now poses a problem intimately tied up with the future of Polish agriculture.

Finally, all the above processes were subordinated to the industrialization drive of the Three Year (1947-9) and the Six Year (1950-5) Plans. Apart from brief pro-consumer periods at points of systemic crisis, the heavy industry-producer goods priority has been maintained (see below), so much so that in 1987 the level of investment in the fuel-energy sector was of 1950s proportions (*Życie Gospodarcze*, 13 March 1988). As a consequence a raw-materials- and energy-hungry investment structure has predominated. It grew to quite unmanageable and ultimately unaffordable proportions during the 1970s as Poland ran up debts in excess of $25 billion to the West and 5 billion roubles to the Soviet Union. The party-state bureaucracy thrived in this pattern of development which gave little autonomy to society and yet appeared to achieve the goals of modernization and economic growth. Since 1956 Poland has gone through the motions of successive economic reforms in order to break the grip of the so-called 'directive-distributive' centralized state. However the underinvested state of agriculture, the poor-relation status of the consumer sector, not to mention the marginal positon of services provision, are all eloquent testimony to the power of the 'redistributors' (Szelenyi, 1979). The 'standard of living' revolts by the Polish working class which have provided the landmarks on the terrain of Polish politics (even the birth of Solidarity was initiated by price rises) are eminently political in that they question the continued primacy of this developmental policy and those who maintain their power through it. 'Societal conflict in the Polish industrial system is not incidental but is a structural conflict immanent to this type of system' (Panków, 1987).

Out of the above social processes has emerged a syndrome of attitudes and actions which define the average Pole as citizen, as employee and as consumer. The division of life into public and private, formal work and informal activity, a passivity in state-sponsored spheres which contrasts with the vibrancy of the family and other milieux outside the state domain, are just parts of it. (Marody, 1987).

The apparent schizophrenic nature of such a life can only be understood in the context of imposed modernization, an artificial political hegemony, the forced social decomposition and its *ad hoc* reconstitution of the social order and the overarching rhetoric of transvaluation contained within an official ideology having little or no basis in the cultural signifiers of that society. Thus it appears that in its forty-year history the Polish regime did violence to its own political roots, rode roughshod over its own working class, relegated the intelligentsia to the status of bureaucratic overseers and sought to collectivize a peasantry with little desire for it, without providing the alternatives to offset the opposition it provoked.

Population Trends

Today one in every five persons added to the population of Europe (excluding the Soviet Union) is a Pole. By the year 2000 it is estimated that almost the entire natural growth in the employed European population will be taking place in Poland. Is this apparent success of fecundity (somewhat abated by 1987) a reason for celebration or a cause for concern? Poland experienced demographic bulges in the 1950s, the 1970s, and most recently in the early 1980s. Most appeared to catch the authorities by surprise, although the demographers insisted that they had made accurate predictions throughout. Anti-natalist policies seemed to stimulate further births rather than even out the cycles. Thus shortages in the provision of kindergartens and schools turned into surpluses only to re-emerge as shortages again. During 1980–1 the state introduced paid maternity and child-care leave up to a child's third year, which promptly took 793,000 women out of the labour market. Since then the declining value of this state benefit has prompted women to return to work, fortuitously coinciding with an apparent labour shortage. The reasons for this sudden upsurge in fertility in the early 1980s are not understood. A declining real standard of living, the crushing of Solidarity causing the return into the family, and the re-emergence of Church authority are all possible explanations. More mundanely, however, the system was responding to the prospect of excess labour power which would be brought about by the putative economic reform of 1982, and not to the dictates of a coherent population policy. In a similar view the offer of early retirement to certain largely skilled industrial employees in 1981–2 prompted a further 600,000 persons to leave the labour market. This in turn came to be regretted. The fact that both mothers and early retirees are being wooed and driven back into employment, albeit part-time in some cases, is evidence that the state's priorities are short-term and manipulative.

In 1986 there were over half a million excess vacancies in the socialized economy, largely for manual workers. Until 1990 the state faces declining entry into the occupationally active population. For some this is seen as an ideal opportunity to carry through the restructuring of industry from its labour-intensive heavy industry bias to a more streamlined, productive and modern model. The prospects are not encouraging (see below) and the central bureaucracy will prefer to juggle with employees in order to maintain the status quo. For even here population pressures have dimensions which are not reducible to natalistic or other concerns.

Qualitative as well as quantitative population changes have made difficult demands of successive Polish leaderships. Currently the prospect of having to feed an extra 3 million persons by the year 2000 (see Table 2.2) has focused attention more upon agricultural self-sufficiency than upon job creation. Added to this is the fact that Poland has over seventy individuals non-productive by virtue of age for every 100 theoretically in the occupationally active group, which poses new problems for planners. Dealing with an ageing

Table 2.2 Population Size According to Census Data

Year	Total	Towns ('000)	Countryside	Urban population as percentage of total
1946	23,626	7,517	16,109	31.8
1950	25,035	9,243	15,792	36.9
1960	29,795	14,401	15,394	48.3
1970	32,658	17,088	15,570	52.3
1980	35,735	20,979	14,756	58.7
1983	36,745	21,922	14,823	59.7
1985	37,300	22,500	14,800	60.3
1986	37,572	22,739	14,833	60.5
	prognosis			
2000	40,300	n.a.	n.a.	n.a.

Source: *Rocznik Polityczny i Gospodarczy*, 1984, p. 52; K. Secomski, 1985; *Rocznik Statystyczny*, 1986 and 1987.

population is something relatively new for the regime. This is made all the more difficult in that it coincided with a catastrophic 25 per cent average drop in the standard of living between 1978 and 1982, which was undoubtedly more severe for pensioners, multi-children families and invalids. At the other end of the spectrum, despite a high of over 700,000 births per annum in 1983–4, the infant mortality rate is stuck at about 18.4 per thousand live births, although it is a lot worse in the industrial and heavily polluted regions. Declining life expectancy for men *and* women (the latter shared with Hungary and Rumania) should not be confused, however, with increased mortality.

An ageing population explains only 25 per cent of the increase in deaths, as shown by the fact that Poland has the highest age-specific mortality rate, for men aged 35 and over, in Europe (*Życie Warszawy*, April 1986; *Trybuna Ludu*, 24–8 December 1986).

Population pressure is most keenly felt in the housing market and allocative system. In 1986, the socialized (cooperative) construction sector produced 127,000 housing units, 5,500 less than in the previous years and equal to the 1965 figure. The shortfall from the planned level of production was worst in the large cities. At the same time prices per square metre of new privately owned accommodation have risen dramatically, standing at 70,000 złoty in Warsaw (or 2 times the average monthly wage). A major obstacle is the lack of infrastructure, sewers, water and electricity. A shortage of building materials, of at least 20 per cent, coupled with waste, poor storage and theft, is aggravated by a chronic labour shortage. Over 80 per cent of urban building workers have to be bussed in from the villages, but even here increased peasant affluence is affecting this form of dual-occupational employment. Whereas in the 1970s the number of housing units (209,000 in 1978) was almost equal to new households as measured by weddings (280,000 or so) by 1985 the divergence between the two, 133,000 and 267,000 was disastrous (*Polityka*, 24 January 1987). As a consequence, the waiting period for the highly subsidized cooperative housing can be as long as twenty years. It has over 2 million persons waiting to join its list, most of them fully paid-up, but both membership and waiting lists are currently closed. The alternative of state-provided accommodation either goes to the very needy or to occupational groups in short supply (for example, dentists in the countryside). It should be noted that, according to official data, expenditure on housing in Poland within the above sectors accounts for about 8 per cent of household budgets. It is a tempting example of the kind of deep subsidy which the regime would like to eradicate and raise individuals' expenditure to about 10–15 per cent. The social distribution of housing can be therefore quite indicative of inequality within the area of collective consumption (*Życie Gospodarcze*, 10 March 1985).

Local governments and factories distribute 55 per cent of all housing. However the most needy and those who have waited in the factory queue are often bypassed for those with desirable qualifications and political newcomers to the area. While 54 per cent of cooperative housing goes to working-class families this does little to relieve the pressure. Overcrowding is a problem: over 14 per cent of the population live two to three per room and 4.5 per cent live more than three per room. By 1985 there were still only 193,000 housing units per annum from all sectors coming into use, which is critical when it is considered that at least 300,000 are needed if the shortfall is to be corrected. As mentioned above, for every 100 marriages entered into there are at best fifty housing units made available. Theoretically there is one room available per 1.03 persons, but homelessness and destitution now figure on the streets of Warsaw (*Przegląd Katolicki*, 14 February 1988).

Private housing provision now produces between half and two-thirds of new living *space* despite a severe shortage of raw materials, and reflects market forces at their most brutal. However, cooperative housing provision is also losing out to factory-funded building, which pays higher prices per square metre. The consequences of this as the economic reform unfolds will be to continue to provide housing to those considered most valuable to the enterprise, while the more accessible and seemingly more egalitarian cooperative sector is in deep trouble (*Trybuna Ludu*, 31 January 1986; 21 March 1986). It may be that the demographic decline in the 20–29 age group during the 1980s will relieve some of the pressure. Nevertheless, Poland provides 10 square metres less per household than the GDR and Czechoslovakia. And, all things considered, its starting point after the war was no worse than Finland, Austria or some of the southern European countries. Housing is now rightly at the top of the regime's official agenda, being pushed by the new unions, social bodies and Solidarity alike.

Population growth affects a whole range of other needs, the satisfaction of most of which is also subject to state subsidy. In 1986, of the 960 billion złoty of state subsidy, food (meat and dairy produce in particular) absorbed 34 per cent. Train and bus services came to over 11 per cent and coal to nearly 16 per cent. The government has cut the level of these and other subsidies under the so-called second stage of economic reform with swingeing 100–200 per cent price increases. This has affected the 9 million persons officially admitted to be at or below the social minimum. Likewise it has struck at the 3 million or so workers compelled to travel considerable distances to work

(40 km in Polish conditions is a long way) in overexploited and under-invested public transport.

Poland spends 21.8 per cent of GNP on social benefits, compared to a COMECON average of 25 per cent. These are either paid in cash or in kind as services. Of the first, retirement and invalidity pensions are the most important. The former now extend to the whole of the population. The latter divide into three categories, the third being the most contentious. This allows for partial early retirement through ill health and is subject to medical examination. For many it appears to provide an opportunity to receive both state assistance and yet engage in second economy activity. The fact, however, that 100,000 persons take such invalidity pensions every year is used as evidence of the effect that deteriorating employment conditions are having upon the work-force. Numbering over 5 million, pensioners continue to be attractive to the state planners as a source of labour. A whole series of incentives already exist and others are in the pipeline aimed at keeping employees on beyond the retiring age (65 for men and 60 for women, although 30 per cent of all employees have the right to retire earlier!) some of which exist in other socialist bloc countries (*Życie Warszawy*, 18 July 1985). Between 1978 and 1984 the number of invalids rose from 2.5 million to 3.6 million putting an increased strain on the welfare system while at the same time pointing to some of the less obvious costs of Poland's crisis (*Tygodnik Powszechny*, 28 February 1988).

Other benefits are generally paid to women in the role of mother, as child care for sick children and as so-called child-training benefits. These allow for a mother (or father) to be paid to look after a child until the age of four when it enters into the pre-school system. At its peak it included 671,000 women but has since fallen to a little over 250,000 (as mentioned above) and in effect is now largely for single mothers, who receive a higher rate of benefit. Sickness benefits from work, various income supplements and non-returnable loans for the very poor make up the rest of the cash transfer payments. Lastly, 73 per cent of the student population receive some kind of grant from the state. Benefits in kind include spending on education and health care which are, formally at least, available free. Arts and culture as well as tourism and physical education also come under this heading. All are being progressively squeezed with possible privatization, increased payments (until now nominal) and stricter rationing.

Other population processes are throwing up further problems for the planners. Patterns of internal migration are making for severe disproportions in the balance of the sexes in the countryside. This may affect food production, the birth rate and the future of individual agriculture in Poland.

For every 1,000 unmarried men in the 20–34 age group and engaged in individual agriculture there are at best 381 unmarried women of the same age. The out-migration of women is just one of the cumulative consequences of underurbanization, which did not generate the kinds of job which would be conducive to keeping women in the countryside and perhaps combining their already onerous chores with some source of independent income. Young women looking at their mothers' burdensome existence are not prepared to tolerate the costs of an underinvested peasant farm.

On a broader scale, during the years 1950–84, over 35 million Poles started life in a new place of residence. Nowadays if they move at all it is usually not beyond the bounds of their *województwo*. This reflects in part the housing shortage which leads people to keep their home and search for a job. It also reflects the declining rates of social mobility. Of the migration that does exist, 17 per cent in 1986 was return migration to the countryside, often seen as a response to the crisis in living standards of the cities, and really a mixed blessing for the authorities who would like to rejuvenate agriculture without necessarily giving it too much permanence in the life plans of the young and ambitious.

For many the frustrations and hardships of everyday life in Poland prove too much. Actual suicides rose steadily during the latter part of the 1970s, a period of relative affluence by comparison to the present, as they did in Hungary. They dropped off quite markedly during 1980–1 from 4,338 to less than 3,000 but have gradually climbed back to over 4,426 in 1986. The rate in Poland, 11.7 per 100,000 inhabitants, is comparable with that in the United States, Canada and other developed countries. But it is quite high compared to rates in such Catholic, less developed European societies as Spain, Portugal and Italy. What was interesting about the 1980–1 figures was that the distribution of suicides and suicide attempts by social grouping changed quite dramatically. Those of manual workers dropped (and shifted in their internal distribution) while those of white-collar and higher-management personnel rose quite significantly (Jarosz, 1981, 1985). Interestingly, the reported suicides and suicide attempts among women seemed to be little affected by the Polish August!

Other forms of death are also quite closely correlated to social class, place of residence and industrial employment. Health and the conditions of work which affect it can be said to be the major source of inequality and discrimination in today's Poland. It is generally accepted that 60 per cent of all occupational diseases are concentrated in the fifty largest factories and some 3 million manual workers function in conditions officially described as being 'beyond the permissible norms of health' (Wojcik, 1984, Vol. 1). In the light of this the fact that manual workers may now on an average earn more than their white-collar counterparts seems to be less than relevant. The spread of food poisoning through poor communal feeding hygiene, of hepatitis, the continuing rates of tuberculosis (22,527 new cases per annum) not to mention the fact that in Silesia 30 per cent of children in the 8–10 age range have respiratory diseases, is more than enough evidence of a major health crisis.

All these health indicators are pointing to a breakdown in the most critical area of so-called quality of life. Where a worker is confronted with a harmful domestic as well as work milieu, which affects the very survival of his or her family, then sooner or later the connection between regime priorities and their consequences for individuals will be made.

Population pressures will continue to be felt through the overstretched pre-school and elementary school system, which is already sending children to school in shifts. Hospitals which are already stretched in terms of beds and buildings, not to mention basic equipment and the supply of medicines (less than 50 per cent of medicines on the official list can be supplied), cannot cope with the growth in alcohol consumption, psychiatric illness (which increased by 20 per cent in 1983) and increasing accidents through motorization, to mention but a few.

The scale of the health crisis in Poland cannot be exaggerated. Every feature of the service is under threat of disintegration. Some examples can only impart a little of the tragedy which is compounded by and compounds the overall societal malaise.

The average age of a Polish hospital is over 65 years with 30 per cent too few beds, the latter having declined per head of population since the 1960s. Those beds that can be found stand in one-third of the area recommended by WHO (i.e. 3–4 sq.m. as opposed to 12 sq.m.) which increases in-hospital infection. There is a shortage of basic materials such as gauze and in one estimate there was one plaster per 40 beds (*Tygodnik Polski*, 13 September 1987). Inevitably this has created tensions within the medical profession and amongst auxiliary staff. The expulsion of religious orders from hospital nursing after the war as well as the undisguised attack by the regime upon the ethos and standing of the profession has had its consequences for the decline in medical ethics and the pervasiveness of bribery, payment for services by all levels of the staff and a general deterioration of doctor–patient relations. Continued underinvestment in the health sector as well as mindless decisions in the pharmaceuticals industry have combined to make even such every-day drugs as vitamin C unavailable, except for hard currency (Kuratowska, 1988). The prevalence of hepatitis A and B is as much due to the absence of disposable needles as to the generally low level of hygiene. In the case of the latter, there are only eight toilet rolls per person per annum, against a calculated requirement of twelve. This matter required the attention of a government minister and is a major indicator of the crisis. No less serious is the inability of Polish industry to supply condoms to the population despite the offer of the ubiquitous Japanese who have offered to construct a plant producing 70 million units per annum for 8 million dollars. With fifty-two admitted cases of AIDS from a test of 400,000 persons considered to be at risk, the prognosis cannot be good (*Życie Warszawy*, 15 January 1988).

Undoubtedly the health crisis goes hand-in-hand with the burgeoning environmental deterioration. The signing of an agreement between Poland, Czechoslovakia and East Germany in early 1988 to cooperate on issues of pollution is a sign of just how grave the crisis has become. Katowice is a major environmental disaster area. Occupying 2.1 per cent of Poland's land area, it receives a quarter of all the dust, gases and untreated sewage emitted into the air and rivers. Over two-thirds of the latter are little more than open sewers, whereas nearly half of all local farmland is toxically contaminated (*Panorama*, 24 January 1988). Chorzów in the Katowice region has the highest mortality rate in Poland, 14.9 per 1,000 head of population, when 10.1 was the national average in 1986.

Talk of a bill to reform the health service will be of little effect in managing the 9 million persons said to be infected with tuberculosis, since in the case of the latter it is the deterioration of living conditions affecting the oldest and the youngest, and thus the most vulnerable groups, which is the chief cause.

The scale of the crisis has found recognition at the highest levels. Speaking at the election meeting of the Katowice party conference in 1986, Jaruzelski bemoaned the shortfall in child-care facilities, emphasizing that the regime had provided in the previous five years 50 per cent more elementary schools, 80 per cent more kindergartens, 50 per cent more nurseries and 70 per cent more medical centres for the region. While this reflects the woeful under-provisioning characteristic of the 1970s, it also serves to signal the regime's rising concern as to the effects of these and other problems in the heart of the working-class constituency (*Trybuna Ludu*, 20 October 1986).

The Peasantry

When searching for a scapegoat for many of Poland's current shortcomings and social ills, politicians and pundits alike look to the enduring peasantness of Polish society.

Inter-war Poland emerged from partition with a highly differentiated peasantry. Apart from the 4 per cent of 'rich' peasants owning as they did holdings of over 15 hectares, there were the middle peasants farming on 5–15 ha and comprising 32 per cent of the total households, while the remainder struggled along at well below subsistence level. The 1921 land reform succeeded in passing 2,800,000 ha (an increase of over 14 per cent) over to the peasantry, which was less than anticipated but still no mean achievement in the circumstances. Unfortunately the outcome was further to fragment the structure of landholding and provide the post-war period with a legacy of overpopulation and unproductive small-scale, often subsistence, farming. Added to this was a growing tradition of political militancy, high levels of religiosity and institutional attachment to land and to the Church (Tomaszewski, 1974).

Following the 1944 land reforms the average size of landholding was still only 6.4 ha, but the parcelling out of most of the estates had created 3,342,000 peasant households, more than three times the pre-war figure. In the wake of the abortive attempts at collectivization in 1949–52, which came with little apparent warning and even less forethought, the agrarian structure emerged even more highly fragmented. Briefly put, in September 1956 there were all of 10,510 collective farms covering nearly 2 million hectares or about 24 per cent of the total. By the end of 1957 only 1,700 remained or slightly more than before the collectivization drive began.

Added to this, 84 per cent of arable land was now in private hands and landholding size had deteriorated to an average of 4.5 ha, some of which were nothing other than allotments. Whereas the 1950s was generally a period where the medium peasant holding predominated, since then a process of polarization has ensued and in its turn become government policy (Mazurkiewicz, 1979).

In its own way, the fragmentation of Polish agricultural holdings is a useful propaganda tool for state collectives. By and large, small is productive in the Polish case. The shortage of agricultural machines and equipment makes it impossible to think of a nation of twenty-hectare farmers. Furthermore, if we exclude the 0.5–2-ha category of farms which cover 5 per cent of area, and exclude the regions of very highly fragmented holdings (industrial areas) then 10–15 ha is in fact the predominant landholding category. As long as the heavy-industry bias starves the peasantry of even basic implements, let alone machines, then it is incumbent on observers to treat the fragmentation theory with caution. Until such a time as the leadership make available the means for developing large scale agriculture other than along the lines of the inefficient collective and state farms, then the continued structure of landholding is the most productive available. Shortcomings in agricultural self-sufficiency should be sought in broader regime policies towards individual farming rather than in the structure, which is an outcome of this policy of discrimination. This having been said the regime policy of 'kulakization' or supporting larger farms is slowly taking shape as Table 2.3 indicates.

Table 2.3 The Structure of Private Agriculture, June 1984

Year	Number of households ('000)	Households as a percentage of total by area group in ha					
		0.5–2	2–5	5–7	7–10	10–15	over 15
1970	3,224	26.9	32.0	14.4	14.1	9.8	2.8
1978	3,065	30.5	30.2	12.9	12.7	9.2	4.5
1980	2,897	30.0	29.5	12.8	13.0	9.7	5.0
1982	2,842	29.8	28.9	12.6	12.9	10.1	5.7
1984	2,844	30.1	28.3	12.5	12.8	10.3	6.0
1986	2,756	29.6	28.0	12.2	12.9	10.6	6.7

Source: *Rocznik Statystyczny* p. 279, table 8(B), and 1987, p. 290, table 7 (398) B.

It should be noted that the revised Polish constitution of 1983 guaranteed *individual* landholding and not private ownership. This is more than a semantic quibble since the ideologues emphasize that the latter refers to a capitalistic social formation with unfettered rights over property, whereas under the former the state cares for the appropriate use of land as a national good (*Kierunki*, 4 May 1986). In its attempts to push through land-concentration policies the state will use this argument more frequently. At the moment it must contend with an inherent suspicion on the part of the peasantry as to its motives which stretches back, some commentators argue, to the experience of collectivization in the eastern territories occupied in 1939 by the Soviet Union as much as to the heavy-handedness of the Six Year Plan period.

For the present, land concentration policies are stalled inexplicably by legislation which appears to make it almost impossible for those who are pressing for a more efficient structure to get their way. Critics argue that peasants sometimes spend more time travelling to their patchwork of fields than they do actually working on them. They use horses since a tractor would be too wide, even if available. Some fields are left untended since they are simply forgotten by their owners. Some of the latter do not even live in the villages whilst many peasants have alternative means of employment and thus feel little constraint to become efficient farmers. At the current rate of progress it would take an estimated seventy years to correct the most glaring examples of traditional attachments to plots of inefficient size (*Trybuna Ludu*, 13 October 1986).

From the above it is clear that the rural population of Poland is not made up solely of peasants. Of every ten non-peasant adults in the countryside, six commute to neighbouring towns to work, one is involved in work which has nothing to do with agriculture, while three are employed in jobs servicing the infrastructure of rural life and agricultural production. The other 50 per cent of the rural population are engaged in agriculture and break down as follows. The state sector with its 1,278 PGRs (Panstwowe Gospodarstwa Rolne) or state farms incorporates 8.3 per cent of this 15 million population. There are also 2,342 collective farms which account for 1.3 per cent of the agricultural community whilst the individual landholding (and leasing) peasants make up the remaining 90.4 per cent. This last class breaks down according to main source of income as follows: 30.2 per cent are full-time farmers (although internally quite differentiated in terms of income size, productivity and market sales), 31.4 per cent are considered to be peasant workers, drawing the majority of their income from agriculture, while 19.2 per cent derive the bulk of household income from non-agricultural work. Employees of various institutions with allotments measuring 0.1–0.5 ha make up the remaining 9.6 per cent (Woś, 1981).

In order to generate an income comparable to that of other socio-occupational groups it is calculated that a farm must usually be over 16 ha. There are 162,000 such landholdings (or 6 per cent) in Poland. These were the target of a *specialization* policy during the 1970s. In return for the necessary raw materials, credits and a guaranteed market from the state, a peasant agreed to specialize in a particular line of production over a number of years. The crisis of 1980 put paid to this form of direct linkage between state and individual peasant. Current land-concentration policies again envisage building on this group of landholdings and creating 450,000 core units covering 50 per cent of arable land and producing three-quarters of marketable produce.

At the other end of the spectrum are the worker-peasants from whom the 'surplus' land would be reclaimed whilst they would be encouraged to become either full-time farmers or workers.

It is generally believed that the structure of Polish agriculture has taken this form because of the availability of alternative sources of income and employment. All the evidence points to the desire on the part of heirs to these dual-occupational smallholdings to continue to bifurcate their activities. Created through forced industrialization and underurbanization, they tend to invest more in housing than farming infrastructure. They are less amenable to state control of production through the use of price policies, taxation, investment strategies and contract purchase since they can maximize income through their off-farm employment when any of the above policies is deemed by them to constitute a disincentive to agricultural production.

Similar forms of vertical integration through the state provision of services and goods ranging from coal to combine harvesters can be ignored by this group if the terms are not right.

The problem remains that any move against this increasingly large group using administrative methods might well be interpreted by the very individual farmers the state wishes to woo as a move against them all. The ensuing economically defensive behaviour would drive down production and shake what trust remained in the regime's attitude to their continued existence. Apart from that it is doubtful whether the economy could provide the investment necessary to make these larger units cost-efficient, let alone provide the urban residence, jobs and services for the millions who by moving out of small-scale agriculture would for the first time find the need for leisure and other urban services confronting them. One could well replace the 2 million horses which act as draught animals for these peasants and consume 1 ha of land for feed per head. Would the tractors and other forms of personal transport be made available? Furthermore, it is easy to point out that 45 per cent of those holdings between 0.5–2 ha produce nothing for the market, but the degree of self-provisioning is enormous and essential, given the inadequate distribution system in the Polish countryside. Currently those with more than 0.5 ha are denied a meat ration card, a recognition of just this fact.

The peasant-worker symbolically straddles a major divide which still finds the countryside chronically underprovisioned compared to urban areas. Contrary to the popular image of a rural scene sprouting with half-finished and new housing, the reality is that in terms of every 1,000 inhabitants, rural areas received 3 new housing units over the last three years, compared to 83 for the towns. These were built largely out of private funds rather than through state subsidy or direct investment. Less than 6 per cent of villages had a water mains system whilst hardly any had a communal sewage disposal. Only half of all villages could be reached by solid roads thus, not surprisingly, only a half of them had a bus stop. In the poorer regions only two-thirds of villages had a retail outlet of any variety.

Since January 1972 the peasantry has been covered by the state medical system, with free access to doctors, subsidized medication and care. The countryside is still 6,000 doctors short and there is a need for at least 1,500 new pharmacies. Only 30,000 peasants made use of subsidized sanatorium facilities, compared to 2.5 million urban residents, despite the fact that their health is now not much better, and for some age groups worse, than their urban counterparts. The advantage of longer life expectancy held over their urban peers has now been eroded and the need for geriatric care will further burden the medical services which have become understaffed largely through the retirement of women doctors who have not been replaced. Whilst rural males can expect to live 67.1 years, for women the span is 75.6, static since 1975–6 (*Rocznik Statystyczny*, 1987 p. 53). All-in-all there is increasing concern being voiced at the extension of the health crisis into the traditionally robust countryside. Despite the obvious gains in life expectancy and morbidity rates since 1944, the gap between town and country particularly in view of the deterioration of conditions in the former is becoming politically charged.

Developmental differences between urban and rural children are being attributed to poor diet in the latter. Accidents, diseases caused through poisoning by chemicals and infected life-stock all contributed to giving rural males between 15–19 and 20–30 years of age a higher mortality rate than their urban counterparts (*Odrodzenie*, 20 February 1988). The fact that as many as 45 per cent of rural inhabitants are of non-productive age combined with the under-supply of medical personnel (only 50 per cent of the required level) makes access to appropriate health care difficult (only one in a hundred private households possessed a telephone). As a consequence rural inhabitants have 2.1 visits per annum to the doctor (often a part-timer and at some distance away), whereas their urban opposite numbers go 11.1 times (*Życie Warszawy*, 17 March 1988). Whereas Poland has the highest rate of growth of heart disease in the world, Polish peasants outstrip their urban peers in both this and hypertension. Thus demands for a parity of incomes between urban and rural populations are primarily aimed at redressing the broader imbalance of deprivation and what can ultimately only be interpreted as exploitation.

In all likelihood the breakdown of the rural extended family is part of the reason for the above-mentioned shortfall in housing for young families, currently estimated to stand at over 500,000 units. Ageing parents place a further strain on the poorly developed social services. According to one estimate 720,000 peasants of pensionable age were still working their landholdings, a good proportion of them women. Since 1962 peasants have been entitled to a state pension in exchange for handing over their land to the State Land Fund. Since 1977 (with various alterations in 1980 and 1982) peasants have received the full range of state benefits on transferring their land to the state or a suitably qualified heir. Others can build up pensions by paying contributions related to the size of their holding and the sale of a minimum of produce to the state purchasing agencies—as opposed to the open market. Thus the state not only wishes to control production but also to speed up the transfer of land to younger, more energetic, farmers. As with most welfare provision it has its intrinsic and instrumental side. Doubtless a state pension will give a sense of security to its half million recipients rather than leaving them at the not too tender mercies of their relatives.

While the above moves may serve to keep some young farmers on the land, the countryside still exports its most able and educated children to the towns and into industry. Not only does it produce most of the populational growth but it hardly participates in nursery and pre-school provision, in multi-child income supplements, subsidized vacations for youth, education grants, and so on. A glance at the statistical yearbook reveals such a disparity in the allocation of benefits as to extract the statement from one official commentator that this is a 'contradiction of the Marxist principle to each according to need' which ostensibly guides the distribution of welfare if not of wages (Woś, 1981, p. 246).

During the periods of crisis, as in 1981–3, peasant incomes sometimes overtake their non-agricultural counterparts. By 1984, however, the ratio was back to 90 per cent and a price scissors was opening between agricultural prices and production means, which deeply angered the peasants and was picked up by 'their' party, the ZSL. (*Trybuna Ludu*, 18 March 1988). Nevertheless a powerful urban stereotype persists which accords high incomes to all peasants, rather than the minority, which is the reality.

Escape from rural hardship is not made any easier by the poor quality of rural education nor indeed by the system of positive discrimination aimed at easing the passage of children from rural backgrounds into higher education. This was introduced in 1965–6 (and is now being cut back) but has in fact seen the proportion of such students *drop* from 11 per cent to 7 per cent over twenty years. While peasants continue to be the strongest defenders of the points system, as it is called, there is evidence that higher education is becoming less and less attractive to what was always a highly instrumentally orientated body of students. Skilled manual and technicians jobs are now more sought after than they have ever been particularly those with earning power in the flourishing second economy or private services sector.

Cultural deprivation is part of the general underprovisioning of the countryside. One-third of villages has no library to speak of, two-thirds have no cultural centre and there are a mere 14 telephones (private and official) per 1,000 persons compared 84 per 1,000 in the towns. Mains gas reaches only 2 per cent of homes, which makes the peasants dependent upon state coal supplies, which as mentioned is frequently made conditional upon grain sales to the state sector (and often not delivered). A further 7 per cent had bathrooms and 21 per cent indoor WCs.

Many of the hardships of rural life are of necessity borne by women. An estimated 2.8 million work on holdings while 1.5 million of these run the farms almost single-handedly, as the wives of worker-peasants, as single parents or as pensioners. Whereas rural women in the 1930s were calculated to work a thirteen-hour day, half a century later sixteen hours is the norm. Not surprisingly, women are turning away from the toil of peasant life and for every 100 men migrating out of the countryside 112 women (half of them in the 15–29 age group) will also depart.

The traditional peasant family inevitably takes on new contours in the face of deprivation. Although between 84 and 98 per cent of the rural population sampled expressed positive attitudes to religion, whether in terms of deep religious conviction or, as is more likely, in terms of the ritualistic or even political meaning which it has, it is likely that the traditional affiliation of peasants to the Church will undergo a form of evolution. The moral authority of the Church in matters of everyday life for the peasant is being eroded in the face of urban secular values but in its place is emerging a form of leadership more suited to facing the problems posed by contemporary economic, political and social processes (Tygodnik Polski, 29 June 1986).

But the Church is not alone in defending the existence of individual peasant agriculture. There are many who are prepared to seize on the most unlikely allies to argue for the survival of this form of production. Indeed such production is not inimical to socialism given developments in China and in the Soviet Union itself, they would argue, and to emphasize their point they quote Gorbachëv himself:

> Genuine economic accounting, linking the income of an enterprise to the end effects, ought to become the norm for all parts of the agricultural-industrial complex, in particular the state and collective farms. Contracts for work done and the piece-work system will be widely disseminated at the level of the brigade, link and family, apportioning to them for an agreed period of time means of production including land. [*Polityka*, 7 July 1987]

The Working Class

As late as the second half of the nineteenth century and early twentieth century the infant working class in a partitioned Poland was still an island in a peasant sea. Concentrated chiefly in industry, mining and transport, it retained strong links with the countryside. Ties of upward social mobility as existed were primarily with the petty bourgeoisie. By the end of the century there were 1.2 million workers outside agriculture located in such places as Warsaw, Łódź, Zyrardów and the Dąbrów Basin. Occupational identity among miners, textile workers, and metalworkers was increasingly evident when rooted in definitive urban status and by the end of the century less dependent upon the peasant influx (Żarnowska, 1973).

Given the presence of alien capital it was not surprising that language differences overlay workplace subordination, so that nascent class conflict often surfaced as nationalistic or ethnic confrontation. Paternalism in some of these industries extended into housing, nursery and even elementary schooling provision (the latter being a distinct privilege). This in turn served to isolate sections of the working class from the less fortunate of its members. Added to this was the entrance of pauperised elements of the petty bourgeoisie and craftsmen which did little to foster the self-esteem of these factory workers and thus impeded the growth of collectivist action. Political events on the broader scale, as in 1905, injected strike militancy more quickly through nationalistic sentiment and in the process gained important rights for the working class chiefly in the Russian partition (Kalabiński, 1973).

By 1931, the number of workers, including the unemployed, domestic servants (415,000) and agricultural labourers, amounted to 4,217,000 or one-eighth of the population with attendant families. At the height of the depression unemployment was in excess of 700,000, with over a fifth of these being white-collar employees. The army of domestic servants comprised 38 per cent of all employed women. Agricultural labourers made up nearly 1.5 million (Ratyński, 1970).

However bad the situation was for the bulk of the proletariat, it compared well with the overpopulated countryside. Nevertheless, during the depression, strikes and occupations (the so-called 'Italian Strike') escalated by 1936 involving over 600,000 employees (Ciechocińska, 1965). The economic upturn and the enactment of protective legislation eased the immediate pre-war situation. By now there were well over 332 trade unions with some 941,000 members in a working class of nearly 5 million but this still only covered 15 per cent of workers in 1935 (Naumiuk, 1985; Hass 1973).

Miners and railworkers had 80–90 per cent unionization, whereas agriculture (26 per cent) and textiles (50 per cent), as would be expected, were lower.

In 1949, there were only 32 centralized trade unions covering over 90 per cent of all employees, whether worker or white-collar. Ten years later, the working class proper numbered 5 million or one-third of the population including their families. In the nature of things it was in every sense a new working class since most of the pre-war representatives had either been casualties of the war or had been absorbed by the voracious appetite of the emerging politicized bureaucracy.

Growing at the rate of 10 per cent per annum between 1947 and 1958, the new recruits from the countryside found employment without the need to raise qualifications or complete education. As a consequence, by 1958, 41.9 per cent had incomplete elementary education, bordering on illiteracy, while 47 per cent had finished this minimal level of education (Rajkiewicz, 1959). In this context the widespread and spontaneous growth of workers' councils between 1956 and 1958 can only be treated as the beginning of a process wherein sections of the working class moved from being objects to subjects, initiators rather than mere pawns within the modernization process. By 1978 only 4.9 per cent of workers had incomplete elementary education, with 54.2 per cent complete, while a new group had emerged, namely those 35.1 per cent with basic vocational training (skilled workers). A further 5.3 per cent had secondary vocational training.

Differences in education have been shown to influence lifestyle, socio-political involvement and the perception of deprivation. Given the same per-capita income, consumption patterns depend to a degree on level of education. However, it is the relatively highly educated workers, those with secondary education, that have given most evidence of a qualitative change in the nature of working-class evolution. It was these workers who came to the fore in 1980, as an analysis of delegates and officers to the 1981 Solidarity Congress indicated (Kulpińska, 1985).

Of those with vocational training nearly half are under 35 years of age. These are workers who are not only better educated and proletarian more by choice than by default but also have grown up in a communist Poland, have not known the pathologies of Stalinism at first hand and, most importantly, have sampled the successes of autonomous association in independent unions and the feel of workers' power.

In a youthful population, young workers predominate among those under 29 years of age and increasingly they are second generation working-class families. Thus of the 15–19 age group, 65 per cent came from working class backgrounds, compared to 49 per cent of those aged 25–29. Given the decline in upward social mobility opportunities (which may briefly reappear during the normalization process after 1981) these workers are all the more likely to be critical of the conditions within which they live and work and of those whose ostensible role it is to represent their interests. Tellingly perhaps, 70 per cent of workers sampled in one study said that they would not wish their children to follow in their footsteps; 95 per cent of the intelligentsia likewise would be averse to their children being downwardly mobile into the working class (*Życie Partii*, 1 January 1986).

This attitude is made all the more comprehensible when the prospects associated with working-class membership are considered. At the last census those occupying manual worker positions (for officially the category 'worker' no longer exists except in ideological debates) numbered 7,893,269 persons in 1978, of whom 2,700,000 were women. This working class can be divided into the 47.8 per cent of its members who are employed in socio-economically and geographically concentrated industries, and the 30.1 per cent employed in the other so-called sphere of material production—building and public works, trade and transport.

Industry has at least 1,200 fatalities at work per annum, 100,000 take invalidity pensions each year, and every day over 2.2 million out of a total work-force of 11.5 million in the state sector are absent. This last figure includes those on maternity leave, taking holidays etc. But those on sick leave account for 22 per cent of the total work time lost each day. In 1982 sickness benefits for the first three days of absence were cut in an effort to counter what appeared to be malingering. Since then the emergence of the real picture of workers' health and the fact that workers themselves rate *health* as *the* major value in their lives (over housing, family, and so on), has put this in its proper perspective. The picture is particularly bleak in those industries euphemistically termed 'light', 'where nearly all the women employed work at the extreme of their physical capacities' (*Związkowiec*, 24 November 1985).

Here, as in other underinvested non-priority industries such as textiles, medical care is geared to lowering the number of days officially taken off and to underreporting in-factory accidents rather than tending to chronic disease. Statistics on health in the Gdańsk area revealed that as many as 23 per cent of male workers had chronic illnesses, as did 37 per cent of female dockers (Wojcik, Vol. I, 1984). The fact that individuals could be disqualified from certain types of work on health grounds (*sic*) in fact lowers the actual statistics. Young workers are already at a disadvantage compared to their white-collar peers prior to taking up debilitating work. Comparisons of students going to vocational as opposed to largely white-collar lyceum schools have revealed a deficit in 'developmental' terms as high as ten months. More graphically perhaps, one study of youths intending to start vocational training in a building school revealed that 36 per cent of those examined required treatment and/or removal of eight or more teeth. Whilst this may well reflect the already mentioned deficit of dentists and health care in the countryside, it also highlights the fact that, in health terms, class membership will be more important a determinant than social origins.

The burgeoning environmental crisis means that the worker has no respite from deteriorating work conditions when at home. It is estimated that 23 of 49 *województwa* in Poland now contain regions under serious ecological threat. They cover 43.6 per cent of land area and house 58.6 per cent of the population. Eight of these are considered disaster areas. These regions have nearly 8,000 factories with untreated sewage waste and 800 doing particular damage to the atmosphere. Most of the 5 million tonnes of dust and gass pollutants emerged from these factories. The worst areas house 2.3 million workers in 13,000 factories or mines.

A large proportion of the land in the most polluted 10 per cent is unfit for food production, given the high levels of cadmium and lead in the soils. This points to a very real threat to Poland's efforts at agricultural self-sufficiency. Schools, hospitals and whole housing estates are accordingly now illegally located but most of the residents have nowhere else to live. With only 200 or so employed to administer a law on the environment which is itself considered ineffectual, the prognosis is not good. The law does not formulate rules of behaviour nor provide for sanctions in cases of infringement. It is little wonder, therefore, that in the words of an official pronouncement surveying these data 'we have found ourselves on the brink of an ecological catastrophe' (Wojcik, 1985, Vol. 5).

It comes as no surprise therefore to learn that 55 per cent of one sample of workers considered themselves to be the worst off group in society, ahead of the pensioner (28 per cent) or the multi-child family (7 per cent) (*Życie Warszawy*, 20 August 1985). Particular deprivation was experienced by those workers with no additional source of income, something which, as in Hungary and elsewhere, is emerging as a new dimension of stratification. This is a society where 45 per cent of industrial workers and engineering staff were officially found to engage in activity generating additional income and which extends their working day to ten hours and a further 45 per cent over ten hours. Often this activity is now aimed at maintaining a particular living standard rather than improving upon it (*Słowo Powszechne*, 31 October–2 November 1986). Added to this, poor work organization loses twice as many hours from the working day as absence through illness. This is a continuing source of frustration to workers who are encouraged to raise their level of productivity and thus their incomes and yet are unable to do so. As a consequence they continue to demand an organization which is exclusively theirs (79 per cent), that is, craft based unions rather than the type of union which represents the whole work-force or a branch of industry (*Związkowiec*, 21 July 1985).

Such representation, as much as trade union pluralism in the sense of the re-establishment of Solidarity in some form or another, is becoming all the more necessary as wage inequalities within the working class open up. The ratio of average to maximum pay for workers was 1:4.64 and 1:7.05 for non-workers in March 1986 (*Perspektywy*, 5 December 1986). For example, miners could earn from 64,741 złotys per month up to 106,000 zł. per month (admittedly for a six- or seven-day week). Note that the average per-capita income for all employee families was a little over 12,500 zł. per month and some 33 per cent of the population received less than 8,000 zł. per month, not enough to keep them above the poverty line as set by the planners (*Słowo Powszechne*, 28–30 November 1986). Whereas much is made of factory managers who earn less than a considerable proportion of their subordinates, this overlooks the fact that such a manager can earn 40,000 zł. per month or 139,000 zł. per month—and this from one job. The situation is further confused by the complex nature of the wages system. Anything from 20 to 85 per cent of the take-home pay of a worker may represent basic salary, whilst the remainder is made up of premiums, piece-work rates and a whole variety of extra payments the calculation of which is often beyond the grasp of its recipient. Enterprise directors for their part receive premium payments which are largely kept secret.

To cap it all, whilst only 36 of the official 46 hours of the working week were actually given over to production, on a national scale work time was overfulfilled by 143 per cent, representing overtime employment. The authorities hope that the further introduction of the Soviet-style work brigades or collectives will make the connection between effort and reward more tangible. For the much vaunted egalitarianism of Polish workers is less concerned with achieving equality of condition or even of opportunity as with the *criteria* of inequality and the regime policies which determine these criteria. In point of fact workers are less egalitarian now than they were in 1980 and 35 per cent (as compared to 8.5 per cent in 1980) expressed opposition to the idea of limiting maximum incomes (Kolarska-Bobińska, 1985). They appear to support income inequalities when these are based on risk-taking in *legal* activities, in which hard work and imagination are essential components. Conversely the exploitation of official position, of shortages or the philosophy of the 'fast buck' draws increased demands for state control.

The same applies to the thorny issue of housing provision (see above) which the regime has had to address by instituting close scrutiny of the correctness of housing allocation. Of manual worker households with school-age children in the 1970s, over 50 per cent lived in one- or two-room units sharing many of the basic facilities such as kitchens and bathrooms (Malanowski, 1981). Since 1978 the size of the average Polish household has expanded from 3.11 persons to an estimated 3.30 in 1984. So great an increase over such a short time span is only in part explained by the birth rate. It was primarily due to the decline in new independent *households* (not families) set up due to the housing shortage.

Herein was to be found an explanation of how it came about that despite the severity of the economic crisis the prevalence of articles such as colour TVs, automatic washing machines and even automobiles *per household* actually increased. The official statisticians, whose propensity to find a silver lining in every cloud continues to receive official censure from the highest Polish authorities, did not differentiate extended multi-family units joining together to survive the crisis from the usual nuclear family. They even had the temerity to suggest an improvement in terms of the number of households actually occupying a single housing unit, despite the self-evident growing divergence between the 300,000 new marriages entered into and the projected construction of 200,000 housing units during 1987 (an optimistic figure by previous experience).

It is not surprising, therefore, that housing provides such a powerful incentive as well as a potent sanction for exacting discipline over those awaiting provision. Of the western industrialized countries only Ireland has more persons per housing unit than Poland but the area of living space is larger (the figures for Poland are given in Table 2.4) Of the socialist countries only the USSR and Romania had a higher concentration of persons per square metre. The private sector produces over half the total living space, despite the chronic shortage of raw materials and land shortage in prime sites, not to mention the absence of infrastructure. Even if the working class were to be given greater access to housing in whatever sector, the tendency towards removing subsidies from most forms of provision will make it increasingly difficult for them to do other than wait. Inevitably they have to therefore sacrifice a considerable proportion of their leisure time on travel to work. While as many as 25 per cent of employee households have a car, they tend to be white-collar households and this, seen against the underinvestment in public transport, signifies yet another area of inequality. Just how important this dimension of inequality is, can be shown by the fact that morbidity rates are affected by distance travelled to work, given the state of rail and road transport. While workers take up the use of sanatorium facilities to offset

Table 2.4 Density of Housing Occupation

	Average no. of rooms per unit	Average no. of persons per unit	Average no. of persons per room	Average living space per unit (²)	Average living space per person (M^2)
1960	2.46	4.08	1.66	n.a.	n.a.
1970	2.87	3.94	1.37	50.7	12.9
1978	3.15	3.66	1.16	53.9	14.7
1984	3.31	3.53	1.07	55.6	15.8
1986	3.27	3.37	1.03	56.0	16.6
Town	3.20	3.13	0.98	51.5	16.4
Country	3.41	3.79	0.90	64.2	16.9

Source: *Kierunki*, January 1986; *Rocznik Statystyczny*, 1987, p. 439, Table 6.

some these effects, almost equally with white-collar employees, their needs as well as their numbers are considerably greater. It is these hidden areas of inequality referred to by Szelenyi and others (Szelenyi, 1979) which are the outcome of state redistributive policies and will increasingly become the object of conflict as the economic stringency measures demanded of Poland by IMF, World Bank and the Soviet Union cut away the panoply of state subsidy.

This is a young working class, 42 per cent of its members being under thirty years of age. Surprisingly perhaps, they show a high level of religiosity, some 70 per cent of them in 1984 declaring a tie to the Church (*Trybuna Opolska*, 31 May 1985). On the other hand, their level of participation in the structures of the PZPR leaves the authorities with a major problem. Whereas the number of workers in the party dropped from over 1,422,000 in 1980 to 810,000 in 1986, as a proportion they declined from 46 per cent to 36 per cent of the total membership. At this point it is wise to remember the strictures concerning the class make-up of party figures which allow for a considerable amount of flexibility (Malanowski, 1981). Of the party membership that remains, only a minority of the 7.5 per cent considered to be young members are in fact workers. This is the third political generation within the post-war working class, each of which has experienced economic growth and crisis (*Życie Partii*, 12 September 1984). What can be expected of them? In a study carried out among these young workers in the 18–26 age range in mid-1984 and drawn from the largest and best-known factories and enterprises, a far from rosy picture was painted of the future. While most declared themselves for socialism, it had to be authentic, democratic and not the state of affairs which had become synonymous with economic problems and social policies gone awry. Criticism of the government was pretty universal and the respondents placed little store by the array of socio-political institutions being constructed by the post-martial law regime. Most feared a return to the traditional centralized model of exercising power and they certainly did not feel that they constituted a ruling class. Over 70 per cent of them were put off participating in societal activities, despite recognizing the need for such involvement. This was partly due to the fact that they felt they had little chance of influencing the course of events—a form of fatalism evident among all youth—while the statutory bodies entrusted to represent their interests did not do so, including the trade unions (*Życie Warszawy*, 7 May 1985). This sense of privatization and withdrawal from public life was underlined by the mere 11 per cent who showed any interest in future political careers, whilst a mere 1.8 per cent looked to the achievement of a managerial position! More and more the need to guarantee financial success does not imply a career within the official hierarchy. Given that the most important material values such as housing or a car are in the gift of state distribution rather than personal attainment, which is in turn related to the official position, this represents a significant rejection of the state-sponsored consumption values of the 1970s and the development of more privatized means of achievement rejecting incorporation and positing some form of self-help. This may merely be a reflection of the poverty of material inducements left to the state or the gradual abandonment of support among the young working class for this discredited reward system, the so called egalitarian-etatist, in favour of inegalitarian-market.

At this point it should be mentioned that many of these values are associated with key 1980–1 attributes. Past Solidarity membership, present membership of the official unions, membership of the PZPR after 1981 all contribute to the formation of a new syndrome of attitudes. Egalitarian, that is to say, pro-centralist attitudes, anti-private sector, anti-self-help, anti-self-management, pro-party, all these 'conservative' attitudes have become clearer in the face of the pro-reform (that is, decentralist) attitudes which seek a loosening up of the 'welfare' and reward system, the introduction of a degree of uncertainty provided it can shorten the deferred gratification time-scale contained within the traditional system (*Tygodnik Powszechny*, 24 August 1986).

All this is part of a process begun during the 1980–1 period which can best be termed the 'renegotiation of the social compact', that tenuous implicit agreement arrived at during the early period of the formation of the regime. In this process, in exchange for relative political passivity, the regime guaranteed a certain level of social benefits, did not exact high levels of productivity or industrial discipline and provided an umbrella of certainty over the hardships of everyday life. Since then this compact has outlived its usefulness to both regime and society, not least due to the constraints of the economic crisis. Political docility in the post-Solidarity generations, polarized as they are (Jasziewicz, 1986), cannot be expected. Likewise there is a tendency to elevate the symbolically powerful institutions such as the Church and self-management over existing state institutions such as Army and Sejm while at the same time promoting social self-organization. Youth religiosity stands at 85 per cent with 40 per cent actively engaged in various church-sponsored organizations (*Zarządzanie*, No. 1, 1988). Although the state is still perceived as the initiator and executor of reform (a reflection of the Solidarity sentiment of 'no responsibility without power'), the doubts as to its effectiveness and indeed likely consequences even if half successful, place a premium on individual, privatized and low-level collective action

(Morawski, 1986). If economic uncertainty in the form of inequality, limited unemployment or industrial restructuring, greater levels of downward mobility, and so on, become more prevalent then in all likelihood political uncertainty will also increase. Vigorous interest articulation both through and outside of existing institutional forms, of which there are many, will have to become routinized if the inevitable social conflict is to be managed. In this the key actor will be the working class although it will be the intelligentsia which may once again provide the clearest message of discontent.

The Intelligentsia

The attraction of white-collar non-manual work carrying the possibility of intelligentsia status and group membership, although slightly diminished in the era of austerity, continues to exert a strong influence on the pattern of social stratification. Most Poles look back to a peasant past and forward to a white-collar future. How otherwise does one explain the fact that of the 49 *województwo* PZPR first secretaries, 48 of them had degrees (one was just completing his in 1987) with at least 3 PhDs, and yet felt obliged to claim some token link with the working class, either through birth or through a brief interlude as a manual worker during their political careers. Forty years of pro-worker ideology coupled with anti-worker practice, overlaid with intelligentsia pretentions, had all but destroyed the self-esteem of the working class. That is until it was temporarily at least salvaged by the projection of the positive stereotypes, emerging out of the Polish August, of an articulate, determined and socially responsible working class.

Before looking at the changing nature of the educational system and career placement a few words have to be said as to the origins of the intelligentsia category and its associated 'cultural coefficient', as Florian Znaniecki would have called it, and the hold it has on the Polish psyche (Znaniecki, 1952).

It was a student of Znaniecki, one Jozef Chałasinski (1946) who provided the most accurate and useful account of the emergence and formation of this elusive social stratum. As a social type, the *inteligencja* was tied to a particular social milieu, to a certain collective lifestyle and contained within the confines of a specific socio-cultural formation. To the social terrain within which the intelligentsia moved, Chałasinski accorded the term 'ghetto'. This captures nicely the sense of social competition and exclusion which underlay intelligentsia mores. It was with the landed gentry and aristocracy that the intelligentsia competed (largely due to their own origins in that society) while the mechanisms of exclusion were employed against the working classes, peasantry and petty bourgeoisie. Through their social manners, emphasis upon proper upbringing and the primacy of 'salon culture', the intelligentsia sought to compensate for their lack of an economic base to their social position. Being a by-product of arrested capitalist development and in the absence of a strong indigenous bourgeoisie, as a group they were often portrayed as parasites of the foreign capital which dominated their partitioned country. They nevertheless saw themselves as essential components of their society for that same reason, charged with the mission of preserving national identity, the Polish soul, in the face of Prussification or Russianization. In this can be found the antipathy to those facets of life related to industry and economic entrepreneurship. Along with the peasantry, they are blamed for the lack of a technical culture and the overemphasis on the humanities at the expense of applied science. This dichotomy between an ideal-spiritual culture, on the one hand, and a material culture, on the other, was a manifestation of the juxtaposition of the intelligentsia to the masses. Elitist elements of the intelligentsia ethos still persist alongside its concern for democractic freedoms (all too often rooted in the *szlachta* or gentry's archaic practice of *liberum veto*, their detractors would claim) (Czepulis-Rastenis, 1973).

The history of the intelligentsia, intertwined as it is with national uprisings (romantic or foolhardy depending upon your point of view), was always concerned with the idea of the Polish nation. The upheavals of the early 1980s have seen the reconstruction of this intelligentsia, or so some Polish commentators would us believe. Comprised in the main of peasants' and workers' sons and daughters, through a curious process of cultural syncretism they have taken unto themselves the values of democracy, patriotism and the moral leadership of the nation with the purpose of formulating and preserving national identity in the new order of things (Jerschina, 1983).

It should be noted that in 1939 they constituted 6 per cent of the total population or two million employees and yet their social weight was considerably greater than their numerical representation. Whereas the tenure of a *matura* or school-leaving certificate was usually a necessary if not sufficient condition for access to the intelligentsia in the inter-war period, the inflation of credentials now requires higher education as the necessary *titre d'entrée*. The 1983 cadres census identified over 1 million people with higher education qualifications employed within the socialized economy or one-twelfth of all employees. Of these 32.5 per cent were engineers, 17.2 per cent were trained in the humanities, while economists, medical graduates and lawyers each comprised 10 per cent of the total. There are, in the nature of things, individuals with higher education occupying positions officially designated as worker, and, to confuse the picture further, in 1983 there were 1,358,000 positions requiring higher education but with some filled by underqualified incumbents. Thus, 68,400 graduates were doing jobs below their educational level (the proverbial well-informed and eloquent taxi-driver), while at least 30,000 held worker positions! Whilst this may come as no surprise to the western reader the potential unintended consequences of such a seeding of the socialist proletariat can be a cause for concern for the regime. More normal is the phenomenon where graduates take up positions which have little or nothing to do with their training, pointing to a quite high degree of flexibility and inefficiency within the educational system (this includes 30 per cent of all pure scientists, lawyers and economists, not to mention the 50 per cent of humanities graduates) (*Rada Narodowa-Gospodarka-Administracja*, 9 February 1985).

If remnants of an intelligentsia culture persist in today's Poland they are usually to be identified in the outward trappings of supposed good manners rather than in the internal predelictions of the soul. Courtesy habits tied to flowers, chocolates and elaborate hand-kissing, not to mention the universal title of *pan* (or 'sir') accorded to those of more distant acquaintance, often compensate for the brutality of interpersonal relations which are the often decried norm. Gift-giving shades imperceptibly into full-blown bribery, fashion, custom and convention all rolled into one. However, the intelligentsia boycott after martial-law of regime institutions may serve to reconstruct a more flattering stance.

Intelligentsia status continues to be signified in part through birth, reflecting an exclusionary mechanism aimed at the practice of the post-war regime, of rapid promotion and educational shortcuts. This was made necessary by the need to reproduce physically an intelligentsia, few of whose 85,000 members trained in the inter-war period had survived. In 1945, the total educated population, that is, those with higher *and* secondary education of some kind, amounted to 100,000 people. Of these 32,000 or so had an engineering technical background. Faced with the task of literally rebuilding Poland, the regime took the opportunity of creating not only its own working class but also a socialist intelligentsia by controlling the channels of upward social mobility.

Favouritism was shown to the active supporters of the infant and largely alien regime. Political qualifications almost completely supplanted educational criteria in terms of access to educational facilities, the former often being read off from an individual's social origins. New schools and colleges aimed at training engineers, lawyers, judges and prosecutors were set up and the burgeoning police and military services opened up new avenues of social mobility. The state administration provided at least 100,000 new positions for those willing and able to express their loyalty to the new order. Between 1945 and 1962, of the 300,000 graduates produced by the higher education system, 55 per cent were of worker or peasant origin, compared to 15 per cent in the 1930s (and 50 per cent in 1984). Children of white-collar families continued to gain access to higher education at much the same rate as between the wars, 40 per cent or thereabouts. It was the children of the 'bourgeois landowning and in some cases petty bourgeois' classes who were replaced by the new arrivals (Hryniewicz, 1985). A major change in recruitment was brought about by the loss of Poland's Jewish population which had provided a significant proportion of lawyers, doctors and other professionals in the inter-war period (since other careers were often closed to them).

The intelligentsia drawn from the masses has continued to place great store by the symbolic value of educational title. From Gierek's much publicized degree received at the Mining and Steel Academy to the present military and party leadership, where fifteen of the 230 members of the Central Committee of the PZPR bear the title of professor, the prime minister and foreign minister amongst them (*Polityka*, 12 July 1986), the marriage of political power and social honour or prestige is consummated.

The penchant of regime leaders to surround themselves with academic advisory committees, propagate consultation through the questionnaire rather than give room for popular democracy does not, however, indicate a reappraisal or promotion of the role of the intelligentsia in Polish society.

By and large there exists a society-wide sense of mistrust between the intelligentsia and the leadership in the wake of martial law (*Tygodnik Demokratyczny*, 13 May 1986). Indicators of regime loyalty such as party membership or recruitment into the new trade unions are particularly low in the universities, the medical service and the artistic professions. Internal migration as well as emigration (20,000 engineers and technicians, 3,000 medical doctors have left since 1981), retreat into the family and close occupational milieu have been accompanied by a visible process of material impoverishment and relegation down the ladder of official wages. Conflicts over control of the universities, appointments of university rectors and interference in the workings of cultural organizations are the more obvious areas of conflict.

During the period 1980–3, the average real monthly earnings of academics fell by 34 per cent, that of manual workers by 21 per cent and that of clerical-administrative staff by 14 per cent. By 1984, therefore, those working in higher education earned 15 per cent below the national average and 25 per cent below that of workers in production. While the situation has improved, there can be little doubt that a major reordering of official incomes has taken place during the last five years. Despite this, the ranks of the working class still advertise many vacancies whilst the white-collar occupations continue to grow much to the annoyance of the former. Although it is too early to write of a divergence of interests between the bulk of the intelligentsia and the regime or the party-state apparatus, internal differentiation along economic lines is being bolstered by political changes. The usual model of the intelligentsia referred to (1) the creators and popularizers of aesthetic and humanistic values; (2) engineers, scientists and those involved in production; (3) the non-technical occupations and professions; (4) the managers and administrators associated with the economic apparatus; and (5) low-grade routine white-collar employees (Widerszpil, 1979). This is no longer a very useful categorization.

The impact of the second economy and market reforms, the decline in educational aspirations caused in part by the economic demotion of certain graduate professions, the cutback of privileges to be extracted from *nomenklatura* status within the party, these and other processes have over the last few years begun to deconstruct the ordered world of the intelligentsia. Catholics, Marxists, Party and PRON membership have all taken on political weight since 1981, and altered the pattern of life chances. Foreign earnings and travel, independent means however achieved, involvement in the flourishing private sector are new criteria by which status will sooner or later come to be accorded. Of equal importance will be the political dimension. There is undoubtedly a regime intelligentsia created through continuing political patronage tied to the party-state hierarchy and amongst the generally accepted 20–25 (*Polacy '84*, 1985) per cent of those considered to be regime supporters. This form of sponsored mobility will continue to recruit individuals into the administrative and apparatus sections of the party-state. At the other extreme it was found that 70 per cent of those considered to belong to the wealthiest group of the population, those with an annual income of over 1 million złotys, were themselves graduates often engineers rather than the stereotype of private sector artisans or service providers (*Polityka*, 15 February 1986).

Another section of the intelligentsia, which either cannot or will not participate in the previous two forms of career development will come to form a political-cultural segment, existing largely outside of the *nomenklatura*, having opposition loyalties or Church affiliation, subject to strong peer-group pressure and working strictly by academic-professional criteria of integrity and propriety. In many ways this represents a routinization of the more extreme cultural boycott enacted in the aftermath of martial law which, while much diluted, still emphasizes certain key values pertaining to professional behaviour. Finally there is a large group of the young intelligentsia (25 per cent) who seek to emigrate.

A more oblique view of the changing priorities of the regime towards the intelligentsia can be found in the area of publishing. Whereas in 1935 the total number of book titles, brochures and journals published was 11,609, in 1985 the figure was 9,690. Of course even this does not signify the very real shortfall, as a brief examination of unsold stocks on the shelves would underline. As for the area of literature proper, 'belles-lettres', the pre-war figure was 2,010 (1938) whereas in 1985 it was 1,517 titles published. In the field of scientific publishing, in 1985 there were 2,635 titles published whereas before the war (1938) 3,491 titles were produced. As for textbooks, before the war there were 1,087 texts available to the 50,000 or so students and few thousand academic staff. Today the figure is 1,557 for a student body of 340,000 undergraduates and 65,000 staff. Poland is in the company of Romania when the quality and variety of books available is taken as an indicator of regime commitment to education (*Tygodnik Powszechny*, 29 June 1986). From this point of view the 690 books published by the underground since 1982 must be seen as a godsend.

Education

Perhaps nowhere were the consequences of Nazi occupation felt more keenly than in the sphere of education. Over 16,000 teachers were lost, 60 per cent of the educational infrastructure and a mammoth 95 per cent of the schoolbooks destroyed. The higher education sector fared little better. The incoming regime was committed to the introduction of free educational provision and the gradual elimination of the private sector of education. At the elementary level, by 1950, 98 per cent of children in the 7–13 age range were being catered for in a seven-year programme. Teachers were mass produced through shortened schemes of intensive training. This, as with similar exercises elsewhere, was to have negative consequences in the future. Secondary schools which had always been rather elitist establishments were taken over by the state and some new ones relocated in working-class areas to make them spatially as well as socially accessible to the new working class. Vocational education was given especial priority and was intended to supersede the more traditional general lyceum. Higher education was opened up and expanded and here once again technical training came to the fore. By 1951 there were eighty-two establishments of higher education with a total of 141,000 students, whereas in 1937 there had been only thirty-two centres dealing with 47,000 students. As previously noted, by 1951, a high point, 35.8 per cent of students came from working-class backgrounds, whereas 24.1 per cent were of peasant origins. These were distributed through the full-time, part-time and 'correspondence' course sectors.

An educational reform enacted in 1961 provided for eight years' compulsory elementary schooling, to which could be added three years' elementary vocational training as well as two years' factory-based training (often remedial to the elementary grades for the poorer students). The major conduit to higher education was the four-year general secondary school or lyceum which provided over 70 per cent of the first-year intake into full-time higher education. In some respects, however, the centre of gravity in education is shifting in the direction of the *technikum*, where a course of between four and six years can be followed, taking students from elementary vocational schools, for example, and providing them with an extra three years' training. This having been said, both the *technikum* and the four- to five-year secondary vocational schools, which between them are becoming the prime socializing vehicle for the future skilled working class, do not really provide for entry into higher education itself, as they were intended to.

During the overambitious years of the 1970s, the regime, in keeping with its propaganda of success, proposed the introduction of a common ten-year system of schooling to replace the patchwork of institutions which had existed to date (Szczepański, 1973). This was considered to be more commensurate with the status of Poland as an advanced industrial society and would also bring it into line with the Soviet system. Along with many other grand ideas, this was scrapped in 1982 and the emphasis shifted to changing the content of the curriculum rather than the structure. This was deemed necessary given the serious shortcomings in political socialization, historical awareness and citizen values as seen by the regime. Along the way to the abortive reform, rural schooling and teacher training had fallen casualty to shortsighted measures not least of which was the closure of all but one of the teacher training colleges by 1981.

As it now stands the educational structure is characterized by certain dimensions of inequality. The non-compulsory kindergarten from age three can cope with 43 per cent of the urban cohort and 19.1 per cent of their rural peers. Given the increasing tendency to impose basic teaching tasks on the pre-school sector (not least the so-called 'zero' level at age six) this is a likely source of disadvantage located at the very start of the educational ladder. As for nursery care, less than 5 per cent of women can avail themselves of this, so that 54 per cent of young married women with children leave work. If they cannot or do not wish to interrupt their careers then they have to look to private child-care or nursery provision which is beyond the means of all but the most affluent of dual-income households. At least 1,600 new kindergartens were estimated to be required in order to make up the projected shortfall for the 1986–90 period (*Polityka*, 29 November 1986).

Of those who successfully complete their eight grades of elementary education (and some 2 per cent or 150,000 rural youth do not) 4 per cent will not go on to any form of secondary schooling, and these are again chiefly peasant children. A full 78 per cent carry on into vocational training, 60 per cent at the elementary level. Of the latter, only 10 per cent will actually complete secondary education while the remainder will emerge as skilled workers with diplomas.

Since 1981 the percentage of elementary school children continuing into secondary education has dropped rather than risen. Increasingly parents and students, and especially those from rural backgrounds, are placing greater emphasis upon immediate skills rather than deferring entry into the labour market. In fact a drop of 30 per cent in aspirations for higher education has occurred over the last few years (*Radar*, 14 February 1985).

Those with *technikum* diplomas now do not feel the need to try for higher education and engineering degrees. Conversely there is some evidence that skilled workers would like *their* children to enter higher education: particularly the 61.5 per cent in one study who had wives with secondary or even higher educational qualifications (*Życie Warszsawy*, 4 April 1985). Technician and skilled-worker status has continued to rise since the 1960s while that of the unskilled manual and clerical worker has declined. Women predominate as the one-quarter of technical graduates grouped in bookkeeping, education and health and welfare (*Rocznik Statystyczny*, 1985, p. 459). New 'skilled' occupations synonymous with large incomes, such as taxi-driving and flower-growing, have along with private sector work disturbed the picture of prestige scales.

Vocational education providing two or three days' practical training per week is closely linked to industry. However, the nature of the tie raises the suspicion that this is simply a way of using students as a form of cheap labour. How else could one explain the 530 narrow specialities being offered by these factories which seem to fit the production needs of the enterprise rather than the educational priorities of worker training? Elsewhere, in an effort to make up for the Solidarity socializing effect, the regime introduced new elements into the school curriculum. Not only has this lengthened the school day to thirty-five or thirty-six hours per week (entailing the extension of the shift system) but some of the subjects are also highly controversial. Not the least of these has been the proposed course on religion taught in a 'scientific' and comparative vein trying in an effort to loosen the Church's grip on Poland's youth. Other new topics relating to the principles of law and legal awareness, ethics and environmental protection are aimed at either inculcating a respect for the civil authorities or else paying lip-service to the problems of Poland's future. Sex education appears to be no less contentious an issue between Church and State.

If the shift from general lyceum schooling to vocational training continues and the working class and peasantry gradually lose the high level of interest in higher education then not only will this serve to harden class boundaries but it will also finally consign to the history books the system of positive discrimination practised over the last twenty years aimed at recruiting a more representative cross-section of the population into the student body.

Introduced in 1965–6 the points system, as it was called, gave additional weighting to specific categories of individual seeking access to higher education after the successful completion of their *matura*. Orphans, conscripts after military service, scout masters, those who had worked as ward orderlies in hospitals or teachers in the countryside, as well as those from manual worker and peasant backgrounds, were given additional credits which could offset poorer exam performance. In a much publicized exercise of social consultation, over three-quarters of respondents were in favour of abolishing positive discrimination (*Kierunki*, 9 February 1986). Paradoxically the greatest opposition to such assistance seemed to come from those who have themselves benefited in the past and who now find that their children are at a disadvantage, due to their self-same success. They, as new entrants themselves, are not sufficiently part of the intelligentsia milieu and are unable to compensate for this now reversed discrimination through environment, contacts and other intangibles of lifestyle. Since 1987 the so-called points system has applied to only a minority of subjects at university and since 1988 been replaced by the rector's 'pool' of 20 per cent of places, which is much the same thing except that now the discrimatory criteria are less clear (*Słowo Powszechne*, 1 January 1988).

There is little doubt that the younger generation of workers have more instrumental attitudes to work than their parents and consequently are more critical of the wages system as it exists. They recognize that work is stultifying, with little scope for development, and they place greater scope on such values as health and housing (*Praca i Zabezpieczenie Spoleczne*, August 1986). This, tied to the emerging patterns of stratification as reflected in educational mobility, will make them more reflective in how they view their position as workers within the workplace and home milieu. Orientation will be less vertical than lateral, something which will pose new problems for the planners, as both workers and engineers express considerably greater satisfaction with family life and social contacts than with so-called 'public life', i.e. relations with authorities (Wnuk-Lipiński, 1987).

Inequality and Poverty

All the above processes are occurring against the backdrop of generally admitted poverty, with Poles being asked directly through a referendum once again to tighten their belts and roll up their sleeves in another exercise in deferred gratification. This time, however, the goal is to achieve not some future standard of living but merely to return to the 1978 level of consumption. The spectrum of expectations, however, the generational and demographic picture, not to mention the political memories, are very different. Not least of these is the presence of a section of the population who are very much the victims of the economic profligacy of the 1970s. Even in those years patterns of poverty were emerging which discriminated against multi-child families, the 2 million invalids, the single parents and the pensioners. In part this was disguised by the propaganda of success which highlighted the technocrat, the artist and the successful private artisan. Where there was redistribution in the shape of health, education, housing and other subsidized facilities these ultimately preferred the higher-income groups (*Tygodnik Demokratyczny*, 9 September 1984), and embellished the already growing cumulative inequality.

In the early 1980s the Central Statistical Office calculated that at least 19 per cent of all families were in a state of poverty, while 7 per cent could be called wealthy. The official unions did their own study and found that 20 per cent of all employee households *and* 40 per cent of pensioner households fell below the so-called social minimum. By 1987, 60 per cent were considered poor, 14 per cent well-off, the remainder surviving (Wnuk-Lipiński, 1988). The social minimum refers to a 'basket' of goods and services deemed by its compositors as necessary within the 'given conditions for correct socio-biological development and functioning for an individual and family' (*Odrodzenie*, 20 April 1986). This instrument has existed for some years but has only become public since 1986. Among its shortcomings are the fact that it does not take into account the availability of the goods and services it stipulates, a major shortcoming in a society characterized by repressed inflation and long queues, both visible and invisible. Furthermore, it is calculated on the basis of actual expenditure rather than in terms of wages and benefits. Savings, charitable contributions by non-state agencies, and donations from relatives living abroad are all taken into account and thus formally recognized. The social minimum is now 12,500 zł. per month (1987), the minimum wage 7,000 zł. per month. The latter is so much lower because it is in part responsible for fixing the level of other social benefits. What it does not deal with is direct redistribution through the workplace, an increasingly important source of inequality. Here various occupational charters or collective contracts accord relative privilege to groups such as miners, bakers, meat-industry employees, and health-service workers. Access to sanatoria, subsidized vacations, allotments and other goods are in the gift of the workplace (either union, management or self-management) and therefore reflect differences between enterprises, sectors of industry and occupational groups. They demonstrate the ability of some to defend their position whilst others go to the wall. At least 40 per cent of families with three or more children, some 4 million persons, are living in poverty, as are one-third of single-parent families. The effect is immediately obvious. It is from the 8 per cent of the population with the lowest per-capita income that 32 per cent of infant mortality derives and among the 2 per cent of families with less than 5 square metres of living space per person that 14 per cent of the infant mortality can be found (*Przegląd Tygodniowy*, 23 November 1986).

However, it is difficult to make sense of inequality indicators. Equal income does not correspond with similar housing situation, to the same access to savings, or the same level of depreciation and dilapidation of consumer durables or even to such factors as the presence of officially defined invalids in the family (present in 20 per cent of all households!). While it is impossible to speak of overt hunger, in a situation where upwards of 54 per cent of household expenditure goes on the purchase of food, then any drop in real incomes must cause undernourishment in essentials such as protein and vitamins. The remainder of income goes on shoes, clothing and housing. As a consequence one in four workers are believed to be under-nourished.

Currently there appear to be two opposing policy positions being enunciated by the regime. The first posits the 'overprotective role of the state' and argues that not only has the state been spending beyond its means, but that it is abused by its recipients. Worst of all, however, is that it undermines the sense of responsibility for one's own fate and puts the burden for all provisioning onto the state. The other viewpoint contends that the state is overprotective towards certain industrial sectors and not towards the welfare system, which by comparison to other socialist countries is underinvested. In the burgeoning crisis the state must care, it is claimed, for the most vulnerable. Pensioners are a case in point. They receive 47 per cent of the average wage, and find themselves severely squeezed both by a rate of inflation projected at 45 per cent for 1988 and a policy which has failed to tie their benefits to the growth in real wages, as promised by the government. More disconcertingly, perhaps, is that the subjective perception of impoverishment appears to be greater than would be indicated by income studies. Not only does this reflect the continued use of 1970s' living standards as a datum point but also that the measures applied by the regime to estimate poverty are inadequate and do not, for example, recognize that the *health* of the head of household increasingly determines income rather than the more traditional measures such as occupation, sector of employment or even family size.

Role Differentiation and Domestic Division

Most of the burden of decreasing living standards is shouldered by women, who make up 51.2 per cent of the population. It is women who have to stand in queues for the goods in short supply; it is also they who serve their irate sisters in retail outlets which amount to 196 square metres per 1,000 inhabitants, as compared to 297 square metres in the GDR and 275 square metres in Czechoslovakia (*Kierunki*, 22–29 December 1985). They had to cope with the decline of the much promised communal feeding and cleaning facilities which raised the hours spent on housework and shopping to 7.5 per day on average. This was aside from the time spent at work, where they earned at best 30 per cent less than their male counterparts, although figures are so apparently shameful that the official statistics do not provide a breakdown by sex (*Życie Warszawy*, 6 January 1986). Decapitalization of durables meant that in one study, for instance, 30 per cent of women sampled could not (or would not) use their washing machine because of a shortage of spare parts and the virtual impossibility of obtaining a new one. Apart from any other conclusion this might inspire, it raises serious questions as to figures indicating the existence of 110 washing machines per 100 households!

Where women found their domestic burden increasing, the impact upon other life chances was immediate. In particular, opportunities for improving education and qualifications have diminished, as shown by the decline in numbers at evening and part-time classes. Women head most of the half million single parent families. Alimony payments are low, cut further by inflation and often not forthcoming from husbands who are as likely as not to find a haven for defaulting in the factory which should be extracting the contribution from them (*Slowo Powszechne*, 31 October 1986). Within the household young families appear to share the domestic burdens more equitably although this depends upon the occupation and qualifications of the spouses. In one case 57 per cent of men from worker family units, as opposed to 20 per cent of those from intelligentsia families, helped with the basic domestic chores such as cleaning, washing and the like although not on a daily basis. It was pointed out that the latter were drawn from the engineering professions, with their exceptionally heavy workloads, where the wife was also likely be employed. Another report published as Women's Day approached showed that while having one of the highest indicators of female employment in the world, 80 per cent cook daily dinners, wash and clean. Only 20 per cent of husbands stand in shopping queues, 1 per cent cook regularly (*Życie Warszawy*, 7 March 1988).

In older families the wife was more likely to be on some kind of child-bearing leave and the father was more often than not involved in the second economy in the broadest sense of the word. Young families had poor housing conditions. Only 44 per cent lived in their own unit, 34 per cent lived with their parents, 5 per cent lived in hostels and student accommodation, while 3.3 per cent had to live separately. One-quarter of them did not take a holiday (*Radar*, 31 January 1985).

In educational terms women have more than closed the gap on their male counterparts. The number completing higher education doubled during the period 1975–83 to 681,000. However, the positions they achieve are euphemistically called the 'specialist shadow'; namely they carry out the background work, preparing the foreground for the male directors' signature rarely getting the credit. There are 1,322,000 such specialists, twice the number of men. As for the skilled manual category, they have consistently declined from a low starting point and have instead fed into the low-status administrative and clerical positions. Women are concentrated in the humanities, economics and medicine and only 15 per cent graduate in technical subjects. A mere 30 per cent of doctorates are awarded to women and academic careers do not follow naturally. One-third or so of the officially entitled managerial positions occupied by women are found chiefly in feminized industries and sectors, namely health, social security, finance and social insurance, education, gastronomy and retail trade all with 70 per cent feminization. Only one in ten desire promotion or a career, although a mere 1.5 per cent wished to be managers.

At the political pinnacle, women comprise 27 per cent of the PZPR membership and saw their representation on the shrinking central committee rise from 23 (8.5 per cent) in 1981 to 34 or (15 per cent) in 1986. There is one woman on the Politburo, as there was prior to the Tenth Congress in 1986. Within the Sejm the number of women has declined to barely 20 per cent. There is only one woman chairing a Sejm subcommittee, one woman member on the Council of State and until the 1988 reform there was one woman minister.

More tellingly, the structure of industrial investment is such that light industry, with over 70 per cent female employment, has 24 per cent of its female work-force exposed to conditions considered injurious to their health. This industry has 70 per cent decapitalization, with many factories occupying buildings over 100 years old.

With the population of non-productive age expected to increase to 1,019 persons per 1,000 of productive age by 1990, the burdens of tending to the immediate needs of those at both ends of the life cycle will expand dramatically. If the state goes ahead and cuts subsidies by 50–75 per cent of 1986 values and allows for only a 5 per cent growth in real income to 1990, then once again it will be women who will bear the brunt of these changes. In agriculture, for example, where the consequences of underinvestment are particularly onerous, the achievement of income parity with non-agricultural employment is to be governed by the principle of 'efficient production'. In all likelihood those farms run by women (that is, worker-peasant households) will suffer from this calculation, based as it will be on optimum, full-time farming practice.

Conclusion

Apart from the vision of a multidimensional underlying crisis within Polish society, the impression must be of a society which has moved from the massified, bureaucratically centralized and monocentric stage of the Gomułka and Gierek Years through the process of coalescence characteristic of the Solidarity era, into temporary atomization after martial law, and finally back to new forms of association. This latter can be seen in the myriad forms of informal and semi-formal associations either existing in a limbo of non-legality or striving for official state recognition under the existing law on associations (*Lad*, 21 February 1988) and which have been loosely termed the 'second society'. Created in response to the multitude of problems facing the Polish population, they mobilize around issues rather than around the formulation of solutions. This latter still lies firmly with the regime, which has not been prepared to loosen its grip on the authorship or the execution of the reform platform, despite the many official committees and consultation devices it has not offered to many the opportunities for officially sponsored organizational participation. Thus although 300 or so new associations have been registered in the last few years, the demand for registration and regime recognition of others continues unabated.

The consensus is that the majority of Poles now recognize that the current crisis will not be a temporary phenomenon and are thus rearranging their life plans accordingly (*Przeglad Tygodniowy*, 28 February 1988). In the process new alliances between social strata are emerging rooted in marketable skills, sectoral power such as that of the miners and metal-workers, or in potentially new forms of interest articulation. Here the relative pauperization of the intelligentsia and the dissatisfaction of the skilled technical groups may yet form an interest bloc as the regime comes to recognize the urgency of technical innovation outside of the existing highly bureaucratized and inflexible state R&D bureaux.

Whereas Polish sociologists write of the monetarization of social relations accompanied by privatization into family-centred life, this is in fact a characteristic outcome of the two forms of power which underlie social inequality in modern society. Max Weber (1978) identified the first as factual power based upon a constellation of interests and regulated through the market. The second is the more familiar authoritarian power of command usually rooted in legitimate domination. In the transition from the first to the second, not only is legitimacy sought by the ruling group but new forms of superior-subordinate relations are articulated and recognized as legitimate in the process. Thus new forms of inequality are established in place of those which featured during the 1960s and 1970s. It is only in this way that we can understand what appears to be a highly fragmented and complex picture of inequality. Based on the twin pillars of officialdom and class (Bauman, 1974) or the twin hierarchies of the bureaucratic-distributive order and the market (Szelenyi, 1979), new forms of inequality arise out of the new rules of engagement between those who inhabit these hierarchies (see Figure 2.1).

The cadre-elite or partyocracy, represented by the various apparatuses, economic, political, repressive, propagandistic, etc., is more highly structured than the diverse mass of direct producers and employees (Panków, 1987). Its power is rooted in the appropriation and redistribution of surplus in the interests of the reproduction of the system. However when that goal is no longer possible under the existing conditions of the directive-distributive command economy, new property relations and market-type mechanisms are invoked. These however have the unfortunate consequence of undermining the basis of power of the *nomenklatura*, which is the trusteeship

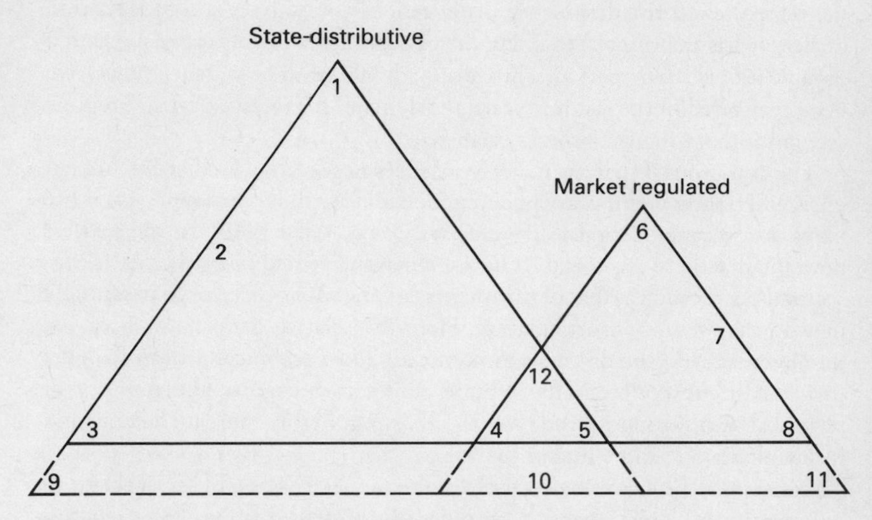

Figure 2.1 Dual Hierarchy of Distributional Inequality
Source: Based on Szelenyi, 1986–7

Key to groups
1 Cadre elites or partyocracy
2 Large, key sector working-class (*Wielko Przemysło*wa Klasa Robotnicza)
3 Light industry, feminized sector
4 Worker-peasants (rural-based industrial workers)
5 Peasant-workers (peasant-farmer with family-household member in non-agricultural, state employment)
6 Private capital (Polonia, or indigenous service/craft)
7 Individual peasant farmers
8 Employees in private sector
9 Industrial/state sector *pensioners*
10 Peasant-worker *pensioners*
11 Retired individual farmers
12 Residual non-agricultural part-time private sector employees/self-employed

(Feher, Heller & Markus, 1983) of the state-owned means-of-production. Hence the internal conflict within the elite which knows that the reform will both succour the system but weaken their grip over it.

The evolution of a *modus vivendi* between state and society in Poland does not overlay this re-alignment of the two power dimensions. As has been shown above and in Chapter 4 key groups of industrial workers are located within the distributive heirarchy and have an interest in the maintenance of the status quo. Likewise not all sections of the intelligentsia or white-collar employees would be served by a shift in system centre-of-gravity to a more market-oriented economy. Four possible economic models and their attendant political ideologies weave in and out of the interests and attitudes of most of the key groups. On the reform platform the tendency towards marketization and the growth of the private-individual sector runs alongside an equally cogent self-management and socialization theme. Whereas the Yugoslavian experience suggests that the two need to complement each other, it is highly improbable that without a major change in the political order this is likely to occur. As for the non-reformers, these likewise fall into the category of the defenders of the directive-distributive system or those with a corporatist-monopolist tilt, where the key sectors of the economy are carved out and controlled by a ubiquitous Planning Commission while the remainder service this sector either in the cooperative or private sector format.

It is against this moving backdrop that the conflicting and merging interests of young and old workers, white-collar and specialist, peasant and worker-peasant, the poor and infirm as well as party and non-party member, have to be studied.

In Poland the market dimension of power is for better or for worse chiefly rooted in the peasantry, the Church and the whole gamut of the so-called second-society, which grew out of the Solidarity legacy providing as it did areas of autonomous existence. More obviously it is also to be located in the nascent Polonia firms and the services and crafts sector. For these and the reasons of crisis spelled out above it is likely to be a more durable and genuinely independent locus of interest coalescence than, for example, might be the case in Hungary.

Finally, the individual and collective strategies of survival within the current crisis in Poland (Marody, 1987) ranging from privatized, second-economy, highly pragmatic behaviour to collective forms of action which exploit the system's own rules, such as strikes, legal actions and low-level non-threatening autonomous association, have different consequences for the system. Some can be incorporated or even cloned by the regime, through policy changes. Others can be tolerated and occasionally purged. Still others are confronted and presented as the limits of the permissible. The key question is how long can such a disjunction exist. It is in the realm of formal politics that the bridge has to be built and, as we shall see in Chapter 3, there seems little scope for optimism.

3 Structures of Political Rule

The Party: Role and Membership

As a communist state unequivocally within the Soviet sphere of influence, whose objectives are determined within the framework of Marxism-Leninism, Poland is subject to the monopolistic rule of a communist party—although the ruling party, the Polish United Workers' Party (PZPR), does not contain the word 'communist' in its name. This is associated with the facts, noted in Chapter 1, that the original Polish communist party (KPP) did not support the idea of Polish national independence, had never secured much popular social support and had been dissolved by Stalin in 1937–8—a successor party (PPR) being set up in 1942 following the German attack on Soviet Russia which transformed the Poles into formal allies of the Russians. The PPR did not secure much popular support either (nor was it in a position to do so under the Nazi occupation), although it grew massively in numbers once it became clear that the development of post-war Poland would be guided along lines acceptable to the Soviet Union. As the Soviet army liberated Poland from the German occupation from mid-1944 PPR membership grew rapidly, increasing tenfold within the year and doubled in size the next, bringing total membership to half a million in 1946 (de Weydenthal, 1986, p. 228). In 1948, following a concerted attempt to neutralize and divide the non-communist parties, the PPR merged with the residue of the non-communist left-wing Polish Socialist Party (PPS) to produce a joint membership of 1.5 million, although the level of membership dropped off considerably over the next three years. Following the instabilities of communist rule between 1955 and 1957 and the continuing unpopularity of the party (although not necessarily of its leader, Władysław Gomułka), the membership totals of the late 1940s were not reached again until 1963–4, while the 2 million level was topped in 1967–8.

A consistent attempt to consolidate the political dominance of the party was made in the seventies by Edward Gierek. There were several aspects to this process. One was the revision of the Constitution of the Polish People's Republic (PRL). The original Constitution had been promulgated in 1952 and there were moves from the Polish party establishment in the mid-1970s, as there were throughout the Soviet bloc, to revise it and give greater recognition to the formal role of the party and the importance of Poland's ties with the Soviet Union, and to make citizens' rights conditional on the fulfilment of their 'public duties'. This formed part of a general attempt to regularize the system of party rule and establish party authority on a stronger legal basis to supplement, and perhaps replace, the principle of coercive government and informal party dictatorship. Initial proposals provoked extensive discussion and much opposition, including formal protests from the Church, but did not prevent the passage of major amendments. In the version of the Constitution passed in February 1976, then, Article 3 began with the statement that 'The Polish United Workers' Party is the leading political force in society concerned with the building of socialism', while Article 6 refers to the fact that the PRL 'strengthens friendship and cooperation with the Union of Soviet Socialist Republics and other socialist states'. The latter formulation is considerably milder in its obeisance to the Soviet link than the amendments made to most of the other Eastern European constitutions, a fact clearly connected with the disquiet expressed by Poles to the original proposals (Raina, 1978, pp. 220–1). Nevertheless, the conflict was responsible for the demise of the independent Catholic group (Znak) in the parliament, its leader losing the right to appear as a candidate on future electoral lists.

A second aspect was the expansion of party membership and its firmer implantation in Polish society. After 1950 party membership did not top the 1.35 million mark until 1962, but then grew rapidly to 2.32 million in 1970. After the shooting of workers in the northern towns in December 1970 and the fall of Gomułka, the level of membership dropped again and did not regain the 2.3 million mark until 1973. It then rose steadily until the end of the decade and stood at 3.08 million in early 1980. The party leadership never stood for the unqualified expansion of party ranks, though. Membership growth had been rapid in the late 1960s prior to the conflicts of 1970, but this had clearly not secured mass support for the party or eradicated the sources of political conflict. The party leadership, Central Committee Secretary Edward Babiuch stated in 1977, now rejected such concepts as 'recruitment' or the 'harvesting of society' for party membership. At the same time, the PZPR was declared to be a 'party of the whole nation' and no real conflict was seen between principles of selectivity and extensive party growth. There was not, said Babiuch, 'any dilemma under our conditions between quantitative and qualitative factors in the development of party ranks' (*Życie Partii*, June 1977). The party was regarded as having significant reserves in this respect and the large numbers of young people entering the work-force in the mid-1970s were viewed as likely candidates for party membership.

A third aspect of the attempt to consolidate the position of the party under

Gierek was the drive to strengthen links with strategic social groups. The prime target here was the industrial working class. In 1971 the Central Committee Secretariat had decided to form direct organizational links with the 164 largest industrial enterprises and exercise central supervision over them, rather than entrusting them to local party committees. Attention was also paid to the numerical representation of the working class in the party membership. Workers had made up around half the membership in the early 1950s (49 per cent in 1951, 48 per cent in 1954) but their level of representation had fallen. In 1971 they made up 39.7 per cent of party members and efforts were made by the leadership to reverse this trend. Babiuch claimed that 1975 had seen the highest proportion of workers among new party members since the establishment of the PZPR. By the time of the Eighth Party Congress in 1980, workers made up 46 per cent of the party members, and accounted for 60 per cent of new applicants for membership (*Życie Partii*, March 1980). Somewhat surprisingly for a party ruling a society at a relatively high degree of economic development and for a leadership emphasizing innovation and technological progress, relatively little emphasis was placed on enhancing the role of the intelligentsia in the party (Kolankiewicz, 1981a). Its place in the party membership fell from 43.6 per cent in 1971 to 32.5 per cent in 1980. The proportion of party members with higher education rose, too, only slowly during the Gierek years: having made up 7.9 per cent of the membership in 1970, their representation rose to 11.7 per cent in 1980 (*Rocznik Statystyczny*, 1985, p. 31; *Życie Partii*, February 1980).

Developments after the VIII Party Congress in early 1980 showed the fragility of the party's social base, despite the level of membership growth and the concentration on the role of the working class in it. When the next wave of political dissatisfaction broke in July and August 1980 it was again centred on the industrial bases and led by angry workers—and even, in many cases, party members and those holding office in local party committees. It was a sign of the protracted crisis that the party lost around a third of its membership between 1980 and 1985—and that workers and young people played a disproportionately large part amongst those who resigned or were expelled from the party (see Table 3.1). Numbers had fallen slightly after the 1970 events, although by no more than 3 per cent, and even the earlier crisis of 1956 had seen a decline in party numbers of no more than 24.2 per cent between 1955 and 1959. Following the events of 1980, numbers continued to fall until mid-1985, and it was only in the latter half of that year that some slight recovery began.

It is clear then that the mere number of party members does not tell us very much about the stability of the party's social base or about its political

Table 3.1 PZPR Membership, 1960–87 (per cent)*

	1960	1970	1978	1980†	1982	1984	1986	1987
Total membership (millions)	1.155	2.320	2.930	3.092	2.327	2.117	2.129	2.149
Women	15.3	22.5	26.2	26.8	26.8	26.9	27.2	
Workers	40.3	40.3	45.7	46.1	40.2	38.5	38.0	38.0
Intelligentsia	42.9	42.3	35.8	32.5	49.0	51.0	51.7	
Age								
18–29	26.0	25.3	23.5	24.8	11.1	7.6	6.9	
30–49	52.5	56.5	53.1		57.1	57.4	56.8	
50+	21.5	18.2	23.4		31.8	35.0	36.3	
Education								
Full higher	5.3	7.9	12.0	12.0	15.8	17.4	18.3	
Full secondary	19.5	27.0	32.5	32.4	35.9	36.7	37.2	

Notes: * State at end of year unless otherwise stated. † Membership total end of year, percentage composition at the Eighth Congress (February 1980).

Sources: *Rocznik Statystyczny*, 1981, p. 31; *Rocznik Statystyczny*, 1985, p. 31, *Mały Rocznik Statystyczny*, 1986, p. 23; *Życie Partii*, 1980, no. 2, p. 14; 1980, no. 3, p. 16; 3 March 1988.

strength within Polish society. The structure of the party organization, the rights and duties of party members and full-time officials, and the capacity of the organization to respond to pressures for change have also had a crucial bearing on the position of the party within society. The relatively small initial decline in party numbers during the first stage of the 1980 crisis is instructive in this respect. During the last six months of that year, as strikes broke out in early July and spread to cover virtually the whole of the northern coast by late August, as the party-state leadership collapsed and the mass independent trade union 'Solidarity' came into being and became officially registered, the party lost officially only 68,000 members. The rate of departure was to speed up later, 401,000 leaving in 1981 and 360,000 in 1982, but the PZPR still had on paper 3.092 million members at the end of 1980, only a little short of its highest total ever. This apparent strength as a mass movement was largely illusory—of the 3 million, 1 million had already become or were about to become members of Solidarity (and many of these were industrial workers). The mood of such workers was expressed in the story of one activist, who had been given extensive publicity only a few months earlier, at the time of the Eighth Party Congress:

> I have been let down. Many times I have spoken out in defence of what the party was doing even though I did not fully agree with it. But I believed that behind every decision were reasons which were deeper than my own or those which my friends and neighbours put forward. So I defended the party line. I accepted that as my duty. Now, not for the first time, I have been let down. And, speaking frankly, I no longer have the strength or the conviction. [*Polityka*, 4 October 1980]

Many party members in early 1980 were, to put it mildly, less than fully convinced by party rhetoric, not wholly committed to the values and objectives espoused by the party, and had severe doubts about the leadership's ability to implement agreed policies. Nevertheless, for a variety of reasons, ranging from pure opportunism and careerism, to measured realism (Polish 'positivism') and a sense of social commitment, and even (on rare occasions) moral and ideological conviction, the party had built up and retained a mass membership. It was located within an elaborate national structure which helped to compensate for the members' lack of political commitment with a range of organizational mechanisms.

Organizational Structure

Members belong to the party through local organizations which 'are established according to production and territorial principles' (Article 38 of the 1981 Party Statute). They normally belong, therefore, to organizations located in their place of work and steps have been taken since 1981 to ensure that national party leaders also have some local party affiliation. At the end of 1985 membership was effected through some 74,000 Basic Party Organizations (POP), 21,000 Shopfloor Party Organizations (OOP) and 31,000 party groups (*Rocznik Polityczny i Gospodarczy*, 1986, p. 158). There is often much doubt, though as to how real the existence of some of these organizations is and official complaints have often been heard that they show little activity, fail to recruit new members and generally do not provide a solid base for party work.

Such complaints were made in 1985, when it was noted that nearly one-fifth of the membership was in groups of less than fifteen (the minimum size for a party group, at that time, was five members; it was lowered to a minimum of three at the Tenth Congress in 1986). This concerned particularly the party organizations in education, the retail and service sector, health and in the countryside (*Życie Partii*, 19 June 1985). The information, contained in a Politburo report delivered by Central Committee Secretary Tadeusz Porębski, reflected the state of affairs following five years of numerical decline, and was accompanied by a clear statement that political revival would be best achieved through the restoration of higher membership levels. The restoration of the party's fortunes, in terms both of membership levels and of activity, was, however, slow and partial. Materials prepared two years later for the Fourth Central Committee Plenum in May 1987 suggested that only a quarter of party members could be described as active. Sixty per cent of the membership carried out the elementary duties of going to meetings and paying party dues, but apart from that showed an essentially passive attitude. Fifteen per cent (some 320,000 members) did not even perform these elementary duties (*Polityka*, 30 May 1987).

Apart from the statutory political obligations of party members, including those of taking an active part in political life, popularizing Marxism-Leninism and the party's programme, and combating all social ills (enumerated in Article 2), the member is directed to play a part in establishing the central institutions of the party by participating in two kinds of elections. The first is for the executive group and secretary of the basic party organization, that is the one or more officials, generally employed by the organization, who act as the full-time representative of the party at local level and who, in view of the indeterminate mood and commitment of the ordinary member, may well act as the only dependable form of party presence in the locality. The second is for delegates to local party conferences (at the level of rural or urban commune, district or plant) which, in turn, elect their own committees and delegates to provincial conferences (see Figure 3.1). At this level the party committee, which acts as the legislative body for party affairs between conferences (held at intervals of two and a half years), may range from nineteen to seventy-five members (the latter in cases where overall party membership exceeds 10,000). The size of the executive body, elected in turn by the committee, which acts to supervise and check the day-to-day work of the party and its officials, ranges from seven to seventeen members (*Krajowa Konferencja*, 1984, pp. 106–7). The executive includes four or five secretaries, who are its senior members. Finally, the provincial committee has a membership whose number ranges from eighty-one to 121 (for provinces with more than

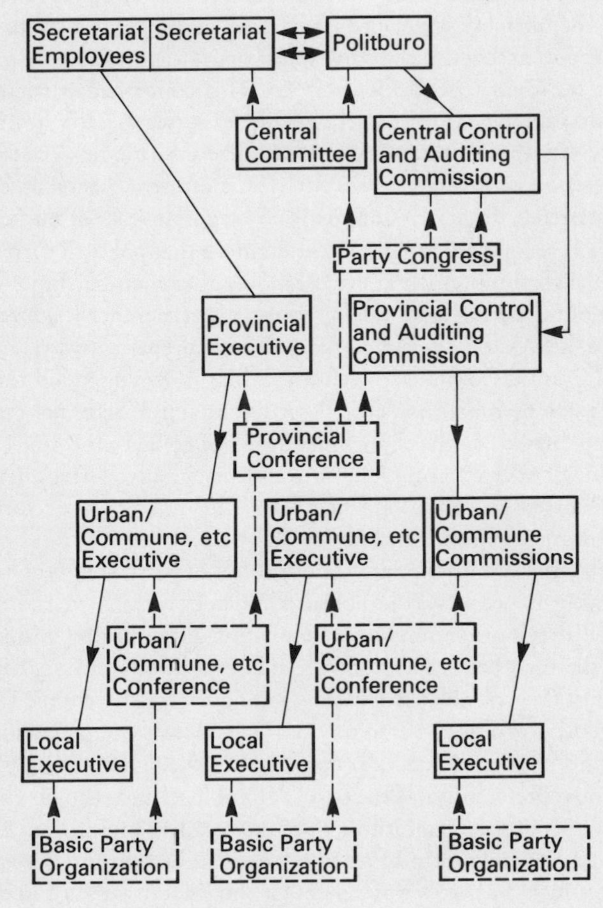

Figure 3.1 Structure of the PZPR

80,000 members). The size of the provincial party executive ranges from twenty-one to twenty-five members, and the larger provinces have seven secretaries, each responsible for a particular sphere of activity (education, industry, agriculture, organizations and other areas depending on the socio-economic and other characteristics of the province). The institutions in these areas are supervised by the various departments subject to the secretariat. Regional Centres to coordinate local work and strengthen party control were set up informally at the beginning of the martial law period. At the Tenth Congress these centres, ROPP, were given the formal status of KW departments. Since 1975 there have been forty-nine provinces, and it is the composition and approach of the provincial committee and its executive apparatus that exerts a major influence on the status and effectiveness of the party in a given area.

It is the provincial conference, too, which elects delegates to the Party Congress, the supreme legislative body within the party organization, normally held every five years. The Congress determines the composition of the party's Central Committee, the membership of its major ruling body, the Politburo, and the leadership of the Secretariat, the major executive body within the national party organization. Following the collapse of the Gierek regime in 1980, and the formation and registration of Solidarity, an Extraordinary Party Congress (the Ninth) was held in July 1981, only seventeen months after the last. The Congress was attended by 1,964 delegates who, under the political conditions pertaining in Poland in the first half of 1981, had been selected by an equally extraordinary process. Instead of the normal process of candidates being identified by the executive and 'elected' without discussion or competition to the Congress, the delegates in 1981 emerged following exhaustive debate and often extensive conflict. Although, for the most part, authentic representatives of their local party organizations (in that they were to a far greater extent than was previously the case elected from below) and largely reformist in orientation (insisting on new democratic procedures during the Congress and amendments to the Party Statute), the delegates to the Extraordinary Congress did not overturn all established party authorities or practices. Stanisław Kania was re-elected First Secretary of the party, although his candidature was contested and the election did not take place at the beginning of the Congress as Kania had wished.

The Central Committee elected by the Congress showed further unusual characteristics. Among the 146 voting members elected to the CC were very few representatives of some groups who had previously played an important part in its membership. There were no heads of CC departments and far fewer provincial first secretaries (eight instead of the twenty-five on the previous CC). Government ministers and vice-ministers were notable for their virtual absence and the CC as a whole was characterized by the drastically diminished representation of officials from the party-state apparatus, a change clearly in line with the amendments made to the Party Statute at the Extraordinary Congress (Kolankiewicz, 1981b). At the Tenth Party Congress (held between 29 June and 3 July 1986) some further changes in the form of the CC were made. The distinction between full and candidate CC membership was abolished and a unified body was established, to which 230 members were elected. In contrast to the 1981 CC, which had not included any members of the central party staff, that elected in 1986 contained sixteen members of this category and twenty-seven provincial committee secretaries. On the other hand, the number of local party leaders elected fell from thirty-six to seven (Lewis, 1986a, p. 434).

The CC is the highest party authority between Congresses (held generally at intervals of five years), and is bound to meet at least once every six months. It is the Committee which elects the Politburo and the key party secretaries, although the First Secretary is elected directly by the Congress. Alongside the CC, and also elected by the Party Congress, is the Central Party Control and Auditing Commission (CKKR) (established in 1986 to cover activities previously performed by two different bodies) which has counterparts at province and town (including commune, plant and district) level elected by their respective conferences. The control commissions and the revision commissions were assigned a considerably greater role in the 1981 Party Statute than in earlier formulations. Instead of being 'called' or 'summoned' (*Statut*, 1978, p. 78) by the CC or provincial conference, the commissions were then elected by the Congress and other party conferences, while overlapping membership between the party commissions and the Central, provincial, urban and other committees was abolished. The control and auditing commissions are concerned with the general effectiveness of party work ('especially the satisfaction of demands made on party bodies and organizations, including letters from the public and complaints') as well as the proper conduct of the party's financial affairs, which had been the main concern of the auditing commissions before 1981. The commissions also direct their attention to the observance by party members of the Statute and to their proper conduct in political, social and moral terms, as well as being involved in meting out party discipline and applying appropriate sanctions.

The most important body elected by the CC, though, is the Politburo. As the leading executive organ of the party it is responsible for the conduct of party affairs throughout the country on a day-to-day basis and, by virtue of the party's leading role, for social and political developments within the country as a whole. Indeed, Politburo members and other CC secretaries have the statutory obligation and right (Article 50) 'to articulate their position in relation to the most important problems of socio-economic and political life in the country.' The Politburo meets frequently, recently every Tuesday, and is one of the major decision-making centres in modern Poland. The Politburo constituted by the CC at the Extraordinary Congress retained considerable stability through the series of political phases that followed the summer of 1980. Numerous changes in its original seventeen-person membership were made, particularly among those with a sharper political profile who were concerned with the central decision-making offices of the Polish state, but the overall balance and character of Politburo membership was not radically changed.

The current composition of the Politburo and the Secretariat is shown in Table 3.2, and the occupations and other offices held by their members also stated. It will be clear that while some of those who figure in the leadership are among the major power-holders in the country (Jaruzelski, Messner, Baryła, Czyrek), others fulfil more of a representative function (Murański, Stępién, Rembisz). Politburo membership has in fact shown considerable stability in terms of the representation of major power-holders. Of the five newcomers to the Politburo in 1986, three were worker representatives, one a member of the national (not central) party organization, and the other the head of a recently established official trade-union movement. They replaced members from similar backgrounds elected during the 1981–2 period. But *all* those who were members of the Politburo before the Tenth Party Congress and who held central party or government posts continued their membership into 1987. For most of them membership had been continuous since 1981 or earlier. A recent recruit, General Baryła (made a CC member in 1985 and elected to the Politburo in 1986), was nevertheless a leading member of the party-military establishment and had been head of the army's Main Political Administration since May 1980. The political elite assembled by Jaruzelski in 1981 showed considerable durability.

Democratic Centralism and the *Nomenklatura*

The contrast within the top policy-making body of the PZPR in terms of its representative and power-exercising members reflects a duality in the position of the party and a contradiction in its role which has crucial repercussions for the entire political system and its mode of operation. The

Table 3.2 PZPR Leadership (April 1988)

		Politburo full members	
W. Jaruzelski	born	1923	First Secretary of the CC, Chairman of the RP and the KOK
K. Barcikowski		1927	Deputy chairman of the RP
J. Baryła		1924	CC secretary (security)
J. Czyrek		1928	CC secretary (international)
J. Głowczyk		1927	CC secretary (propaganda)
C. Kiszczak		1925	Minister of Internal Affairs
Z. Messner		1929	Chairman of the RM (Prime Minister)
A. Miodowicz*		1929	Chairman of the OPZZ
W. Mokrzyszczak		1938	Chairman of CKKR
Z. Murański*		1952	Foreman
M. Orzechowski		1931	Foreign Minister
T. Porębski		1931	CC secretary (general affairs)
M. Rakowski*		1926	*Sejm* vice-marshall
F. Siwicki		1925	Minister of Defence
Z. Stępién*		1939	Textile Worker
M. Woźniak		1936	CC secretary (economy)
		Politburo candidate members	
S. Bejger		1929	Gdańsk first secretary
M. Gorywoda*		1942	Katowice first secretary
Z. Michałek		1935	CC secretary (agriculture)
G. Rembisz*		1937	Foreman
		Other secretaries of the Central Committee	
S. Ciosek*		1939	Administration, also head of CC Socio-legal Department
K. Cypryniak*		1934	Organization, also head of CC Political and Organization Department
A. Wasilewski*		1928	Culture, also publishing-house director

* New members in 1986 or after

duality is best summed up by the party's dominant operating principle of 'democratic centralism'. This is discussed in the Party Statute (Article 16) with reference to the following features: all party authorities are chosen by democratic means according to the Party Statute; the minority acts according to the decision of the majority; and the commitment of members and organizations to positions not in agreement with formally agreed majority decisions does not release them from the obligation to implement those decisions. Somewhat cynically, although not unrealistically, the principle may be summed up thus: members may hold whatever opinion they like and even, within limits, express it—but they should not endeavour to put it into practice if it conflicts with the policies and decisions arrived at (supposedly democratically) by the leadership. Much, then, depends on what is meant by 'democratic'. As a great many countries, including the great majority of modern states, claim to be democratic in some way, the term is open to a variety of conflicting interpretations. There is, indeed, a tradition of political thought that can be identified with 'totalitarian democracy', a paradoxical term that indicates the variety of political thought and practice that democracy can encompass (Talmon, 1961). Democracy involves *some* conception of decision-making and policy formulation in keeping with the will of the majority, but that will may just as well be imputed as one defined by the expressions and behaviour of the majority itself. One is tempted to the conclusion that, while the Polish party and overall political system is clearly a centralized one, the complementary claim that it is also democratic is virtually meaningless.

The view that the application of the principle of democratic centralism gives little indication of the actual operation of the political or party system is supported by developments within the party in 1980 and 1981. Following the fall of Gierek and in the face of the apparent inability of the party leadership to cope with Poland's serious economic and political problems, a grass-roots movement for party reform and political change developed within the party. This followed, and appeared fully to be in accordance with, the Kania leadership's call for political change and renewal (*odnowa*). The movement spread and gained particular force during the preparations for the Extraordinary Congress and the elections at the successive party conferences which eventually produced the delegates for the Congress. It encountered, however, considerable resistance, particularly from the incumbent party authorities who were accustomed to a slower pace of change and one whose course was determined by the national party leadership, and incurred the displeasure of the Soviet leadership, who condemned developments in the PZPR in their letter of June 1981. While there were clearly different views on the legitimacy of the party reform movement, it was generally sanctioned by the national party leadership and not regarded as contrary to the Party Statute (at least under the political conditions prevalent in Poland prior to the holding of the Extraordinary Congress). Reformers were generally calling for greater elements of constitutionality in party life and more accountability on the part of the PZPR authorities. Their actions were in keeping with Article 18 of the existing Statute (*Statut*, 1978, p. 55), which enjoined all party authorities to work in 'constant and close contact with the party *aktiv* (activists) and basic party organizations', to consult with them and provide full information on all major current issues. One problem was that such a clause was ill-defined and difficult to enforce. It was significant that the new Statute, drawn up at the Extraordinary Congress, contained whole new sections on the 'PZPR in the System of Socialist Democracy' (Part 5) and on 'Electoral Principles' (Part 4), the latter introducing new limitations on office-holding within the party and restricting incumbents to two terms of office. In the absence of such provisions and, it must be said, the political capacity to enforce them, the 'democratic' qualification of 'centralism' may be very tenuous indeed.

The fact that the tenor of party life could switch, within the same formal framework, from the centralized authoritarian mode operated by Gierek to the democratizing, rank-and-file-driven movement characteristic of late 1980 and early 1981 directs attention to coexisting features in the party structure and to a duality in party life. It is, as noted above, reflected in the party's leading body, the Politburo, which includes male and female workers (typically, one token woman since 1981), and a trade-union leader, as well as key power-holders such as the Prime Minister and CC secretaries. This contrast is also evident in the structure of the PZPR itself. We have so far outlined the constitutional structure of the party which builds on the mass membership of over 2 million and emphasized the sequence of elections which determine the membership of local and provincial committees, delegates to the Congress, the composition of the CC and the form of the Politburo. In Figure 3.1 this upward flow, representing the democratic procedures outlined in the Party Statute, is shown in terms of processes and party gatherings by the dotted lines. This aspect of the party, its role as a mass democratic movement, is reflected more in ideological statements and formal statute than in political practice. In terms of actual process and the exercise of party power the centralist principle is dominant and the flow of authority is downward. This is represented in Figure 3.1 by the processes and executive bodies bounded by the unbroken lines, which reflect the dominance of the Politburo as an executive agency closely linked, in terms both of function and overlapping personnel, with the Secretariat.

There are several reasons why the executive functions of the party dominate its formal, mass democratic character. The executive bodies are led by full-time paid party officials with privileged access to organizational resources and information. They are often party-trained and educated, with extensive experience in the executive bureaucracy, or apparatus, of the party. They are generally from a well-integrated group and have often held a number of party posts in combination with related jobs in other hierarchies. They therefore form an experienced and well-organized central core of the party organization. At the level of the CC the number of political workers (that is, party officials as distinct from secretarial and support staff) is around 600. At the Fourth CC Plenary Session in May 1987, the decision was taken to cut back on central party staff by 20 per cent. At the same time the number of CC departments in which they worked was reduced to a total of twelve: Political and Organizational; Cadres Policy; Ideology; Propaganda; Culture; Science, Education and Scientific and Technical; Socio-legal; Socio-Economic Policy; Agricultural; Foreign; Party Management; and the Secretariat Chancelry. About 3,500 people are attached to provincial committees: a full-time staff of around seventy for each committee. A further 7,000 are concerned with work in local and factory committees. The total number involved in full-time party work announced at the Extraordinary Congress was 11,003 (*Nowe Drogi*, August 1981). Despite the fall in party membership, the number of those employed as political workers in the party apparatus had increased to 13,000 by 1987 (*Życie Partii*, 3 June 1987). Of those in the Politburo who reflect the role of the party as the repository of centralized power, most have had experience as party officials and some have spent considerable time in the party apparatus. By 1987 CC Secretary Woźniak had spent six years in the party apparatus, and before that had held various posts in the government hierarchy for fourteen years. Secretary Porębski had been a party official for eighteen years, although for part of the time he had also held academic posts, and had earlier held office in the communist youth movement. A Politburo member like Messner, who also holds office as Prime Minister, had also spent two years as a provincial first secretary. The forty-nine provincial (KW) first secretaries had, at the end of 1984, spent an average of 10.7 years working full-time in the party apparatus and thirteen of them had spent more than fifteen years at work in the apparatus. This, however, reflected a lower level of career specialization than had been the case under Gierek, at the end of whose period of rule the average provincial first secretary had spent 15.3 years working in the apparatus (Lewis, 1986b).

The body of full-time party workers therefore represents an integrated group with extensive shared experiences, whose career and prospects have been dependent on the judgement of their superiors and employers in the CC Secretariat. It is not surprising that their outlook and behaviour have reflected the character of the party as a centralized power structure rather than as a mass movement determined by the commitment of its local members. Following the party's loss of central control in 1981 the Jaruzelski leadership has paid serious attention to the selection, training and behaviour of party workers. A second complete review of all apparatus workers was reported to have taken place by the end of 1985 and by that date, according to an announcement made by General Honkisz (then Head of the CC's Cadre Policy Department), over 80 per cent had higher education. The number who had received training in Soviet party schools had doubled over the previous three years and a ten-year plan had been drawn up to improve the qualifications of party staff and double the number of those graduating from party schools (*Życie Partii*, 6 November 1985). The filling of responsible party posts was clearly not a haphazard affair to be left to the vagaries of party members' votes. In 1987 Honkisz moved from the CC Cadres Policy Department and responsibility for it was taken on by Świderski, up to then the secretary-general of PRON. This suggested the adoption of a less restrictive view of cadres policy appropriate to the coalition approach to exercising power.

But at the same time the leading positions in the party apparatus, the secretaries elected by the CC and the committees at province, town and rural commune level, are formally subject to the will of the members of those committees. The offices are supposed to be filled by election rather than appointment from above. This is one of the areas where the contradictions within the concept of democratic centralism are particularly sharp. It is significant that conflict within the PZPR in 1980 and 1981 focused initially on the persons of some local secretaries held to be corrupt, dictatorial and inefficient, and then on the processes of election to secure extensive personnel change within the apparatus and to incorporate restrictions in the Statute on the length of tenure in leading apparatus positions. For this reason the reformist forces in the party were often referred to as the anti-apparatus movement. This raised grave doubts in the Soviet Union and the unacceptability of such practices was made quite clear in the 'June letter' dispatched to the PZPR. In connection with the development of 'counter-revolutionary forces' in Poland, explicit reference was made to the fact that the local party leaderships were being constituted by 'people chosen at random, openly expressing opportunist views' (*Nowe Drogi*, June 1981, pp. 30–1). Much light is shed on the orthodox conception of democratic centralism by this suggestion that secretaries chosen and elected by a local party conference are thereby 'chosen at random' and that secretaries who reflected the views of their electorate rather than acting on orders from above were opportunistic. Nevertheless, developments at this time, involving the spread of a 'horizontal movement' within the party (Kolankiewiez, 1989), helped sustain the commitment of the rank and file and delayed the further dissolution of the party.

The conflict between the elective principle, the party as a mass democratic movement, and the practice of appointment and central cadre planning, associated with the practice of the party as a hierarchical power structure, is generally reconciled by the nomination of a first secretary at, say, a provincial party conference attended by a Politburo member or CC secretary. The nomination is not contested and the new secretary is confirmed in his position by the conference delegates' casting a vote. He is thus 'elected' and the democratic component of democratic centralism is duly observed. This confirmation is not automatic: the candidature of nine prospective provincial secretaries was not confirmed at the provincial conferences held in the autumn of 1986 after the Tenth Congress. It is important to remember that we are talking of election by a self-selected group of party members, who have agreed to act within the terms of the Party Statute and abide by the principle of democratic centralism. They therefore accept to a higher degree than average the need for party unity and discipline and may well not perceive any contradiction between democracy and centralism so long as appointments made by this method are not seen as giving rise to serious inefficiencies or sanction extensive corruption, a distortion that became evident towards the end of the Gierek period. Such defects are not necessarily inherent in this appointment system, at least not in the pronounced form they took under Gierek. The choice of the particular official is not an arbitrary one, of course, and a carefully vetted file of suitable candidates is maintained. It is from such a file that a selection is made when an appointment is needed or thought appropriate to a range of responsible positions.

This is the essence of the *nomenklatura* system, which became extended and gained particular notoriety in Poland under Gierek, as those identified as suitable for appointment to *nomenklatura* posts accumulated a range of privileges that appeared to bear little relation to their efficiency, technical qualification or integrity (Smolar, 1983). A major feature of the *nomenklatura* system is that both the list of individuals suitable for appointment and the set of key posts to be filled are determined by the leading executive organs of the party, which greatly enhances the power of the central party organs over the party hierarchy and over government and social organizations, whose staffing they also control (Lewis, 1985a). Thus the Central Committee Secretariat, particularly its Cadres Policy Department, exercises control over appointments in the provincial committee secretariat and in a whole range of party and formally non-party bodies; the provincial committee secretariat determines appointments at lower levels of the party hierarchy and in other local organizations (see Figure 3.2). The *nomenklatura* system is therefore a major pillar, if not the foundation itself, of the party centre's executive authority and the key to its rule over the party as a whole and the whole framework of non-party institutions—and thus to its domination over Polish society. The number of appointments controlled by this system has generally been estimated at around 160,000, although it has probably been reduced under Poland's military rulers. The extent of the party's supervision of employees goes even beyond this, however, and the head of the CC Cadres Policy Department noted that over 1 million had been covered in the 1985 staff review (*Życie Partii*, 6 November 1985). While party organs have direct control over appointments to the most important posts, they also exercise more general supervision over employees, both by virtue of the fact that more important staff are likely to be party members and through the influence of the party organization in the place of employment.

Organs of State and the Government

By such means the party leadership is generally able to exert wide-ranging control over the national organization and to maintain its formally proclaimed leading role in Polish society. It is also well placed to maintain a dominant position over the organs of state power. It is not the only political party represented in the Sejm, the Polish legislative organ. There are also the United Peasant Party (ZSL) and the Democratic Party (SD), which in 1986 had respectively 498,000 and 117,000 members. The ZSL naturally has a predominantly rural membership, that of the SD is primarily urban, aiming to represent white-collar workers, artisans and members of the intelligentsia. Neither competes with the PZPR or acts as its political opponent; both are allied with it and form subsidiary channels of political support for the leadership. On this basis Poland's party system is formally described as a hegemonic one, rather than being a typical one-party system (Wiatr, 1967). In practice, the political implications of these arrangements have varied over time. During the Stalin period and after the early phases of Gomułka and Gierek's rule, the influence of the 'allied parties' was very limited. During periods of change and political instability they had greater opportunities to

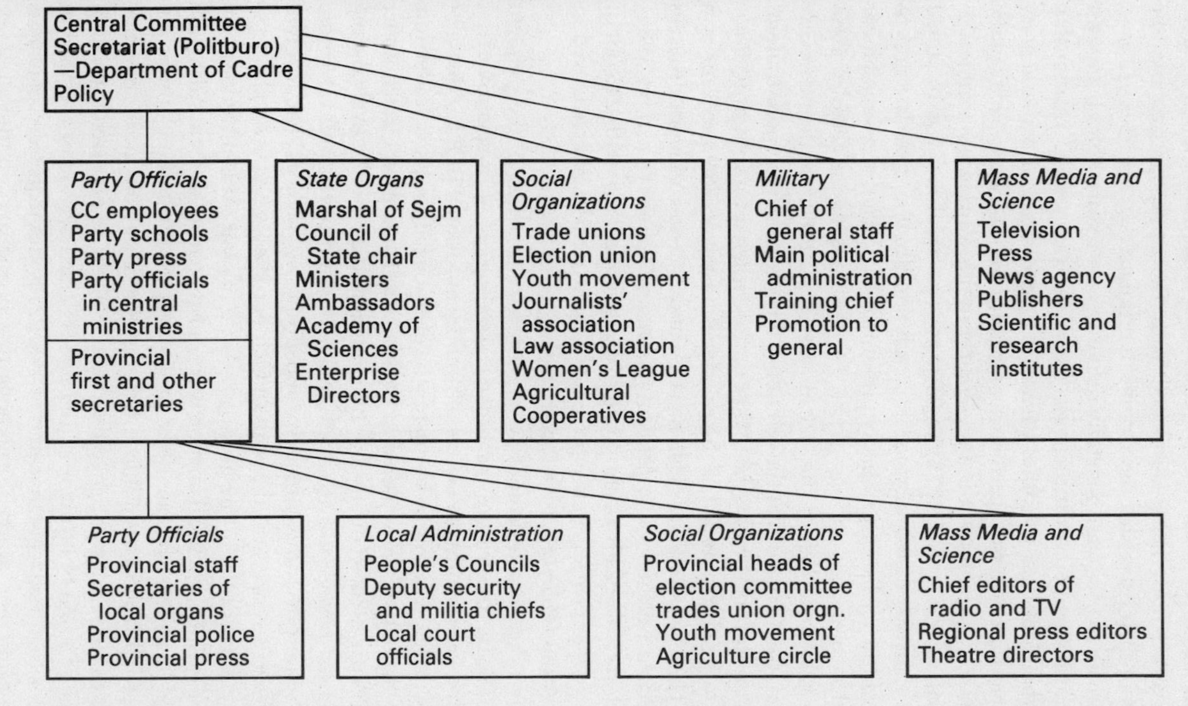

Figure 3.2 System of *Nomenklatura* Appointments

The above lists represent a brief selection from each category.

Source: based on material from *Aneks* (London), no. 26, 1981, pp. 44–50.

exercise some influence. Jaruzelski's attempts to neutralize opposition and increase social support in the post-martial law period have also led to more consultative relations being developed with the minor parties and the possibility of their exercising more political influence.

Elections to the Sejm are generally held every four years, votes being cast within multi-member constituencies. As in the case of the relationship between the PZPR and the other parties, the significance of parliamentary elections has varied over the period of communist rule and the capacity of the population to register its political preferences in this way has been subject to change (Sakwa & Crouch, 1978). In 1985, the electoral law was modified to ensure that two delegates stood for each constituency mandate and to introduce a further list of nationally prominent candidates as a supplement to those elected on a constituency basis. The elections held in October 1985 were the first since before the fall of Gierek in 1980, the Sejm having extended its life in order that the elections could be held in a more tranquil political atmosphere. Unlike the 1980 election, when a turnout of 98.9 per cent was officially recorded, a more modest total of 78.9 per cent was claimed. This, however, was challenged by underground Solidarity sources who estimated a turnout of 66 per cent (*Uncensored Poland*, December 1985). The result gave the PZPR a continuing majority in the Sejm with 245 out of 460 seats (53 per cent), which represented a fall from the level achieved in earlier elections (*Polityka*, 26 October 1985).

Although the Sejm does not have the capacity to act as an independent legislative body, the parties' candidates standing on a cooperative, not competitive, basis within the electoral front organization, PRON, it does not always act merely as a rubber stamp for the decisions of the party leadership. The 'long Sejm' that was replaced in October 1985 had been elected under Gierek in April 1980; its discussions became more than usually lively during the Solidarity period and its questioning of government officials more pointed. Some government requests and proposals, such as that to grant special powers to cope with the crisis in October 1981, were rejected.

When military rule, in the guise of a 'State of War', was introduced on 13 December 1981, the proclamation was not issued from the Sejm, although this should have been the case if the procedures set out in the Constitution had been strictly followed. While critical interventions were made and some continued to vote against the government, in 1982 the Sejm passed legislation demanded of it and built many of the powers characteristic of the State of War into the standard legislative framework. PZPR members were, of course, the most numerous group throughout this period and continued to be subject to party discipline.

Sejm activity and shifts in the independence of members' behaviour have tended to follow a cyclical pattern since the consolidation of communist rule in the late 1940s. The lowest level of activity was shown by the Sejm elected in 1952 during the Stalin period and, with the change in political climate in 1956, demands were made for an extensive review and upgrading of the institution's status. Particular criticism was made of the widespread use of government decrees, which meant that the Sejm was sidestepped and its formal status as the 'leading organ' of the Polish state undermined (Terry, 1981, pp. 29–30). Although a considerable increase in Sejm activity did take place, the more far-reaching demands, for example that the group of PZPR members should have some independence from the central party leadership, were not accepted and both the level and significance of Sejm activity declined towards the end of the Gomułka period, a process that broadly repeated itself under Gierek. There is considerable evidence to support the suggestion that the status of the Sejm has varied according to the perception of the party's leadership of the need and usefulness of more extensive political participation, and that the Sejm is thus best regarded as a 'minimal parliament' which is relatively weak in its relation to the leadership of the party and the state bureaucracy (Olson & Simon, 1982, p. 48).

Considerable care is taken to give the Sejm a representative character, although, of course, the decisions as to who stands as a candidate are taken under party leadership within the electoral front rather than the electorate itself having the power to decide who its representatives should be. The major political authorities have generally been well represented (in the 1970s the whole of the Politburo, all provincial first secretaries of the party, and over half the CC were elected), as are other spheres of public life, including the arts, science and education.

The Sejm elected in 1985, though, contained far fewer representatives of the party establishment (only 28 of the 460 deputies were also members of the CC) and more political novices. Some members do not belong to any of the three parties and a few have a formal Catholic affiliation, although the qualified independence of the Catholic members has been steadily reduced since the controversy over the amendments to the Constitution in 1976. Some criticism has been expressed of the lower political temperature that has characterized the Ninth Sejm (that elected in 1985) and the fact that most major political initiatives have been issued from other areas of the central leadership (*Polityka*, 6 June 1987). Members of the different party and non-party groups are represented in somewhat different proportions on the Sejm's permanent committees, now numbering over twenty. These bodies can be of some importance in view of the very short period during which the full Sejm is in session, generally not more than a dozen days a year. The PZPR does not have a majority on all committees, although it is, of course, the largest single grouping. Its representation has been strongest on committees which can be seen to lie closest to its interests, such as those concerned with national defence, communications and the machine-building industry. Heavy industry, mining and foreign trade have also seen extensive PZPR representation. The ZSL has, not surprisingly, had higher representation on the forestry and agriculture committees while the SD has been most numerous on internal affairs. Non-party members have been concentrated on the foreign affairs and science committees, but have been absent from the national defence committee and that concerned with mandates and rules which govern the political regulation of Sejm membership (Olson & Simon, 1982, pp. 71–2). But the role of the standing committees should not be exaggerated, either, as the frequency of their meetings is also less than that of their equivalents in Western parliaments. Many of the more contentious issues are not taken up in full committee and are dealt with in informal *ad hoc* subcommittees.

Sejm members formally determine also the composition of two other major organs of state. One is the Council of State (RP), which takes on the Sejm's legislative responsibility when it is not in session and exercises its power to appoint and recall government ministers. It also acts as Poland's collective presidency and its chairman takes on the role of head of state, the function fulfilled by General Jaruzelski (in conjunction with his role as party leader) since November 1985. The former chairman of the RP was Henryk Jabłonski, who did not manage to be re-elected to the Politburo at the Extraordinary Congress in 1981. Jaruzelski's transfer to this post therefore brought it back within the ambit of the senior party leadership. The RP nominates the vice-chairman (its chairman being elected directly by the Sejm) of the Supreme Control Chamber (NIK) responsible for supervising and checking the activities of the entire state administration and a great array of social organizations.

The second major organ is the Council of Ministers (RM), whose chairman acts as Prime Minister. The Prime Minister is nominated at the first session of a new Sejm. The proposal of Zbigniew Messner for this post in November 1985, given Messner's extensive experience at the Katowice Academy of Economics and related institutions, suggested a greater concentration of government attention on the recovery of the Polish economy and its further reform. The chairman of the RM then presents his proposals for the composition of the government to the Sejm for ratification. That proposed by Messner involved a reduction in the number of ministers from thirty to twenty-six, including the retention of four generals.

The issue of further change in the institutions of central government remained very much on the agenda. The protracted and generally ineffective process of 'economic reform' fed the conviction that the main barriers to change lay in this area. Published evidence showed that staffing in central government institutions had grown by 7 per cent during the 1982–5 'reform' period and that the rate of growth had been greater at the higher levels of government service (*Polityka*, 10 January 1987). The Polish government was larger than that in comparable capitalist and developing countries and was surpassed in size only by those in some other communist countries, particularly the Soviet Union (*Polityka*, 12 September 1987). Proposals emerged for a radical change in the central government apparatus, reducing the number of central resorts from twenty-nine to sixteen and bringing the number of permanent ministers down from twenty-five to eleven. By these means, it was claimed, the government could devote itself to governing rather than involving itself in administration (*Polityka*, 25 July 1987). In the event, a specially convened session of the CC was followed in October 1987 by the passage through the Sejm of legislation which appeared to introduce major changes, eliminating seven ministries and reducing the size of the central governing group from thirty-two to twenty-three. A 25 per cent cut in the 12,000-strong central government bureaucracy was also projected.

Following the proclamation by the RP on 13 December 1981 of martial law (the 'State of War', *Stan Wojenny*, alluded to in Article 33 of the Constitution) until it was lifted in July 1983, the established institutions of political rule (and of PZPR dominance) were overridden by a Military Council of National Salvation (WRON). It was headed, as was the government (in his capacity as Chairman of the RM) and the party (as PZPR First Secretary), by General Jaruzelski, an amalgamation of roles which made it unclear at times precisely which capacity he was acting in. This was probably a major reason underlying his accumulation of the posts—since he had become First Secretary of the CC eight weeks before the military pronouncement it could at least appear that the party leader was in command. The WRON comprised four deputy defence ministers, three commanders of military districts, three service chiefs, the three generals who were cabinet ministers, two other generals and four colonels.

While the WRON was dissolved in July 1983, the legacy of military rule retained some practical significance. First, not only did General Jaruzelski retain his other offices of party and state, relinquishing some of the latter at a later stage, but many other military personnel remained in key positions. Second, extensive legislation was passed during the period of military rule which extended the range of repressive measures available to the state in times of political 'normality' (Sanford, 1986, pp. 180–3). The necessity to resort to the constitutionally awkward formula employed in December 1981 was now no longer necessary if the party-state leadership felt an immediate need to increase its security capability. Third, a National Defence Council (KOK) (*Komitet Obrony Kraju*) remains in existence whose composition and status are a matter of some speculation. Its importance, however, has been emphasized by some analysts (Morawski, 1985, pp. 29–30). Certainly, its powers with reference to defence and matters of state security were extended in November 1983, and General Jaruzelski took over as its chairman at the same time as he resigned from the Ministry of Defence.

Centralism and Self-government

The structure of rule in Poland has therefore not only been a centralized one (although it has not always operated effectively and has on occasion been relaxed) but has seen further tendencies to the reinforcement of central state power following the Solidarity period. Both democratic centralism and the principle of self-government have been promoted, but the development and perpetuation of centralized party-state power has been favoured. This has not left much scope for autonomous action on the part of the official organs of local and self-government, the People's Councils (RN). According to Article 46 of the Constitution, they are responsible for directing the 'total configuration of cultural and socio-economic development and exert influence on all units of administration and the economy within their area'. On the other hand, their influence is far from being sovereign: RNs may be overruled by superior authorities in any case where their decision is illegal or 'incompatible with the state's basic line of policy' (Article 54).

In practice, self-government has never been strong and was further weakened under Gierek. The existing three-tier system was replaced by a two-tier one, which was intended to strengthen central control over local government and eliminate the local centres of independence and opposition to central power that had previously developed within the state hierarchy and, particularly, the party apparatus. One measure concerned the abolition of the Praesidia of the RN, which had a cumbersome and ambiguous role as both organs of formal self-government and of central government, and their replacement in the latter function by local governors (*wojewody*) at province (*województwo*) level appointed by central government (Figure 3.3). The governors appointed analagous executive agents at the lower level of government. The self-governing functions of People's Councils were supposedly enhanced by local party secretaries being placed to lead the RN,

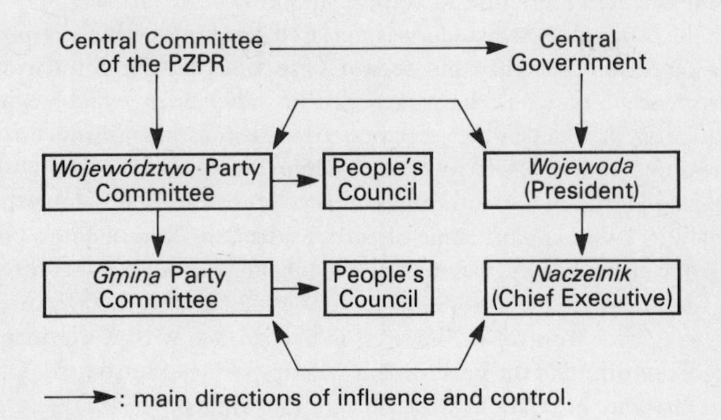

Figure 3.3 Post-1975 Structure of Local Government

although it was never very clear how this innovation tallied with the notion of *self*-government. This arrangement was quietly dropped in 1980, when national political developments had raised far more significant issues. In practice, the administration left little room for self-government and the state executive even tended to dominate party organs and their apparatus (Lewis, 1982).

Gierek's slogan that 'the party leads but the government governs' had been accepted as one of the guiding principles in the structural changes made in local government and administration during the 1970s. It underlay such measures as the party's assumption of direct leadership over the RN and the establishment of a separate state executive, and aimed to reduce bureaucratic complexity and the doubling of administrative functions. By emphasizing the separation of state and party activities, moreover, it was intended to strengthen party control over state organs and thus enhance party leadership. As was the case with other policies pursued by the Gierek regime, though, this aim was not achieved. Centralization was enhanced to the detriment of administrative and economic efficiency, and nowhere was this truer than in the case of the economic administration and the central ministries—although their deconcentration had been part of the original conception of reform. The economy remained highly centralized, however, and the increasingly massive economic production units (WOGs) occupied a dominant position, contributing to a weakening of local party control and an overburdening of the state executive. This was accompanied by the misuse and abuse of state funds that accompanied the progressive collapse of the economy and the growing inability of the regime to maintain its position.

Local elections were due to be held in Spring 1982 and were postponed under the State of War, which was declared not long before the proposed voting date. Solidarity had put forward proposals for the reform of local government which would have increased its independence and enabled the introduction of independent electoral commissions, promising further to undermine conventions of party leadership. The need for reform was also recognized by the Polish authorities, although obviously not along the lines proposed in 1981. The principle of party leadership, exercised now through the agency of the PRON, was maintained but some changes were introduced in legislation passed by the Sejm in July 1983. RN were to gain greater freedom in their control of finances, in accordance with the principles of economic reform that the government was struggling to introduce. They had increased rights in relation to local economic enterprises and were able to make greater claims on them in relation to the planned provision of local services and facilities. They were also to have greater powers in connection with the appointment and supervision of those exercising state executive authority, that is the provincial governors and local administrative leaders (*Rocznik Polityczyny i Gospodenczy*, 1984, pp. 102–6).

When the postponed elections were held in June 1984 they were treated, by the authorities and opposition alike, very much as a trial of political strength and a test of the regime's authority, which remained open to considerable doubt following the lifting of the State of War the previous year. In the event, the authorities claimed a turnout considerably lower than the usual figure within a hair's breadth of 100 per cent, although one that reflected a clear 'majority' if that is how the proportion of those voting was to be interpreted. It was claimed that 75 per cent in fact voted, which meant at that nearly 7 million of the electorate had not. Solidarity representatives claimed that 60 per cent had voted (which meant that, on Solidarity's own calculation, in 1985, the regime had succeeded in encouraging a higher turnout for the Sejm elections). To gain election, candidates had to capture the votes of at least 50 per cent of those so entitled (each elector had as many votes as the seats available for that constituency). This was not achieved in 330 cases and new elections had to be held (*Polityka*, 30 June 1984). In the context of the election it was clear from the declarations on both sides that it was not so much the character of the local government organs that was at issue or any public appraisal of the reforms introduced the previous year as popular willingness to become involved in the official machinery of political participation established by the regime. The main issue was the legitimation of the structures of political rule the authorities deemed appropriate during the period of military rule and under the slightly changed conditions that followed the lifting of the State of War.

Questions surrounding the nature of local government, though, could not be ignored and the new party programme, in preparation prior to the Tenth Congress, came under some criticism for its relative neglect of conditions that would make more effective the operation of representative institutions like the Sejm and RN. More effective decentralization was called for and options like one-member constituencies discussed as ways of increasing public interest in the operation of the RN and raising the level of involvement in election campaigns (*Polityka*, 24 May 1986). A year after the Tenth Congress, though, the slow pace of change was the source of some complaint, and faster progress in improving electoral procedures was called for in preparation for the 1988 elections to RN (*Polityka*, 18 July 1987). New proposals for the RN election procedures were presented to the public at the end of 1987. While failing to arouse much popular enthusiasm, they were welcomed for obliging voters to enter a ballot booth as standard procedure and eliminating the practice of 'passive voting' (*Polityka*, 16 January 1988). The maintenance of a preferential list of candidates for the provincial councils was generally criticized, but the new regulations were broadly approved as first proposed.

Auxiliary Organizations

The strained relationship between the communist authorities and the Polish population led the Jaruzelski leadership to establish and encourage the development of a range of socio-political structures, which lay officially outside direct PZPR control but which sympathized with and acted to facilitate the achievement of the leadership's objectives. Against a backdrop of falling membership, not just in the PZPR but also in a number of official regime-sponsored organizations, the struggle to wean Poles away from identification with the Solidarity organization and to involve them in the activities of auxiliary organizations supportive of the central party-state institutions was the focus of the regime's attention. As the previous discussion of PZPR experiences might have suggested, this task has not been an easy one, although it has been pursued with persistence and some subtlety over the years.

The process began early in the period of military rule with the formation, along the lines of Jaruzelski's WRON, of Citizen's Committees for National Salvation (OKON) intended to promote national unity and dampen down social antagonism towards the military leadership. These were later termed Citizen's Committees for National Rebirth (OKON) and, in the autumn of 1982, formed into the Patriotic Movement for National Rebirth (PRON). By

1986, over 150 social organizations had affiliated themselves to PRON, which had also taken over the functions of the former electoral front organization, FJN.

PRON was credited with a number of political initiatives, including the lifting of the State of War, the proclamation of various amnesties and the introduction of the 1987 referendum. It was clearly intended to be viewed as a kind of surrogate pressure group—one in which the level of pressure could be regulated by the authorities and which was not the expression of uncontrolled social forces. Nevertheless, in 1986 PRON had 1.2 million individual members, only 30 per cent of whom were not already members of political parties. This, it was officially admitted, did not give PRON a very strong claim to be socially representative (*Nowe Drogi*, September 1986, p. 53).

A number of new bodies were also set up by the Sejm early in the period of military rule. A Constitutional Tribunal, Tribunal of State (a constitutional court), and Commission for Constitutional Responsibility (designed to investigate affairs brought before the Tribunal of State) were all established in 1982. In combination with the large amount of legislation brought before the Sejm in 1982, these initiatives demonstrated the intention of the military leadership to normalize the political situation by underpinning their unconventional rule with a range of new legal powers and procedures and a network of auxiliary political institutions.

The context in which these institutions were to operate, though, and the restrictions that were placed on their activity were evident not just from the conditions imposed by a 'State of War' but also from the vehement objections expressed to a proposal made in the party journal that a form of 'socialist pluralism' might help counteract the negative features that had tended to recur in Polish political life (*Nowe Drogi*, September 1982). Pluralism of any sort, it was countered, involved some idea of a free play of forces and as such identified the concept as one belonging to the world of contemporary capitalism.

It was permissible to talk of and encourage the formation of a plurality of political organizations, cooperatives or unions (as indeed the military authorities had set about doing), but this was not to be confused with any form of political pluralism (*Nowe Drogi*, December 1982). Proposals for the retention or reactivation of political pluralism could be identified as attacks on the foundations of the socialist order (*Nowe Drogi*, October 1983). The extensive discussion this provoked showed, though, that the idea of a 'socialist pluralism' had broader support in the party and that the necessity of coming to terms with the diverse forces within Polish society through frameworks less restricted than those of obvious communist front organizations was also recognized. While there was evident disagreement about the autonomy that should be permitted to organizations outside the central party framework and their relationship to the diverse forces in Polish society, it was agreed that a range of such institutions was not only acceptable but politically quite essential.

Following the experience of Solidarity and other autonomous trade union organizations in 1980–1, it was clear that the future form of the trade-union movement would be one of the first issues that had to be faced. All existing trade-union organizations, suspended since the announcement of military rule, were declared illegal in October 1982 and legislation was passed to permit the creation of unions on a new basis. They were organized, in the first instance, at enterprise level and then by industrial branch but not, like Solidarity, by region. They were obviously designed to be more amenable to party-state control than the former union, and there was no great enthusiasm amongst workers and employees to join them.

In contrast to the membership of 9.5 million which Solidarity achieved in a matter of weeks in 1980, the new unions had mobilized 4.299 million by the end of 1984, after two years of existence. Party members showed little greater inclination to join than those outside the party organizations and it was clear that the new organizations had only lukewarm support, although public sympathy was by no means completely lacking (Mason, 1987). In November 1984 a central union organization (OPZZ) was set up and in 1986 its Chairman, A. Miodowicz, was elected to the Politburo.

But the new unions were certainly not presented as just a tool of the government or party—and they would have had little capacity to perform any useful function if it was clear that that was all they were. The actual degree of union independence has naturally been very difficult to establish, though. The OPZZ is certainly reported to have been critical of matters like food supplies, economic planning, housing and work safety, while its chairman at the Tenth Party Congress attacked the 'violent rebirth' of arrogance among economic administrators (*Polityka*, 29 November 1986). Price reform and the government's counter-inflation policy were the major bone of contention and the unions were reported to have made the government retreat over price rises planned for 1987 (*Polityka*, 28 March 1987, and 4 April 1987). Their views appear to have evolved from opposition and scepticism towards the reform economic programme on those grounds to support accompanied by a strong emphasis on the need for administrative reform and the reduction of bureaucracy (*Polityka*, 4 July 1987). In this, of course, they were in agreement with central leadership policy as it developed in the second half of 1987.

Careful attention was also being paid to other sectors of society by the Jaruzelski leadership, and a novel attempt to institutionalize relations with opinion-formers and the intelligentsia was made with the establishment of a Consultative Council (RK) in 1986 to advise directly the Chairman of the RP (Jaruzelski at the time of the Council's formation). Two-thirds of the Council's members had professorial status and a quarter were or had been Sejm deputies. Only a third of the 56 members were party members and a number had a strong affiliation with the Catholic Church (*Polityka*, 20 June 1987). It was difficult to establish the degree of influence such a relatively informal body could have on policy-making, but it certainly opened up channels of influence that have been unusual in Marxist regimes. In 1987 the process spread further through the political system and RK counterparts were set up at province level as 'Consultative Conventions': OKK (*Polityka*, 28 November 1987).

But these new institutional arrangements and possibilities of social influence were established, it must be noted, in a situation where participation in existing officially constituted organizations had fallen dramatically and where many groups and professional associations which had formed or reconstituted themselves and acquired extensive autonomy in 1980 and 1981 had been radically reorganized or disbanded under martial law. Like participation in the PZPR and other workers' organizations, membership of youth associations fell sharply in the early 1980s. Against the 1.993 million membership of the Union of Polish Socialist Youth (ZSMP) in 1980 and 2.361 million in analagous organizations in 1970, there were 1.504 million members at the end of 1986; numbers in the Scouts' association (ZHP) fell from 3.149 million in 1980 to 2.050 million in 1986 (*Rocznik Statystyczny*, 1987, pp. 31).

While the central structures of political rule came under severe criticism in 1980 and 1981 and ultimately survived only with the support of a military intervention which succeeded in pacifying their socially hostile environment, the democratic façade of social support and the quasi-popular characteristics they had acquired were obliterated. Military rule therefore found the official, tolerated political structures at a low level of popular support which continued to decline, while recently established or rejuvenated organizations which had developed autonomously and had extensive social support were now suspended or abolished. The range of new structures established since 1982 was clearly intended to bridge this gap and to blur the sharp contrast between official and popular institutions. It is doubtful whether the regime has had a great deal of success in this endeavour.

Nevertheless, the leadership has continued to place considerable emphasis on what has more recently been termed the 'coalition method of exercising power', whose basic condition was identified as the class structure of Polish society which, while not monolithic, was nevertheless numerically dominated by the working class (*Nowe Drogi*, September 1985). Similarly to the previous formulation of socialist pluralism, this conception also evoked criticism decrying the abandonment of the party's leading role and calling for the reassertion of the dictatorship of the proletariat (*Nowe Drogi*, January 1986). Further discussion in the party's theoretical journal was this time accompanied, though, by editorial comment affirming that the 'coalition method' was not to be identified with any kind of political pluralism implying tolerance of anti-socialist forces and that it had already been practised extensively in communist Poland (*Nowe Drogi*, August 1986).

It seems clear that by this stage the leadership was determined to stick to its policy of political inclusion and was not inclined to be intimidated by charges of Marxist-Leninist heterodoxy (Kolankiewicz, 1988). Certainly, at the Tenth Party Congress the need to continue with a policy of 'national understanding' was reaffirmed, as was the desirability of cooperating with 'all who accepted the Constitution' and wished to work for the development of Poland (*Polityka*, 18 July 1987). The weakness of the PZPR and its associated organizations had clearly impressed on the leadership the advisability of maintaining and developing a broad network of socio-political structures over which central party-state control might well be very light but which could, by their very existence, serve to buttress the position of the central leadership. In this sense, the role of the more recently established auxiliary organizations was recognized to be growing and their political significance far from peripheral. The experiences of the post-1981 period had nevertheless impressed on the leadership the long-term nature of the plan for political recovery this represented and the limited nature of the political improvement it had so far brought about. In the autumn of 1987, as the emphasis on political reform was again growing stronger, and a referendum was held to extend the scope of consultation, the priority of change in terms of extending democratic practices surrounding elections to representative institutions like the RN was recognized (*Nowe Drogi*, September 1987).

Overview

Despite the obvious contrasts between the different periods of recent Polish history, from Gomułka to the Gierek regime, through the Solidarity period to the State of War and Jaruzelski's militarized form of normalization, it is possible to detect a certain continuity in terms of the central structures and themes of political rule. There have been variations and differences in emphasis, but party leadership, democratic centralism and the dominance of Marxist-Leninist ideology have been lasting principles of political action. What is specific to the Polish situation is that they have also been weakly expressed themes and that they have clearly not been strong enough to sustain the authority of the party-state leadership at certain crucial junctures in the post-war period.

Ideological fervour and Marxist-Leninist dogma were objects of contention under Gomułka, they were not strongly promoted by Gierek, they largely disappeared from view during the Solidarity period, and they were also played down under military leadership. During the Gierek period democratic centralism within the party became transformed into bureaucratized authoritarianism, was replaced within much of the party in 1980–1 by a democratizing reformism, and was effectively sidestepped by the militarized leadership. Similarly, party leadership has been persistently proclaimed but never fully practised or proved capable of existence as an autonomous principle of political rule: under Gierek it was supported and largely supplanted by the administrative bureaucracy, with the rise of Solidarity it became effectively submerged, while Jaruzelski proclaimed it only with the support of the steel corsetry of the military.

It is, then, the inadequacy of the conventional components and structures of communist rule that has proved to be most striking in modern Poland, while the specific characteristics of the successive phases of recent Polish history have been largely concerned with the mode of entry and operation of the supplementary institutions of political rule. The recent emphasis placed on the 'coalition method of exercising power' represents one further way of approaching this problem and an attempt to replace military structures and personnel as agencies of political rule. It is notable that the PZPR has continued to play a relatively limited role in this process and that growing emphasis is placed on non-party structures.

4 The Economics of Crisis

Nowhere is the complex relationship between politics and economics, so characteristic of the Soviet-type society, made more evident than in the history of Poland's successive crises. To the extent that political interests can be identified, they are also articulated within the economic arena. The place of work, the industrial relations network, the economic administrative hierarchy become forms of political as well as economic interest aggregation and integration. Even where a multitude of outlets have been created by the regime to channel political demands, these are usually judged by society to be inadequate and thus ignored.

What is evident is that the state of organizational affiliation rooted in the place of work, such as trade union, party or management identity, is a key element of political integration. It thus makes little sense to deal with the economic system of management, administration, directive planning and allocation in isolation from the political and social processes which underlie it.

A political economy of 'real socialism' has to recognize that the systems of eastern Europe were *ab initio* different in kind from their western capitalist counterparts. Capital accumulation, markets, economic incentive and motivation, and indeed the whole range of actions and attitudes extant within capitalism, are perforce absent. Instead, the indigenous regimes, committed first and foremost to political consolidation and only then to economic transformation, substitute a variety of structures and mechanisms to perform these self-same functions. Often these are linked to structures of domination extending beyond the physical boundaries of these nation-states, for example into the CMEA, and bilateral relations with the Soviet Union. Economic reform, with its search for higher productivity, within this context has shifted from an emphasis upon refining these mechanisms to introducing the 'radical methods of profit and loss accounting and . . . competition' as General Jaruzelski put it during a trip to Japan in June 1987. Echoing Gorbachëv, he claimed that these, however, were simply tools like multiplication tables (*sic*) for making the economy more effective without, by implication, altering the fundamental principles of the socialist system. It could be argued, however, that to the extent that these market mechanisms are effective they will reshape these founding principles. Competition implies capital flows, bankruptcies, unemployment, and income inequality before it can provide the supply-demand equilibrium so much sought after by these regimes. That all the above are now being actively canvassed, by reformers and regime alike, is generally accepted. What the political consequences will be is difficult to surmise. The 'right to work' has been left as the only slogan to which the regimes of 'real socialism' can convincingly point in their ideological confrontations with the West. If this is now sacrificed in the search for 'restructuring', then it is impossible, in the Polish case, to predict what, if any, level of additional 'glasnost' could compensate in a society still imbued with the living legacy of Solidarity and all the freedoms which the period of its open existence brought forth.

The Context of Crisis

Poland is a country whose employment structure is still overly biased towards agriculture, heavy industry and raw materials—the primary sector. While agriculture is relatively efficient, given its structure and resources, its products are highly subsidized as much through the intermediary state organizations as to the prices paid to peasants and present the regime with a hard political, as well as economic, nut to crack. Industry is still energy- and materials-intensive in use, with poorly developed export capacity. With inflation running at approximately 23 per cent, and forecast to rise to 60 per cent during 1988, meat is still rationed, whereas 'invisible' as well as visible queues exist for consumer durables. Poland's hard currency debt at the end of 1987 was in excess of 39.2 billion dollars and rising. No less significant is the 6.5 billion rouble debt owed largely to the Soviet Union (but being tackled more forcefully), which the latter is now using as a lever to impose conditions of cooperation upon the Poles which will fundamentally affect the future structure of economic production, export orientation and ultimately political and social change. During the early 1980s debt servicing exceeded foreign currency earnings by more than half and Poland was *de facto* bankrupt. Whereas Poland may well be in the same financial position as, for example, Argentina, the fact that only 8 per cent of Poland's national income derives from export earnings, compared to 13 per cent for Argentina, makes the latter far more vulnerable. And yet Poland's light industry, with its low pay levels and some international quality productions (admittedly declining) earns 'curiously little' from export (*Polityka-Eksport-Import* No. 2. 1987). At root has been the continually frustrated attempts by successive Polish leaders to reorientate Poland towards efficient export only to find themselves more firmly than ever in the grip of the traditional heavy- and machine-industry lobbies.

Worst-case scenarios predict a debt exceeding $60 billion by 1995. Currently little is on offer from the West in the way of new credits after the much awaited partial normalization of Polish–US relations in 1987. Positing a policy of step-by-step re-engagement based on 'prioritized political and economic conditionality' (Hardt and Boone, 1987), the scenario of events in Poland loosely associated with economic reform has done little to inspire new confidence in creditors or debtors alike.

While the initial decline appeared to have been halted in the years up to 1985, since then economic reserves of a simple kind have been exhausted, and the twin evils of decapitalization and underutilization have advanced to centre stage. Whether the economic reform which was formally initiated during the early stages of martial law will gather the critical mass necessary to break down the bureaucratic structures of central distribution and intervention located in the ministries and associations is an open question. The regime is currently embarking on what it has euphemistically called the 'second stage of reform' after a period when most of Polish society could be excused for asking what the first stage consisted of, other than massive price rises overlaid with reform rhetoric. Some interesting proposals are being mooted. Changes to the banking system, shareholding in state enterprises, new forms of worker collective and 'communal property' held by local councils, are all intended to extract initiative, productivity, market-orientation and economic vitality out of the mire of apathy and passivity which came with martial law. (*Rzeczpospolita*, 13 April 1987). These proposed changes will probably only affect a small segment of the economy, since large parts appear to have already been committed to long-term cooperation agreements with the Soviet Union and other CMEA countries. Joint ventures with both capitalist and bloc partners (which are qualitatively different entities despite the use of the same term for both), widespread private and individual sector growth, and 'Polonia' firms (based on émigré capital) are all intended to inject new forms of property relations into the system and thus generate new material interests and hopefully appropriate economic action. Elsewhere enforced bankruptcy of certain enterprises (largely confined to some much publicized building enterprises), projected cutbacks in state subsidy (which literally eat up 45 per cent of the state budget), raw-materials and energy-saving campaigns are intended to signal the arrival of a new discipline in the economy. The Five-Year Plan for 1986–90, however, raises more questions than it answers. It is difficult to say to what extent the lessons of the 1960s and 1970s have been learned and economic restructuring is in sight. Whether the hold of the traditional lobbies has been broken is unclear. The dominant air seems to be one of pessimism (*Życie Gospodarcze*, 25 January 1987). Machinery in the state industrial sector is calculated to be 49–60 per cent decapitalized, despite the fact that over 50 per cent of the machine park, for example, date from 1975 or later, that is, that machinery has not been replaced or spares are not available. The decision to commit 85 per cent of available investment funds over 1986–7 to the completion of projects commenced in the 1970s does not appear to signal a shift from the traditional profile of investment. In this matter the role of the Soviet Union has been critical in providing the means to complete a number of projects such as the much criticized Huta Katowice (and, more controversially, the outdated 'Peace' steel works), thus maintaining and expanding production in steel, electro-mechanical engineering, chemicals and shipbuilding. Poland's total reliance upon the Soviet Union for gas, oil and other raw materials, the bulk of Soviet exports to Poland, as well as its poor creditworthiness, have made it more than usually vulnerable to *ad hoc* offers of Soviet assistance. Shortages of foreign currency, capital and raw materials, whether linked to sanctions or Poland's poor creditworthiness or not, are presented as making the establishment of far-reaching, direct and fundamentally *new* forms of economic (followed by cultural, political and ideological) cooperation unavoidable (see Chapter 6).

Per-capita national income produced in 1986 is still 13 per cent lower than in 1978. Real incomes grew by a mere 1.7 per cent on average, compared to 3.8 per cent in 1985 and were 12.4 per cent lower in real terms than in 1978. Investment was running at 69.8 per cent of the 1978 level (see Table 4.1).

Economic uncertainty, fuelled by inflation and large rises in nominal incomes, has created tensions in the consumer goods market. The target of a return to the living standards of 1978 has now been pushed back to at least 1995. Real poverty currently affects nearly a quarter of the population and the crisis is no longer simply economic but is often referred to by official spokesmen as the 'degradation of civilized existence' (*Życie Warszawy*, 7/8 March 1987).

As the rest of the world gears up for 'deindustrialization' and/or 'post-industrialism' Poland continues to feed its mining, steel, shipping and other 'anachronistic' industries. Services, light industry, pharmaceuticals, tourism, artistic products, optics—all these and other areas of possible expansion trip easily off the tongues of reform-minded economists and yet are even now not treated as serious alternatives (*Kurier Polski*, 27 February 1987).

Table 4.1 Basic Indicators (1960 = 100)

	1970	1975	1978	1980	1982	1985	1986
National income produced (at constant prices)	180.2	287.2	331.7	304.7	253.4	293.2	307.6
Cost of living index	120.3	135.5	161.8	188.3	471.9	768.9	909.9
Consumption of goods and services	162.1	243.0	284.3	299.9	245.0	278.0	291.9
Average monthly wages in state sector	119.5	169.0	176.8	187.8	144.2	152.2	156.3
Investment in national economy	204.5	458.7	487.9	394.1	268.8	347.2	364.9

Sources: Rocznik Statystyczny, 1986; *Rocznik Statystyczny*, 1987; (author's own calculations).

The Genealogy of Crisis

Poland's post-war reconstruction, assisted as it was by aid both from the United Nations Relief and Rehabilitation Administration (UNRRA) and later, to a lesser extent, from the Soviet Union, was initially an *ad hoc* process. Although the Central Office of Planning was set up in 1945 under Czesław Bobrowski (who was to be a major figure in the post-1981 reconstruction) and was then abolished in 1948, the role of the state was still largely in the area of goods distribution. The Three-Year Plan of Economic Reconstruction (1947–9) was aimed at just that, rebuilding that which had been destroyed, and it is to this period that many of the images of Poland arising phoenix-like from the ashes refer. On 5 March 1947, after the manipulated 'victory' in the January election, the Polish government signed an agreement in Moscow which set the seal on in-depth Soviet involvement in Polish economic development. A special commission was set up to oversee scientific and production exchanges, meeting twice a year. This could be seen as a natural consequence of the Polish–Soviet Treaty of Friendship, Aid and Mutual Co-operation signed on 21 April 1945. The economic inheritance of Stalinism in Poland as compared to the political-cultural inheritance has proved more durable and immune to restructuring than in any other bloc country save Romania. (*Prawo i Życie*, 9 April 1988).

After 1949 and during the Six-Year Plan, accumulation priorities predominated, and Soviet involvement in creating Poland's industrial base was almost total. Soviet specialists designed the Lenin Steel Works and most of the 150 large industrial complexes built during those years. Likewise, $1 billion of credit from the Soviet Union helped pay for this investment. These enterprises are currently responsible for 30 per cent of industrial production, 57 per cent of all steel, and the bulk of iron, oil and other products. Over 35,000 Polish specialists have been trained in the Soviet Union since the war (*Trybuna Ludu*, 5 March 1987) and 22,000 Soviets have assisted in Poland. In the later 1970s Poland was to reciprocate and supply the materials and know-how to equip or refurbish 150 enterprises in the Soviet Union. Half of the sulphuric acid produced by the Soviet Union (or 10 per cent of the world total) would come from some of these projects (*Trybuna Ludu*, 16 April 1985). It is important to keep this external reference of Poland's industrialization policy in mind when explaining the apparent irrationalities of such a direction of development or 'imposed modernization', as it has been aptly labelled (Morawski, 1980).

A glance at the indicators of growth for investment and consumption sectors during 1950–70 reveals increases of 958 per cent and 549 per cent, respectively. It becomes apparent that Poland's subsequent inability to foster export-led growth was rooted in the structure of specialization. Central was the predominance of the electro-mechanical engineering industry (with its obviously military connections). Not only did it require high inputs of materials and energy but it was later seen by some economists as the worst possible 'choice' of specialization which could have been made given the degree of competition in this sector which existed within CMEA countries at the time (Landau, 1985). Despite this, Poland is reported to be considering expanding the share of this sector as a proportion of industrial goods sold from 23.6 per cent to 25.6 per cent by 1990, much of this being accounted for by a planned 70 per cent increase in exports to the Soviet Union of machine-industry products (*Czerwony Sztandar*, 12 August 1986).

Of course, there are other reasons for the particular contours of Poland's economic development. Between 1950 and 1954 over 15 per cent of national income was given over to arms production and indeed the Korean war and the cold war helped to consolidate the ascendancy of the machine-building sector which acted as coordinator for the military-industrial complex. Developing at the expense of infrastructure, housing, agriculture and services, it took the Poznań riots and Polish October to call a brief respite to this lopsided growth. During the 1956–8 interlude attempts were made to halt the aggrandisement of bureaucratic power rooted in extensive growth and in a centralized command economy. A shift in the balance away from heavy industry as well as an adjustment of the uneven development of the

Six-Year Plan period was called for. Also, the unequal trade relations which had persisted between Poland and the Soviet Union since 1945 came under criticism. Poland was in effect paid compensation for, among other things, the artificially low prices paid for coal delivered to the Soviet Union since August 1945, although this compensation was largely in the form of release from payment of outstanding debts (Landau & Tomaszewski, 1985). These conditions should have made for a more flexible foreign trade policy and allowed for alternative growth strategies.

Despite propitious political and social conditions for introducing radical economic reforms as well as pushing consumption growth, by 1958–9 some elements of old pattern had reasserted themselves. At the same time the effects of infrastructural neglect and of so-called 'social considerations' were becoming more noticeable (the underdevelopment of health, leisure, culture, and so on). Productivity remained low, growth stagnated and western export markets were still inaccessible (Brada & Montias, 1985). A policy which during the 1960s had sought to reorientate Poland's exports through specialization along selected lines quickly ran into opposition from the heavy industrial-military lobbies. Being only partially introduced, it affected real wages (which were growing at a slower pace than anywhere else in the Soviet bloc), cut back housing and neglected working conditions without producing the necessary countervailing results in consumer goods production. Consequently the workers' riots of December 1970, in reaction to retail price rises, were the political consequence of economic policies rooted, however, in politically determined priorities.

Taking the mechanical engineering industry again, its share of Polish exports grew from 20 per cent in 1957 to 38.5 per cent in 1970, and accounted for 52.7 per cent of total exports to the socialist bloc countries (chiefly the Soviet Union) (Landau & Tomaszewski, 1985). This was hardly the stuff of a selective export strategy, but simply more of the same. The entry of Gierek and Jarosziewicz onto the scene produced policies which sought to resolve the double problem of achieving export-led growth and greater productivity in the absence of indigenous resources for restructuring and modernizing the economy. Foreign credits would be used to provide the necessary goods and services as well as capital investment, thus both incentives for higher productivity and the means for such production would be available at one and the same time. Higher real wages and large-scale investment, often with long lead times, was a risky policy but, with the ready availability of foreign credits, the buoyancy and optimism symbolized by the slogan of 'building a second Poland' and initial good fortune, expectations were high.

Gierek's policies involved no reform of the existing economic mechanisms (except for a failed attempt in the second half of the 1970s, the so-called 'economic manoeuvre' and the WOGs). Indeed it could be argued that 'turnkey' modernization, grounded on imported licences and technology, was a strategy eminently suited to the maintenance of the existing directive-distributive bureaucracy since it involved a minimum devolution of autonomy and responsibility to R & D centres, enterprises, local councils or society at large. It was inevitable, therefore, that investment policies would respond not to market forces or to the real capacities of the Polish economy but to various lobbies and pressure groups (not the power of argument but the argument of power, as a popular saying would have it). The grand gesture, prestigious projects, such as the Katowice steel works, the growth of motorization from 453,000 private cars in 1970 to 2,219,000 by 1980, western cigarettes and consumer durables, all provided the veneer of success, disguising from view the underlying crisis and the failure of strategy.

A brief period during 1972 saw a rapid growth in consumption goods. This then declined and by 1975, 'A' group (production) investments had a higher share of investment over 'B' group (consumption) than was the case in 1970 (68 per cent). It has been argued that the onset of the oil crisis and consequent recession in the West undermined a basic assumption of the regime's strategy, namely to pay for investment with exports. Be that as it may, 70 per cent of the trade deficit was generated during 1973–7 and the symptoms of crisis were clearly apparent in early 1976, when debt servicing alone amounted to over one-third of total income from exports. Nevertheless, whether it be due to economic romanticism, 'voluntarism', traditionalism or a host of national characteristics, despite the declining tempo of growth after 1976, investment still grew at excessive rates (2.5 times during 1970–80).

By the late 1970s, the Poles were effectively eating their credit (due to a failure of ill-conceived agricultural policies) or using it to cover mounting interest repayments. Infrastructure had been ignored, *overinvestment* had outstripped the abilities of an overstretched economy. Some one-third of all investments were stalled due to a shortage of building capacity (which accounted for 40–60 per cent of costs of new investments). Rather than modernizing existing stock (a lesson apparently learned by Gorbachëv's reformers) new capital goods were hastily and prematurely purchased while credit existed, often being kept in store (a euphemism for the actual conditions which allowed precious materials to deteriorate). As early as 1975, 60 per cent of all projects were behind schedule, tying up capital investment while real wages growth generated dangerous inflationary pressures.

Rather than being export-orientated, Polish industrial production, due to its poor quality as much as to shrinking markets, succumbed to import substitution. In the end Poland finished up taking credit (for licences, investment goods, etc.) in the West and exporting to the East (Monkiewicz, 1983). Turning, for example, once again to the mechanical engineering industry, by 1980 it provided for 47.8 per cent of all exports, and contributed nearly two-thirds of total exports to the CMEA countries (a quarter of exports to capitalist countries) (Müller, 1985), 'International obligations' are often cited for the disproportionate development of the Polish economy as much as to the indigenous 'centralized anarchy' or wild investments outside of the plan (Kaminski, 1985). As a consequence of these policies the demand for energy during the 1970s grew sevenfold and for cement twofold. And yet Poland used 2.5 times the energy per dollar of GNP as did France or Japan, and even 40 per cent more than Hungary. The same applied to steel and other materials. Poland's energy- and materials-dependent economy was in a worse state than before it had embarked on Gierek's modernization. In 1987, alongside lower market production and poorer quality goods, Polish industry still used more fuel and energy than in 1978 (*Życie Gospodarcze*, 14 February 1988).

By the 1980s, 10 per cent of enterprises accounted for 75 per cent of the means of production, employed 50 per cent of labour and accounted for 58 per cent of industrial production (Raport, 1986). It showed clearly where resources had gone: 'to those that have shall be given'. At the same time small scale production (e.g. bricks for housing) had been sacrificed on the altar of gigantism.

All of this makes reform, either in physical resource terms or in structural terms, very difficult. The presence of giant enterprises creates monopoly producers, whom the reformers have been decidedly loath to cut back. That these large enterprises are not only located in the fuel and heavy industry sector but are also the site of the most potentially militant sections of the working class, gives the economic bureaucracy good reason as they see it for not challenging them on prices and wages. Monopolies make pricing and wage reform equally ineluctable. Under the Gierek regime, during periods of relative support for the leadership, prices were not raised while wages forged ahead in an obvious policy of buying off discontent. Between 1970 and 1979 average wages rose by 116 per cent, prices by 77 per cent. Indeed during the whole 1950–79 period, wages had risen elevenfold, whereas commodities purchased in the socialized sector had risen by 170 per cent. Not surprisingly, therefore, by 1981, something like a quarter of the money in circulation was not covered by the goods available in the marketplace. That this produced a black market rate for the dollar at nearly 800 per cent of its official value is not surprising.

Martial law, if it did nothing else, raised prices by a swingeing 76 per cent during 1982 and produced a cut of 25 per cent in the average standard of living. Nominal incomes grew by 63 per cent during 1982, while during the days of alleged 'rampant wage demands by Solidarity' they had only increased by 27 per cent (Fallenbuchl, 1986). Martial law and its aftermath also presided over a mammoth drop in industrial production which in most areas is only just struggling back to 1980 levels and still falls short of the 1978 high levels. (see Table 4.2). Furthermore the regime has done little to date to attack subsidies, either in industry and agriculture or in various communal services, although post-1988 reforms promise to change this. It has had to defer to key sections of the working population in respect of large pay rises and at the same time has felt obliged to compensate (however inadequately) the weaker sections of the population, in receipt of a variety of benefits. As a consequence, inflation and dollar black market rates are such as to make rumours of a currency exchange (last enacted in 1950) sufficiently credible to warrant repeated government denials.

Inflationary pressures, monopolistic gigantism, foreign trade 'errors' and excessive rates of investment have not been the only legacy of the 1970s. The most emotive issue referred to the 447 licences for technology and know-how acquired by the Poles (90 per cent for the machine, heavy machine and chemical sectors). Only 342 of these licences ever came into operation and of these 166 never achieved anything like their planned production targets (*Życie Partii*, 16 September 1981). When, in 1982, a halt was called on over 1,600 investment projects (whose average level of completion was 27 per cent) the situation was grim. By 1983, 444 of those had been given the go-ahead and have soaked up what remains of the investment funds. The Soviet Union, in response to the effects of this putative western 'credit trap' came to the rescue and selected those enterprises with which it would cooperate either through the provision of raw materials and semi-finished products, or through the completion of investment. Thus was the policy of Polish reintegration and dependence on the CMEA put onto a new footing. *Ad hoc* measures were soon to turn into a full-blown policy coinciding with the emerging Gorbachëv reform platform.

By 1980 31.3 per cent of Poland's huge credits had been spent on investments (electro-mechanical engineering, construction, and so on) nearly 14.6 per cent on imports of grain and feedstuffs, and 18.3 per cent on other goods. A further 35.8 per cent was financing credit, some of which went on the purchase of raw materials and semi-finished products, unwittingly often

Table 4.2 Polish Industrial Production, 1970–86

Product	1970	1978	1980	1982	1985	1986
Electricity (TW/h)	64.5	116	122	118	138	140
Coal ($\times 10^3$t)	173	234	230	227	249	259
of which hard coal	140	193	193	189	192	192
Natural gas ($\times 10^6$m^3)	5.18	7.9	6.3	5.5	6.4	5.8
Zinc ($\times 10^3$t)	209	222	217	165	180	179
Copper (electrolyte) ($\times 10^3$t)	72.2	332	357	348	387	388
Refined oil ($\times 10^3$t)	7,471	16,970	16,126	13,405	14,067	14,300
Rolled steel ($\times 10^3$t)	8,136	13,565	13,551	10,477	11,845	12,300
Cement ($\times 10^6$t)	12.2	21.7	18.4	16.0	15.0	15.8
Passenger cars ($\times 10^3$)	64.2	326	351	228	283	290
Agricultural tractors ($\times 10^3$)	38.7	59.5	57.5	53	59	61.8
Ships, over 1000 dwt ($\times 10^3$dwt)	518	742	392	358	343	536
Washing machines, automatic ($\times 10^3$)	n.a.	273	360	232	303	277
Refrigerators and freezers ($\times 10^3$)	444	890	694	509	579	572
Radios ($\times 10^3$)	987	2,569	2,695	2,175	2,690	2,731
Tape Recorders (th)	184	912	806	373	384	406
Colour TVs ($\times 10^3$)	n.a.	60.6	147	144	158	173
Paper ($\times 10^3$t)	764	1,070	1,033	965	1,071	1,100
Shoes, non-rubber ($\times 10^6$ pairs)	108	136	140	126	148	147
Meat and fats ($\times 10^3$t)	1,376	2,452	2,459	1,856	1,973	2,261
Butter ($\times 10^3$t)	127	258	253	225	275	259
Cigarettes ($\times 10^9$)	69.2	90.8	93.4	87.5	90.0	94.2

Rocznik Statystyczny, 1986; and *Rzeczpospolita*, 3 February 1987.

following on from the initial capital investment, and later credits went more and more into debt servicing. However, even as late as 1976, when the so-called 'economic manoeuvre' was announced with the stated aim of cutting back on investment growth, the second stage of Huta Katowice was embarked upon, along with the huge PVC factory complex in Włocławek and the chemical plants in Police to name but three (Rydygier, 1985). Disconcertingly, efforts have again been directed at glossing over the reasons for Poland's indebtedness, particularly where these point to the bankruptcy of the directive-distributive economic apparatus or the economically irrational structure of Polish industry. Agricultural policy, with its current drive for self-sufficiency, reflects at best a partial lesson learned, since the $8.5 billion spent in the 1970s on the import of grain stands as a constant reminder of a quite palpable policy failure.

In short, the experience of the 1970s appeared to set the agenda for any future economic reform, so much so that in the mid-1980s some pro-regime economists were already arguing that the solutions generated in response to the mistakes of the 1970s were no longer applicable to the deepening crisis of the 1980s.

Reform and Crisis

Perhaps the major dimension of Jaruzelski's normalization strategy in the aftermath of the imposition of martial law was his stated commitment to economic reform. Growing out of the reform commission's proposals produced with Solidarity participation, in June 1981, it was adopted by the Party Congress in July 1981. As such, it could not very easily be dropped since it addressed the whole range of pathologies which had afflicted the economic system during the 1970s. After a trial run which involved the state farm and artisan craft sector, followed by the more controversial attempt at introducing an abridged transitional version of the reform in November 1981, a package of nine laws was eventually passed in February 1982, with effect from that July. Although the spirit of the reform had been effectively extinguished, the regime had few other modes of discourse through which it could communicate with a suspicious and alienated society.

The economic reform was popularly presented in the form of the 3 S's acronym (*samorządny, samofinansujący, samodzielny*), postulating a self-managing, self-financing and independent enterprise. At the same time the role of the centre, that of the RM, its all-important Planning Commission, as well as the branch and functional ministries, would be redefined. The Sejm, its commissions and local councils would be accorded greater legislative and control powers whilst the abolition of the middle-level tier of management, the association (*zjednoczenia*), and its replacement by largely voluntary associations of enterprises (*zrzeszenie*), was to be a sign of anti-bureaucratic good faith on the part of the regime. Planning was to be long-term and strategic, and socialized through a maximum of 'consultation'. Production would be profit-orientated, emphasizing quality, productivity, energy and materials conservation as well as being innovative, flexible and cost-conscious. The use of fiscal policy would replace direct intervention by the centre. A mixture of political changes were to be initiated since most commentators were aware that, if production enterprises did not do their job, then the state would do it for them, which in turn diverted the authorities from purely political tasks and entangled them in the day-to-day mire of administration (*Życie Gospodarcze*, 11 January 1987). Centralized distribution and hierarchical direction would be replaced by enterprises disciplined through the market. Bankruptcy was to become commonplace, while the role of diversified banks would be pushed to centre stage.

As mentioned above, the conditions under which reform was eventually introduced differed significantly even from the scenario of crisis under which it was fashioned. In particular the *price* element of the reform, a veritable corner-stone, was undermined. Shortage of foreign currency and of raw materials and high inflation provided the bureaucratic centre (ministries) with leverage over enterprises as well as with convincing arguments for deferring price reform until a more auspicious time. In part the 'propaganda of crisis', which replaced that of 'success', served the purposes of the anti-reform centre. Furthermore, with trade unions first suspended and then wound up and finally 'reborn', and with self-management organs suspended and then encompassed by transitional post-martial law legislation and the party reduced to ineffective 'social commissions', there existed no possible organizational champion of the reform ethos. The bureaucratic centre exploited these represssions to the full in order to reconstitute its power with a new guise, that of reform.

Given this scenario, it was not surprising that enterprises reacted to the stalled reform and uncertainty in a rational way. They sought to maximize their own access to centrally distributed resources, while paying lip-service to reform, chiefly through raising the prices of products and thus playing into the hands of the centre. In fact the centre, while wielding market-type instruments, such as credits, taxation and amortization, still decided upon the profitability or otherwise of an enterprise. What emerged was an *ad hoc* system of negotiating exemptions, privileges and special treatment on the part of enterprises, which was worse in its final consequences than the traditional centralized system. A legislated reform was apparently no more a guarantee of its successful implementation than previous less formalized solutions.

The Formal System: Informal Consequences

(i) *Centre–Enterprise Relations*

It quickly became apparent that the legal independence of the enterprise was in no way synonymous with its *economic* independence. Informal bonds of dependence upon the centre had been growing. In particular freedom in matters such as employment levels and mix, financial discipline, and levels of output were curtailed. The use of so-called 'operational programmes' and subsequently 'government orders or contracts', presided over by the Planning Commission, was a favoured device in bringing enterprises to heel, providing as they did more or less guaranteed access to scarce resources without the headache of recourse to the market. In 1983, 8 per cent of the total production within the Ministry of Light Industry and Chemicals was subject to such programmes; by 1986 the figure was 22 per cent (*Trybuna Ludu*, 10 July 1987). To shelter under the umbrella of a programme was easier than breaking out into entrepreneurship, particularly in such a transitional period when only a minority of co-producers were willing, let alone able, to play by the emerging rules. It was no surprise therefore that, in 1984, over 52 per cent of enterprise directors felt that their independence was severely restricted by the ministry (*Przegląd Ustawodawstwa Gospodarczego*, 1 January 1985). The remainder presumably did not mind such close tutelage.

Attempts at reforming the centre have also been deflected by camouflage tactics. While the number of branch or sectoral ministries had been successively reduced between 1981 and 1987, culminating in one Ministry of Industry, the accompanying and much-publicized loss in personnel had not been accompanied by a change in *function*. Rationalization in 1982–5 was generally reduced to changes in form rather than content. In fact there had been an increase in personnel overall, particularly in the so-called functional ministries, such as Finance. Here again, there had been an upturn in numbers of managers rather than in technical and auxiliary personnel, signalling *interventionist* functions rather than the strategic planning tasks of reform. Perhaps asking a bureaucracy to reform itself without legislation (the last appropriate law regulating the structure of the ministries dated back to 1954) was too optimistic. The promised loss of 3,000 employees from the centre, coupled with a change in function, is intended to address bureaucratic transmogrification.

Left to itself, the centre had adopted the rhetoric of reform while adapting existing practice to the new conditions. The fact that a law defining the powers of ministers, the RM and Praesidium of government, had been constantly deferred was just one sign of the defensiveness of the centre against reform. Despite high-powered committees entrusted with the task of streamlining these bureaucracies, the so-called *attestacja* (or job certification), the powers of the functional ministries such as the State Planning Commission, the Finance Ministry and the Ministry of Foreign Trade, all of which were critical to a reform programme, remained largely undefined and indeed became more fudged as time passed.

As for numbers, the bureaucracy is now wise to this and can appear to be cutting back while in fact creating a whole series of 'auxiliary bodies' (*Polityka*, 10 January 1987). Seeing the old return as the new is not confined to the ministries. The middle-level associations, the epitome of all that was wrong with the previous system of management, were ostensibly wound up in mid-1982. Since then they have resurrected, phoenix-like from the ashes of reform, in almost the same numbers, 616. While the vast majority are voluntary associations (only 31 are compulsory), they encompass nearly all the 6,065 state enterprises. The fact that many were set up while self-management was suspended may have been symbolic of the way in which transitional power was abused, since formally self-management had to assent to such associations. It was, however, now largely irrelevant, since self-management bodies, once seen as the institutional guarantor of the reform programme, were themselves pressing for membership of bodies which appeared to be the epitome of anti-reformism.

Here again this was perfectly rational behaviour. Those enterprises which could not include themselves in an operational programme joined together to maximize their access to scarce resources, and to negotiate from a position of strength with the centre. Thus what on the face of it appeared to be an institutional form favourable to centralized control was often in fact an attempt to limit it. Yet the outcome was monopolistic, anti-market and in consequence compounded the redistributive nature of the system if not the actual power of the centre. Evidence of the latter was provided in the creation of other conglomerates, the 'Kombinat', the *gwarectwo*, large units intended in part to counter the influence of the associations (*Ekonomika i Organizacja Pracy*, no. 1, 1986).

Thus, when looking at the administrative structure, it is essential to distinguish between the manifest and latent functions of particular entities. All in all, public pressure for a reform of the centre has continued to mount, with defensive reactions from the regime, which recognizes that all the low-value reform cards have been played and now is the time for aces. And yet it is possible to surmise that the progress of reform must also include *external* references. In 1985, of the ninety-three categories of consumer goods subject to centralized allocation by *województwo* or region, at least fifty-five were considered to be amenable to market allocation. Introduced as a temporary measure in 1981, the system has expanded rather than contracted (*Rada Narodowa, Gospodarka, Administracja* no. 10, 1986) Found to be costing an estimated 1.5 billion złoty per annum, the Supreme Control Chamber (NIK) forced a revision downwards to 55 of those categories subject to central distribution.

Perhaps the continued existence of this anti-reform structure (five of the Ministry of Internal Trade and Services departments, and eight national trade organizations, not to mention local bodies, were involved) was not simply bureaucratic inertia but was tied to an agreement signed on 15 October 1986, between the Polish and Soviet trade ministries. This called for the mutual unmediated exchange of goods of everyday use between enterprises and trade organizations, to the value of 80 million roubles, double the previous year's level (*Trybuna Ludu*, 9 January 1987). Such direct exchange is one example of the kind of activity which served to foster the distributive apparatus and ran counter to monetarized, market relations. In this context, further conglomerations of enterprises, whether comprised of electronics, steel or energy-producing units (for example, the Megat energy consortium and 'Elpol' the electronics group) were also to be orientated towards export (only a part of which was to go to the West) and in all likelihood were intended to correspond to the new associations and similar structures being set up in the Soviet Union and involving bilateral relations. When it occurs the opposition of self-management bodies to such conglomerations may in fact be unwitting opposition to the consequences of Polish-Soviet cooperation (*Tygodnik Powszechny*, 2 November 1986; *Trybuna Ludu*, 5 January 1987) as much as, for example, to the concentration of profitable with unprofitable enterprises, a traditional bureaucratic ploy. In October 1987 the Sejm created a set of new ministries and central offices as part of the reform of the centre. On closer examination it would be fair to ask whether this was reform or merely reorganization. Some new ministries were set up, namely the unified industry ministry and those of national education and transport-marine-communications. Others were reconstructed, such as that dealing with internal trade and foreign economic cooperation. This left seven other ministries dealing with the environment, construction, work and social policy, finance, culture and the arts, health and welfare, foreign affairs, respectively. At the same time a major review of personnel was intended to drop one in four of these employed by the centre. This is proving to be a controversial and painful exercise in organizational slimming-down (*Przegląd Tygodniowy*, 7 February 1988).

Part of the reform is to release enterprises run from the centre to the control of the local councils. This would then supply the latter with revenue to finance their more independent role under the projected local government reform. The RN have put in for 1,800 such enterprises, over one quarter of the total, to be handed over to them. The centre has responded by passing over 300, with 500 promised later in the year.

Despite the publicity accorded to the reform of the centre there exists considerable scepticism amongst those who believe that such reforms are now part of the system's *modus vivendi* and do not presage a shift over to the greater influence of market forces. On closer examination they argue, key distributive functions have been retained by the centre over twenty-five major products such as coal, steel, paper, transport means and the like as well as over sixty-four major resources imported from the West (*Tygodnik Powszechny*, 20 March 1988). There can be little doubt that this prevarication has drawn the impatience of that part of the elite which has believed since 1986, and more so given the dismal production figures for 1987 (a 2 per cent growth in National Income, 4 per cent drop in real income, 13 per cent lower level of production than in 1978), that radical reform is necessary. To this end the Sejm will provide powers to the vice-premier, Sadowski, enabling him to deal with enterprises and organizations not conforming to reform guidelines, chiefly through greater personnel policy powers (*Polityka*, 2 April 1988). A consequence of this is likely to be the allocation of greater powers to enterprise directors.

(ii) *The Enterprise Director*

The connecting thread between the centre and enterprise has always been the director. Since 1946 this position has been highly ambiguous in terms of responsibilities, prerogatives and lines of subordination and accountability. This ambiguity was brought out clearly in 1956 when the director was seen as responsible to both the emerging workers' councils and to the central ministry which appointed him. From 1958 until 1980, the director functioned in harness with the Conference of Workers' Self-management (KSR), the party secretary and the union chairman, which in no way interfered in his exercise of 'one-man responsibility'. During this whole period, appointments were subject to *nomenklatura* procedures and the usual personal ties typical of cadres policy in communist countries.

There was little say on the part of the work-force over such appointments. The ministry and *zjednoczenia* (association) bosses had personnel policy all to themselves. However both the economic reform proposals and the 25 September 1981 law on the enterprise (with attendant regulations) introduced the principle of *competitive* selection of *some* enterprise directors. This was done both in response to self-management demands that accountability be anchored in the enterprise and not higher up, and in order to raise the quality of direction and diminish the political factor in their appointment, that is, overcome 'negative selection'. The director was now a representative organ of the enterprise, alongside the general meeting of the work-force and the employee council (*rada pracownicza*). As with most things in the summer of 1981, the final version of this law was the outcome of a compromise, which allowed for non-competitive appointment by the minister in the case of enterprises deemed to be of 'fundamental significance to the economy'. A list of affected enterprises was to be submitted later and was not generally envisaged as including more than 200 or so units, perhaps the 203 enterprises already subject to direct CC scrutiny! During martial law, over 1,000 enterprise directors were replaced, particularly those deemed to be sympathetic to Solidarity, often without recourse to competitive selection or self-management agreement. The transitional legislation out of martial law exempted 1,370 enterprises, employing 80 per cent of the work-force, from the competitive election of directors, and the exception thus became the rule. In 1987–8 the list of key enterprises where ministerial prerogative of appointment held sway, was reduced to 400.

Since then, despite admonitions that access to key posts be opened up to non-party candidates, there have been attempts to strengthen the position of the director over self-management and thus to subordinate both more fully to the centre. Over 80 per cent (*Życie Gospodarcze*, 30 November 1986) of enterprise directors are party members, 10.3 per cent are less than 35 years of age, 33.7 per cent are 36–45, 40 per cent between 46 and 55 and 19 per cent over 55 years of age (*sic*) (*Trybuna Ludu*, 26 January 1987). Despite the so-called 'carousel' (where incompetence is rewarded by transfer to another equal or higher position) 30 per cent of directors have held their positions for over fifteen years and 13 per cent for between eleven and fifteen years. The majority come from outside the plant, although competition has more recently favoured internal candidates. Whilst their official monthly pay is in the region of 56,000 zł. for a top-flight enterprise, on top of this come earnings from 'profits', which in theory have no upper limit. Concerned to raise the earnings of their employees, particularly in order to stop them leaving in a situation of artificial labour shortage, directors prefer to bargain for privileges, preference and 'special case' status, rather than push for higher productivity.

In general, factories can be divided into two groups. The first of these are the 'strong and heavy', those in steel and energy, having the highest pay levels and belonging to so-called 'obligatory associations' of groupings of enterprises deemed by the authorities to be of special significance to the country; they are monopolistic and have high levels of party and official trade-union membership. The second group consists of the lower-paid industries, such as food, paper and light industries, which have to be generally more market-orientated, are highly feminized (for every 1 per cent of growth in female employment there is an average wage decline of 53 zł.) and geographically poorly placed, away from larger cities and with no umbrella organization such as those mentioned above looking after their interests. This affects the behaviour of directors themselves. The 'traditionalists' in mining, electro-mechanical and energy industries are strong and monopolistic and simply seek to increase production but not productivity. Those within the chemical and light industries struggle to lower costs and utilize reserves. The weakest industry directors, with the poorest-paid and least strategic position, seek subsidies and waivers in order to survive very much like their stronger, traditional counterparts. Significantly therefore, pay is not related to productivity, but to structural location (*Polityka*, 31 January 1987). Both the weakest and the strongest sectors are therefore tied to central distribution but for different reasons, while reform impetus can only be seen to be emanating from the less significant but potentially most important light/chemical industry sector.

Already it appears from key statements that the 'reform' will apply differently to two commodity markets—one which can be seen to be coming into equilibrium and one which will be disequilibrated, for whatever reasons, for the foreseeable future. Thus the discrepancy between original and actual reform aims will become institutionalized (*Ekonomika i Organizacja Pracy*, no. 1, 1986). In all of this the strategy of price reform further compounds the separation and atrophy of reform. *Officially fixed* prices apply to food (except to the 'green'—vegetables—market), energy, transport and communications, and include mostly, but not exclusively, subsidized goods. *Regulated prices* were seen an intermediate category, affecting 1 per cent of goods sold, which sought to keep down excessive growth in *contractual* or *agreed* prices which the regime would like to present as the norm. Here subsidies still figure, as does control of certain indicators by the finance ministry, but in general the planners hope that by 1990 prices will need to be increased by no more than 10 per cent per year, although this is deemed highly unlikely.

In return for price increases, the population are being constantly assured that inefficiency is being squeezed out of the system, and that high earnings are related to higher productivity, which they clearly are not. Nevertheless, the law on bankruptcy passed in 1983 appears to be being invoked, even if not to its full extent. Over 300 enterprises are under especial bank scrutiny, sixty have been put under the control of commissars, while two building firms have been declared bankrupt and many others simply wound up (*Życie Warszawy*, 10–21 December 1986). Whether this attacks the subsidies to the large monopoly producers is another matter although tax on excessive wage payments can put large enterprises into trouble. Bankruptcy, as much as the consequences of pricing policies, subsidies, and profit calculations, has focused attention on the central role of the *employee councils* and the allied questions of prerogative, collective management, group ownership and responsibility.

(iii) *Employee Self-Management*

Despite a rather chequered career, some form of workers' council (RR) or self-management function has existed in Poland since the war, particularly in early 1945 (when the role of syndicalistic trade unions was crucial), but with the exception of the Six-Year Plan period. A kind of participatory ethos has been apparent in all the proposals put by workers and employees to their rulers. Paradoxically for a workers' state, 'self-government' has been more prevalent in professional and intelligentsia circles than on the shop floor, where the homogeneous branch unionism of the communist system sought to destroy occupational and craft identity.

The largely spontaneously formed workers' councils, legally established in November 1956, highlighted the close affinity between economic reform, enterprise independence and workers' self-management. Reform legitimacy, as presented to the working class, had henceforth to address the issue of workers participation as much as the introduction of market mechanism. As it was, the 1956 reform attempt was partial, since many powers remained with the planning centre, in areas such as investment decisions, price-setting and materials distribution.

As has been well documented (Hirszowicz & Morawski, 1967) these powers of self-management were subsequently delimited by the institution in December 1958 of the Conference of Workers' Self-management, which coopted the trade-union council as well as the party committee into a larger structure and gave the unions tutelage over the workers' council (RR). The latter remained as the only body elected by the employees and had an obligatory two-thirds worker majority. Since the directive-distributive state remained untouched it was highly unlikely that planning and production management could devolve to the enterprise, let alone to self-management.

During the 1970s, decentralization became synonymous with 'techno-cratism', with authority shifting from the centre to particular managers in the form of the unsuccessful 'large economic organizations' (WOG) reform. More than anything this underlined the declining significance of self-management, in that these new management structures had no appropriate organs of worker participation. In response to the 1976 workers' protests at Radom and Ursus the regime responded with its so-called 'economic manoeuvre', an attempt to cut back imports and shift resources from investment to consumption. However, by 1978 the factory party first secretary had formally assumed the leadership of the KSR Conference of Workers' Self-management, which in effect cut down the 'Big Four' (Director, Union chief, RR chairman and Party First Secretary) to a triumvirate. Self-management became ceremonial, mobilizational and by 1980 RRs had all but ceased to exist.

Not surprisingly, the workers' protest of 1980 took the trade unions as their vehicle, since self-management was well and truly compromised. Suspicion of the easily dominated self-management structure was only gradually replaced during the Solidarity period by the recognition that if the broader economic reform was not to be again neutralized by the centre, then the question of enterprise independence and self-management had to be confronted and not dismissed as a needless dilution of Solidarity's effort (Kolankiewicz, 1982). The laws relating to employee self-management and to the status of the enterprise, passed after much overt bargaining and compromise on 25 September 1981, reflected most of the problems facing the system at that time: the position of the director and his accountability, the principles of the *nomenklatura* and party involvement, the nature of 'socialist' property, its alienability or otherwise, the function of local self-government, of trade unions. These and many other neuralgic points were touched upon by the legislation. In the background, the outcome of 1956–8 loomed large.

Less overt in its activities, the so-called 'Network' (Sieć) of seventeen leading enterprises, emerging, not without opposition, from within Solidarity itself in early 1981, saw in the existence of employee self-management the broader guarantor of economic (and inevitably political) reform, which Solidarity within its trade-union straitjacket could never aspire to be without seeking the reins of state power. As it transpired, the 'self-governing republic' thesis tied to a second chamber of parliament rooted in employee self-management, horizontal inter-factory ties between employee councils (mooted in 1956–7) all ultimately provided a more satisfactory scenario of societal transformation (and were therefore more threatening to the authorities) than the more confrontationist Solidarity versus party-state formula. Self-management would seek to go beyond the factory gates, to overcome the fragmentation and segmentation of branch-sectoral divisions of the economy, and even try to rejuvenate parliamentary authority from the grass-roots upwards. The reform wing of the PZPR also felt that it could ground party authority within an overt *nomenklatura* system based upon self-management. Thus self-management was all things to all people.

Article 16 of the Decree on Martial Law effectively suspended self-management. Subsequent transitional legislation severely limited the powers of the enterprise and of self-management in its authority over the director and both of these in their respective dealings with the centre. For example, 1,371 enterprises were restricted as being of 'fundamental significance for the economy', although in statements leading up to the 1987 referendum the authorities suggested that this number would be cut by 900. (*Rzeczpospolita: Reforma Gospodarcza*, 10 March 1983; *Trybuna Ludu*, 16 October 1987). Many of the 'experienced' directors were reimposed and by 1986 in only 15 per cent of enterprises with self-management bodies did they exert any real influence on the formulation of decision. Whilst 5.5 million employees had the right to set up self-management bodies, 3.5 million were deprived of such a right through a variety of legislative enactments (Morawski, 1986). Many of the rights contained within the 1981 law on self-management, in particular Article 24, relating to powers concerning planning, investment and management, were not fully utilized. A more optimistic statement from the government claimed that 30 per cent of self-management bodies were active (*Życie Warszawy*, 12 March 1988).

Put under the special tutelage of a commission of the RP, in 1985, after the martial law transitional legislation formally expired, self-management matters came under a Sejm Commission, interestingly headed again by former First Secretary Stanislaw Kania. Currently matters related to self-management and indeed trade unionism are gravitating ominously back to the centre, in the shape of the Ministry of Work, Pay and Social Affairs. Attempts to impose enterprise directors and bypass competitive selection of such managers were the order of the day and were even supported by the Supreme Court in a highly publicized case concerning 2,000 or so such directors. Furthermore, when seeking to increase the power of managers the ostensible reason given by the centre was that it was needed in order to 'clarify' their rights and provide them with the authority necessary to participate in a reformed economy (*Polityka*, 3 November 1986). In fact the intention was to shift the managers back into centre's orbit of influence. On a different tack, the aggregation of enterprises into larger units, such as the Kombinat, was intended to introduce a new level of authority where there would be no place for the enterprise-based self-management bodies or where their powers would be severely restricted (*Tygodnik Mazowsze*, 23 October 1987). Conversely, the adoption of workers brigades, similar to the Soviet workers' collectives, seeks to displace downwards rather than upwards the focus of workers' self-government (and is anyway self-disciplining rather than self-motivating). In both cases enterprise councils would be left to inhabit a formalized empty shell of rights, without an overt, frontal attack on their rights as contained in law.

To dilute self-management further without again formally altering its legislative edicts, trade-union rights have been extended through legislation and amendments, such as the 'collective contract', while in a divide and rule strategy, the typical 1970s division of labour, or segmentation of interests, is re-emerging. The PZPR, the unions, the PRON, the ZSMP and employee councils will each in all likelihood take on roles relating to propaganda and ideology, pay and bonuses, sport and culture, housing and 'technological development', respectively.

For all this, self-management is not compromised, but as the gravity of the economic crisis deepens, so employees have looked to self-management for help of a more immediate kind, rather than becoming involved with the broader issues of investment, of cooperation agreements with the Soviet Union or financing and credit, and so on. Despite this instrumentalization, the desire for a second parliamentary chamber, based in part on self-management, is still alive and attempts to forge horizontal links with other active employee councils (recognized in law) continue despite regime opposition. However, in the majority of enterprises, a major obstacle is sheer exhaustion, as the pressures of everyday life mount up, becoming more time-consuming and depriving self-management of the zestful characters available in 1983–4. Over three-quarters of employees in a group of large factories studied had little or no idea what the employee council was doing. Symbolically evocative, self-management was nevertheless seen as weak, transitory, and at the mercy of centralizing forces. Older directors, who are a majority, saw self-management in its consultative, transmission-belt role, looking rather to the party and trade-union chiefs as partners. Only non-party directors, a small minority, expressed aspirations to co-management

(*Biuletyn CBOS*, no. 3, 1986). The legacy of the 1970s, antithetical as it was to self-management rights and as transmitted through older enterprise directors, was not conducive to nurturing a spirit of genuine employee participation. The co-optation of self-management is most plainly evident in the high proportion of chairmen with higher education, management, party and most interestingly, trade union affiliations (Table 4.3).

Table 4.3 Characteristics of Employee Councillors and Chairmen of Employee Councils (per cent)

Age			
Less than 30	11		
30–39	45		
40–49	30		
Over 50	14		
Education			
Elementary	29		
Elem./vocational	23		
Secondary	36		
Higher	12		
Occupation			
Workers	54	PZPR members	37
Management	19	Trade-union members	44
Engineering/technical staff	11		
Chairman of Employee Councils			
Education		*Function*	
Elementary	1	Worker/chargehand	8
Elem./vocational	5	Foreman	10
Secondary	44	Manager	5
Higher	50	Engineer specialist	17
		Administrative staff	4
		Other	10
PZPR members	55		
Trade union members	50		

Source: *Tygodnik Powszechny*, 7 December 1986.

As the dependence of enterprises and thus of managers upon the redistributive centre continued to grow despite reform claims to the opposite, so also was self-management drawn into the search for subsidies, special treatment and other forms of 'non-market' behaviour. At the same time, the stratification of enterprises according to 'formal' self-management rights had also become apparent. From those such as the state railway, telephone, airline, banking and other monopoly enterprises involved in security and defence, to those enterprises working partially or fully abroad (which presumably includes 'joint venture' enterprises) self-management had been tailored to fit the restrictions which the authorities felt were required. A further group were those precluded from the right to participate in the appointment of the enterprise director, as mentioned above. Finally, stratification occurred through less formal means, whereby small, provincial, low-priority sector enterprises had weaker employees' councils than their Warsaw-based, key-industry opposite numbers. It is the unskilled, both manual and non-manual, who support self-management least, a natural consequence of the corporatist tendencies in factory management. Pay and conditions of work are uppermost in employees' minds and this is not the prerogative of self-management (*Tygodnik Polski*, 4 May 1986). In a further contentious move, legislation at the beginning of 1986 allowed for the compulsory extension of work-time by an extra four hours per week. This affected some 2,000 enterprises or 4 million employees and was a clear extension of the transitional martial law legislation (*Polityka*, 12 April 1986). This was an obvious affront to both self-management and trade unions alike, the latter in particular suffering another humiliation at the hands of their ostensible patron, the state.

(iv) *Trade Unions without Solidarity*

Poland's trade-union tradition goes back at least as far as the 1880s, although laws allowing such forms of association within the Austrian and Prussian partition were enacted in 1867 and 1869, respectively. Limited trade-union activity was permitted in the Russian partition only after 1906. After World War I, freedom of union activity was promulgated by the Decree of February 1919. Branch-sectoral, craft, regional and all-factory unions emerged while conflicts among communist, socialist and national religious affiliated unions was not uncommon. The fortunes of the communist-led unions declined after the Polish-Soviet war. In the aftermath of the Piłsudski coup of May 1926, various umbrella organizations were set up to consolidate syndicalist, socialist and so-called 'class unions', the Union of Trade Unions of 1931 being the most obvious. In the 1930s trade-union militancy took on extreme forms, such as the threatened mass suicide in February 1935 of a group of miners who barricaded themselves underground for twenty-five days in protest against the closure of their pit. The struggles at the Wujek, Manifest Lipcowy and other mines in 1981–2 in the aftermath of martial law presented an element of obvious continuity. During the 'Rule of the Colonels' (1935–9) attempts at unifying and politicizing left-wing trade unions provoked bitter anti-government strikes and sharp confrontations with the police (Tymieniecka, 1981).

Communist rule brought with it the rapid creation of a Soviet-style—centralized and unified—union structure limiting workers' powers. By the time of the Second Congress of the Trade Unions and the formation of the Central Trade Union Council (CRZZ) in July 1949 the pattern of trade unions as schools for socialism, mobilizing for production and efficiency, had been laid down.

From 1954 until 1958, the 'thaw' witnessed a criticism of bureaucratized trade unionism, a cut in the size of the apparatus of the CRZZ and an open recognition that the unions were neither representative nor defensive of working peoples' interests. The workers' councils provided the stimulus to reform within the trade-union movement. In May 1958, the Fourth Congress of the Trade Unions heard proposals for far-reaching trade-union powers in such areas as law-making and limiting management prerogatives, but these never came to fruition and were subsumed under the Conference of Workers' Self-management (KSR) formula. Thus instead of a law on the trade unions, a law on self-management emerged. Gradually, through the use of non-legislative instruments, such as resolutions of the CRZZ or the Politburo, the trade-union factory council subsumed the workers' councils (RR) under its control. At the same time, trade unions crystallized into twenty-three branch unions and became increasingly managerial (Karczewski, 1982).

After the 1970 workers' protest, demands for greater union democracy and a more representative and accountable leadership were diluted by Gierek's 'Second Poland' strategy (of buying off discontent). Not only was the party now almost in complete control of factory unions but the concern with employees' problems came a long way down the list of union priorities. Concomitantly, the local government reforms of the mid-1970s integrated the unions more firmly into the web of the party-state apparatus. Prior to 1980, there was evidence of mounting opposition from within the mass of workers as well as from some of the lower levels of the trade-union hierarchy. An account of events of that summer of 1980 posits a manipulative scenario which contains a revived union movement limiting the technocratic power of ministries and directors and supported in this by a radicalized party rank-and-file. Of course, all options were preempted by the entrance of first the Inter-factory Strike Commission (MKS) and subsequently NSZZ Solidarnosć onto centre stage. The structure of the pre-1980 branch unions, based upon sectors of the economy and embracing all employees, was important in that it served as a negative stereotype for the post-Solidarity unions. Where much store was placed by the regime in seemingly evenhandedly distancing itself from both pre-1980 and pre-1981 distortions, trade-union structure and organization provided a ready shorthand for promoting the regime's apparent commitment to reform.

On 31 December 1980, the hegemony of CRZZ formally ceased to exist. During 1981, there were five basic forms of union extant in Poland. NSZZ Solidarność; the Coordinating Commission of the branch unions (with at most 3.9 million members, compared with 12 million in 1980), and the Confederation of Autonomous Trade Unions with a million or so members. Apart from these there was NSZZ 'Solidarność' of Individual Farmers (some 70 per cent of all peasants) and the regime-orientated Central Union of Agricultural Circles and Organizations as well as the Branch Union of Agricultural Employees located primarily on the state farms. Within the largely regionally-based Solidarity union, branch tendencies were soon apparent and in due course became formally recognized. This territorial principle, which had been present in the pre-1980 branch unions, in the shape of the WRZZ, has constantly vied with the branch structure of unions. Likewise, after 1982 these regional structures were again to re-emerge in an effort to coordinate factory unions not included in federations and to become the object of double contention—being features of pre-1980 and pre-1981 unionism (*Nowe Drogi*, October 1985).

The fact of branch union membership was to become a major line of political cleavage after the imposition of martial law, determining attitudes as strongly as party membership or managerial position. That the future head of the new 'reborn' trade unions was a former Solidarity member did little to undermine this finding. Solidarity's brief existence as a legal entity has done much to shape the future of trade unionism in Poland and the other countries of 'real socialism'. It is to this legacy that we must now turn. This is not to deny the broader impact of Solidarity membership across the whole range of issues. In particular attitudes to the party, political and economic reform, democracy and legalized opposition, equality and egalitarianism, are all closely tied in with the experience of 1981 (*Polacy '84*, 1986).

The Decree of the Council of State declaring martial law also suspended the trade unions and other associations. By 24 February 1982, however, a committee of the Council of Ministers for Trade Union Affairs was actively considering the manner in which trade unions could be reintroduced into Polish society. In the interim the party initiated so-called factory social commissions to fill the vacuum. It is generally accepted that at this stage the eventual reinstatement of Solidarity under the constraints of the long-awaited law on trade unions was feasible. However, whether it was the continuing pro-Solidarity demonstrations and the organized power of the underground or some other complex of causes, on 8 October 1982, the Sejm passed a law which wound up all pre-existing trade-union structures and allowed new trade unions to be registered at the factory level as from the end of December 1982 (the date of suspension of martial law). The law anticipated the growth of both national and inter-union organizations. It left open the question of trade-union pluralism, or 'competing' union organizations as they were presented. This was to be resolved by a resolution of the RP. Despite vigorous pressure from the new unions to preclude the possibility of two unions functioning in the same place of work (*Głos Wybrzeża*, 24 April 1986), the trade union law as revised in July 1985 allowed the ambiguous situation to persist. Whether this portends the possibility of something like Church-based unions being allowed to recruit and function in the future is a matter of speculation. However, the fact that a significant core of employees remains outside of the new unions and thus constitutes a potential force of opposition is a cause for regime concern. Likewise, the legal ambiguity is exploited by the opposition in the form of regular demands for trade-union registration, even where an official union already exists (Kolankiewicz, 1987).

After an initial burst of recruitment, which saw over 4.5 million members join in the first year and a half, by 1986 the figure was 6,121,500, including some 15 per cent or so disabled or pensioners, and had just touched 7 million by mid-1987. They were dispersed amongst 25,786 units. By 1987 over a half of those who could still join had not and the tempo of recruitment has declined sharply (*Polityka*, 11 October 1986; Mason, 1987). There exist 130 federations encompassing 92 per cent of all unionists who go under the banner of the Polish Reborn Trade Unions guided by a governing body, the All-Polish Trade Union Coordinator, OPZZ. The opposition to centralized control by the former and the desire to maintain a loose federal structure as well as not forcing individual unions into the larger body, can all be traced back to the fact that the new union's legitimacy lies as much in distancing itself from the old CRZZ as its acceptability to the regime rests on not going the Solidarity way. That only 38 per cent of its membership are 'workers', that at best a quarter are 'young' employees less than thirty years of age, that one in three party members has not joined, all adds up to a dismal picture for the regime. Ideological barriers to joining have weakened and sheer poverty is compelling many workers to join in order to have access to the increased welfare benefits disposed of by the factory unions (*Życie Warszawy*, 27 October 1986).

Of course the fragmented nature of the trade-union movement, with large nation-wide occupational unions (not federations)—such as teachers, agricultural workers and miners—of around one-half million members juxtaposed to the smallest comprising 116 members, is presented as a form of 'pluralism' by the authorities. That 80 per cent of unions belong to twenty-three national organizations is ominously symptomatic of a natural gravitation back to the branch structure. The pressures to adapt to the then existing administrative profile of ministries and associations, where 'large is strong', act against fragmentation. However, with the overt demise of branch ministries in 1988 it is difficult to surmise what form union—employer relations will take. Suspicions held by many as to the reproduction of old forms and practice were confirmed when the OPZZ was housed in the same building as its predecessor, the CRZZ (*Sztandar Młodych*, 19 February 1986). The fact that some industrial regions (Łódź) and key factories (Gdańsk shipyard, Lenin steelworks) have low levels of union saturation is disconcerting for the regime (*Sztandar Młodych*, 4 January 1985). But when factories join wholesale then the effect can be equally disturbing to the authorities who are nervous of reinjecting the spirit of Solidarity into their well-groomed structures (*Tygodnik Mazowsze*, no. 189, 26 November 1986).

Recent legislation has given the unions the right as well as the obligation to represent *all* employees, whether or not they are members. That some activists would like to be the *only* representatives was made plain at the Second Congress of the reborn trade unions meeting on 27 November 1986. There are the usual incentives to join the new union, with travel abroad being a key perk (*Tygodnik Powszechny*, 12 August 1986). Relations with the employees' councils are not good, since self-managements hold a higher position in the scale of esteem due to their democratic credentials and marginally less comprised past. The unions have been able to occupy the same space as self-management in dealing with work-related concerns. This has divided the activists, with the bureaucratic centre winning out. In their confrontation with the government, chiefly over price rises, the extension of the working week and the nature of collective contracts, the unions have sought to gain credibility as independent entities, but in nearly all cases they appear to have been choreographed, even in the most recent conflict over food, energy and transport prices (*Polityka*, 4 April 1987). Apart from direct negotiations with government, the unions now have a lobby of some fifty-six representatives in the Ninth Sejm, higher than in any previous period. Although without the right to initiate legislation, the unions have considerable powers of 'consultation'. Needless to say these are often abused (*Metalowiec*, 11 May 1986).

Opinions as to the authentic nature of the new unions are divided. Some commentators see in them the genuine heirs of the Solidarity union legacy, with committed activists combining the class nature of the branch unions with the stubbornness of Solidarity doing a thankless task in an increasingly critical situation and who may yet find themselves in confrontation with the regime. Others can never acknowledge that they are anything other than stooges dancing to the regime's tune, who, despite the NSZZ prefix, are a mere shadow of Solidarity. While angry statements over price rises (Metalowiec, 26 April 1987) may look convincing, breaking with anti-strike mentality (strikes, in a highly circumscribed form, are legal) wrought by the post-Solidarity regime will be more difficult. Likewise, the authorities appear to have downgraded the significance of the trade unions from relations at deputy prime minister level to the Office of Cooperation with the Trade Unions, attached to a department director in the Minister of Work, Wages and Social Affairs (*Polityka*, 29 November 1986). The OPZZ has deferred its threatened departure from the International Labour Organization, voiced after being found guilty of violating the latter's Conventions 87 and 95 (on freedom of association). In response to this charge they claim that 500,000 of its members are not formally subordinated to the central union authority. This does not include the 5 million or so state sector employees outside any union. Underground Solidarity using the existing ambiguities in the trade union law still pushes for formal recognition in such bastions as the Warski shipyard, and many factories have gone to the courts over the question union pluralism. If the 1988 second stage of reform is (even in part) true to its stated intentions then the coming years will see the new unionism put to its severest test.

The Non-socialist Sector

As the consultations over the second stage of the economic reform occupy the headlines, so terms such as capital market and capital flow, property relations, equal treatment for all sectors, become more prominent. The influx of a new generation (post-1982) of entrepreneurially-minded, well-qualified young persons into Poland's 'private' sector, combined with the hopeful signals (family and cooperative enterprises, agricultural family groups, and so on) from the Soviet Union, have all helped force the regime to look long and hard at its relationship with the craftsmen, artisans, shopkeepers and taxi-drivers who make up the non-agricultural, non-socialized sector. Used very instrumentally to bail out the system in previous crises, there is now a feeling that if Italy and Japan can use the small-scale detail production sector then so could Poland. The shortages generated by 'real socialism' have been accepted as being more system-destructive than is any threat from renascent capitalism. With the appearance of joint ventures, mixed capital enterprises, 'Polonia' firms (that is, firms employing émigrée capital) the notion of bankruptcy, shares and bonds, collective property, and so on, the old demarcation lines of state, cooperative and private property are being blurred. Equal treatment for all sectors, private, cooperative and state, whether agricultural or otherwise, is now the watchword.

At its Thirteenth Congress in 1986, SD called for an increase in the private sector's share of the economy from some 7 per cent of GNP to a possible 25 per cent (*Tygodnik Demokratyczny*, 8 March 1987). Their case is pretty unassailable. As an example, for every 100 zł. of capital, the state employee provides 41 zł. of product whilst the private sector provides 173 zł (*Życie Gospodarcze*, 8 March 1987). There are now 326,000 individual workshops, 152,000 service or retail outlets, 90,000 taxis and baggage transporters, 16,000 heavy transport and 683 Polonia firms which go to make up the private sector. Sixty per cent are single-person businesses, averaging 33,000 zł. per month, which is less than the average manager's wage. Some millionaires, earning as much as 113 million zł. per annum (23 million after tax) sustain an already distorted stereotype (*Kurier Polski*, 7 July 1986).

Here the activities of the 'second economy' or illegal private activity serve to provide fuel for those who, while formally supporting the private sector, none the less insist that it be legally pristine in its dealings. This is, however, impossible in a sector working from the rejected materials and cast-offs discarded by the state sector (1 million tonnes of unwanted raw materials) which in turn is far from law-abiding in its own dealings. While the regime encourages private activity in breadth, it has stopped short of any growth in the depth of individual successful enterprises. The uncertainty generated by a policy which is euphemistically termed 'a flickering green light' (neither red nor green) results in a 'hit and run' strategy on the part of private entrepreneurs, who after three years or so wind up a successful business, having made the most of all the tax concessions available, and start up elsewhere.

In all likelihood the younger generation within the private sector (35 per cent are in the 25–35 age group, double the proportion in 1976) will be more aggressive and skilful in promoting individual entrepreneurial activities, since they will be unencumbered by the complexes of their predecessors, who were treated by the regime often as a pariah class. It is an open question as to whether years of anti-private sector activity propaganda have not taken an irreversible toll. There is also a recognition gaining ground among the leadership that Poland has skills, intellectual and craft, whose current hourly rate is lower than South Korea, Taiwan and many Asian countries and that it is here, not in the gigantism of Katowice steelworks, that a beginning should be made to any economic turnaround. In this context, the progressive 'deculturation' of Polish society, affecting the quality and type of education, its accessibility, the degeneration of the quality of leisure and entertainment, particularly as it affects the working class, could undermine this very real opportunity (*Literatura*, January 1987). Poles purchase $150 million worth of alcohol in the so-called dollar shops or PEWEX, which total half a billion dollars in sales (including motor cars, computers, VCR's). Further, it is calculated that 80 per cent of the so-called 'inflationary overhang' (money for which there are no goods) is concentrated in the hands of 14 per cent of the population (hence making generalized price rises pointless), who in turn convert this into dollars or luxury goods which hold their value (over $2 billion is held in dollar accounts in Poland, a further 2-3 billion under the proverbial mattress and over one billion in foreign accounts (*Gazeta Pomorska*, 18 December 1987)) The regime, with IMF and World Bank support, would like to put this money to better use. Thus the idea has gained ground for the sale of bonds and shares in state companies to employees and others but also the stimulation of private enterprise which could be genuinely export-orientated. This will require a greater shift of policy than that envisaged in the much vaunted Soviet blueprint if only because of the existence of the 'other' non-socialized sector—agriculture.

Agriculture

Although Polish agriculture is the one comparative reform success story it nevertheless provides the regime with little comfort: first, it is individual family farmings, not collective or state farming; second, it has had extraordinarily and unprecedented good weather since martial law; and third, reform has been largely about removing obstacles to the market, rather than the conscious application of mechanisms designed to elicit higher growth and productivity.

In 1986, an exceptional year it should be noted, gross agricultural output grew by 4.6 per cent, the grain harvest was up by 20 per cent, whilst meat production was reminiscent of the early 1970s (now often referred to as the 'good old days'). Food exports to both the West and the Soviet Union have increased by as much as 32 per cent over the last five years (*Rzeczpospolita*,

20 April 1987), although the severe weather of 1986–7 has slowed this down somewhat. The stated goal of agricultural self-sufficiency is close at hand. So what are the problems?

While family agriculture functions according to clear economic rules, it nevertheless coexists with *de facto* rationing for most producer goods. Furthermore, state-determined and fixed purchase prices for agricultural produce fall behind contract prices (i.e. prices which are by definition variable) for those producer goods essential to farming, such as ploughs, tractors and fertilizer (in 1987 agricultural produce prices were raised by 20 per cent, while that of machinery, etc., by over 40 per cent). Likewise, considerable subsidy, chiefly to food-processing enterprises and other intermediary state organizations it should be noted, ensures that food prices do not reflect costs of production (often being lower than purchase prices). Rationing of meat and meat products is likely to continue at least until 1990, although a free market and demonopolization of meat processing (other than of pork and beef) is envisaged a lot earlier, while the current market for fruit, vegetables and eggs will be extended. Economic reforms do, however, anticipate the rapid abolition of subsidies for fertilizer and production machinery etc., balancing supply and demand (*Rzeczpospolita*, 21 March 1987). How is this likely to affect the relationship between state, collective and family farming?

Regime propaganda claims that since 1980–1 in that most sensitive of areas, namely landownership, it has followed an even-handed approach to all sectors. Indeed, in 1982 peasants purchased 234,000 hectares from the State Land Fund (PFZ), or ten times the amount disbursed by individual farmers in exchange for pensions and the like. By 1985, however, peasants had passed on a mere 7,000 ha more to the state than they had bought. While the State Land Fund currently holds 800,000 ha, of which 50 per cent is leased to peasants, the latter appear loath to commit themselves to increasing landholding (*Tygodnik Powszechny*, 3 May 1987). The reason appears to be that the state now uses economic rather than political means to halt the transfer of land to peasant farmers. In this sense, whereas in 1982 one hectare of land bought from the Land Fund cost the equivalent of 7 quintals of rye, now it is exchanged for 26.2 quintals. Coincidentally, this is the same real price as in 1975, when land in effect ceased to be transferred. Elsewhere, access to tractors and combine harvesters has been administratively delimited, implying a clear government land policy whereas, in the same vein, access to fertilizers and credit seems to indicate the existence of a stratified policy towards the state-collective-individual agriculture sectors in declining order of priority. This is disconcerting if it is remembered that in the past, government policies towards agriculture have been seen to go in stages. The first stage is one of renewal and regeneration after crisis, for example, dropping collectivization (1957–61) and compulsory deliveries (1971–4) (Lewis, 1973). The second is gradual erosion of reform and the growth of societal tension, for example adverse pricing policy (1962–6) and 'specialization' (1976–7). The third is the crisis phase (1967–70, 1978–81) as evidenced by the events in Gdańsk in 1970 and the 'Ustrzyki-Rzeszów' accords (*Nowe Drogi*, February 1986; Szurek, 1987) signed with the Polish farmers in 1981.

Following this schema, the renewal phase after 1981, in response to food shortage, was to raise procurement prices, to promise an increase in share of agricultural investment to 30 per cent of the total and to ensure a parity of incomes, while removing subsidy from state farms. The second phase of erosion of gains can now be discerned by the growth in subsidy to the state sector, procurement prices dropping, price scissors closing, income parity between agricultural and other sectors waning and investment share declining. While pork inventories were high, there was a worrying downturn in dairy produce (with 32 per cent of holdings now having no milk cows due to the exit of women from agriculture). This in turn affected 'natural' manure-fertilizer production and led to further deterioration in land quality (*Życie Warszawy*, 5 February 1986). Incidentally, state farms use 3.4 times the fertilizer for the same increase in productivity as the individual sector. The shortfall in tractors (1.5 million or 53 per cent of holdings have no tractor) is compounded by the decline in agricultural circles which were the major supplier of draught power, form 130,000 in 1978 to 78,000 in 1983. As a consequence, a horse on an average holding of 5 ha will consume a hectare's worth of produce. While the tractor situation is improving for the family farm, it is likely that deterioration of state sector equipment will soon reverse this trend as farmers in this sector seek to re-equip.

The withdrawal of the Church from the proposed agricultural fund in September 1986 (intended to pump western capital into Polish agriculture) and its replacement by a much smaller-scale venture is perhaps the best indicator of the shift from the first stage to the second. Whilst World Bank and Rockefeller Fund efforts will continue, it clearly indicates the limits to regime tolerance of individual and autonomous peasant production (*Tygodnik Mazowsze*, no. 180, 1986; *Życie Warszawy*, 14 September 1986). In all likelihood, under the guise of the second stage of economic reform, economic instruments such as higher taxation, higher producer goods prices, higher peasant pension payments (increased by 180 per cent since 1985) based upon land size, and a tougher contract purchase policy and tied sales (of, for example, grain to the state in return for coal) will seek to achieve what administration-led collectivization could not, namely the elimination of the small peasant farmer (*Sztandar Młodych*, no. 5, 21 July 1987; *Rzeczpospolita*, 14 November 1986). The creation of agro-settlements in eastern Poland, with decent housing and infrastructure to tempt peasants into collective farming, is evidence of regime intention. Until now, 50 per cent of landowners or households have needed to express consent for land concentration to be enacted. In all probability this limit will decrease to 30 per cent (*Życie Warszawy*, 11 January 1986). While attention is focused on the non-agricultural sector of the economy, it is perhaps instructive to read carefully Article 15, para. 3 of the much vaunted Constitutional amendment of July 1983, referring to peasant property:

> [The State] protects the individual family agricultural landholdings of working peasants, guaranteeing their permanence; proffers assistance in increasing production and raising their technical-agricultural standard; supports the development of agricultural self-management, in particular agricultural circles and collectives; supports the development of cooperation and specialization of production; and broadens the ties of individual agricultural landholdings with the socialist national economy. [*Dziennik Ustaw*, No. 39, Section 175, 22 July 1983]

The individual sector is 'protected', the cooperative is 'supported' while the state sector is 'developed and strengthened'.

The Reform of Reform

During the latter part of 1986 and early 1987, the regime sought to breathe life into its reform platform by announcing the start of the 'second stage of economic reform'. By most accounts, the original reform had witnessed only high inflation levels, price rises (up to ten times in some cases), and the emergence of a hybrid system of centralized distribution to client enterprises, seeking success in the face of raw materials and other shortages, a drop in exports to the dollar (but not rouble) sphere, increased subsidies and deficits in the state budget, a shortage of goods and a decline in their quality. After the Third Plenum of the CC in December 1986, and in the wake of the so-called 'Kubiczek' case where the bureaucratic centre sought to smuggle onto the statute books overtly anti-reform measures, the reform was again reanimated (*Życie Gospodarcze*, 17 May 1987).

Announced in April 1987 and published a month later, the so-called 'Theses' were to be discussed and subsequently consulted and decided upon by means of a referendum by the end of the year. They did not hold many surprises for those familiar with Hungarian experiments nor indeed with

Poland's own economic-reform debate (*Rzeczpospolita*, 12 May 1987). The 'theses' emphasized continuity with the 1981 reform programme but admitted that the by now compromised economic system had proved more durable than expected. The reform would introduce market mechanisms (though not to all sectors), remove subsidies (with some compensatory payments), change the function and organizational structure of both the centre and the enterprise and their respective mutual relations, boost exports, allow in small firms, introduce a heterogeneity of ownership relations (shares, bonds and mixed capital) stimulate innovation, break monopolies, allow the horizontal movement of capital, permit bankruptcies actually to happen and make labour more mobile. The rate at which the price reform was to be imposed remained the biggest problem, with a variety of scenarios ostensibly up for discussion, although the short sharp shock of the two- to three-year period was the option favoured by the regime and the one rejected by the 1987 referendum. Wages, pensions, insurance, sickness benefit and temporary unemployment pay would also undergo radical redefinition, with, for example, an index-linked pension (itself novel) being supplemented by a *voluntary* contribution for higher returns. Taxation would mitigate the differentiation of pay that will be inevitable in such an environment.

Pessimists pointed out that the Five-Year Plan for 1986–90, passed prior to the announcement of the 'Theses', seemed to doom the reform from the outset (although the new head of the planning commission, Sadowski, indicated in 1987 that the Plan might be altered) (*Życie Gospodarcze*, 8 November 1987). Under this Five-Year Plan investment commitments (tied largely to fulfilling Soviet–CMEA trade agreements entered into since 1984) allowed for zero real wage growth, provided for little modernization or restructuring and thus undercut the motivational element so necessary to reform success (*Życie Gospodarcze*, 31 May 1987). Price transformation over a period of two to three years, it is hoped, will create a 'strong currency' (like the Czechoslovak crown). Liberalization of economic life can only be achieved by sharpening the conditions of economic existence, claim the economists. Profit must be the key determinant of wages. One industrial ministry ostensibly replacing all the branch ministries, and backed by an analysis-based Planning Commission and served by a Finance Ministry employing indirect measures of management, are other corner-stones in a retinue of prescriptions all too reminiscent of 1981—an opening-up to world markets, direct enterprise trading links and technology transfers are also essential (*Trybuna Ludu*, 25 July 1987). Most surprisingly perhaps, the regime now insists that 'personal economic success' must be rehabilitated and promoted in the scale of values (*Polityka*, 23 May 1987).

In all likelihood, a segmented economy will emerge, one segment where market mechanisms, new RN 'communal property' forms, mixed capital, small and large firms and export-led innovation combine to satisfy the essential consumer demands. Alongside this sector, however, will coexist a group of enterprises and infrastructure organizations (rail, road, power, gas, coal and petrochemicals) which will be excluded from market pressures. In between will be the 300–400 large-scale enterprises engaged within the so-called CMEA division of labour, tied by long-term agreements on economic and R & D exchanges, which, while drawing benefit from the previously mentioned sectors, will nevertheless be ruled by a different economic logic. While these segments may to some extent coincide with traditional branch structures of the preceding period, the underlying principles will be very different.

The success of this second stage of economic reform will be conditional upon regime political credibility, otherwise stage three may as well be prepared.

5 Power and Policy: Dilemmas and Challenges

The course of Polish history and the geopolitical position of the Polish nation, the nature of Polish society and the transformation it has undergone in recent times, and the persistent problems experienced regarding economic development have all shaped the power base of the leadership and influenced the political challenges it has had to face. The governmental and political structures of communist Poland, and the capacities and strength of its economy, have helped condition the way it has confronted these challenges and determine the resources at the leadership's disposal. The structures of communist rule and the nature of the socialized economy (and particularly its politicized character: Morawski, 1986) have, however, themselves presented leaders with their own problems and produced challenges that stemmed from the operation of the communist institutional structure itself. We may suggest, indeed, that the specific nature of the dilemmas and political challenges that have arisen in communist Poland can be traced to the close relationship between these two sets of factors.

The major historical factor that has governed Poland's recent history is the nature of the post-war settlement in Central and Eastern Europe. This is, of course, true for all countries that form part of the Soviet bloc but it is a factor that has been particularly keenly felt in Poland. There is evidence that the establishment of Soviet control over Poland had been one of Stalin's leading war aims from an early stage and that the elimination of Polish autonomy was a deeply entrenched Soviet objective (Mastny, 1979). Sustained further by the consequences of historic Polish-Russian enmity and the meagre popular support afforded the Polish communist party in the inter-war period, Polish resistance to the imposition of communist power in the years immediately after World War II was considerable. Estimates and official statements on the number of casualties that occurred as a result of conflicts during the establishment of the communist regime have varied. One recent estimate has been that 20,000 died, a high loss in comparative terms for this period of Eastern European history (Korbonski, 1982).

The major conclusion to be drawn from these experiences was that communist forces encountered strong resistance (passive and active) to the establishment of a Soviet-orientated regime and had limited *political* resources (in distinction to the military capacity of the Soviet Union which it was clearly advisable to leave in the background) which they could use to achieve their objectives. This has been the principal cause of some of the special characteristics of communist rule in Poland and the source of the particular dilemmas its leaders have faced. It is a condition that has generally received due recognition in the Kremlin throughout the post-war period.

Thus relatively high levels of tolerance have been shown during such different periods as the 1950s (when major show trials were avoided, Gomułka's life was spared, and a relatively slow pace of collectivization permitted) and the 1980s (when Solidarity was allowed some sixteen months of existence, various social forces were given fairly free reign, and pressures for direct Soviet intervention apparently resisted: Kukliński, 1987). It has, indeed, been suggested that some of the problems encountered by the Gierek regime were attributable to the fact that Brezhnev and his entourage became less mindful of the nature of their 'Polish problem' (Fikus, 1984).

The special conditions of communist rule in Poland have, of course, been fully recognized by the successive leaders of the PZPR. Władysław Gomułka, certainly no liberal or parliamentary democrat, held decided views on the inappropriateness of conducting a Soviet-style collectivization in the Polish countryside and encountered major political resistance from more orthodox quarters precisely for this reason (Bieńkowski, 1971a). The Gierek regime toughened significantly around the time of the 1976 demonstrations, following a relatively relaxed start, but held back from a full-scale clamp-down on the growing underground opposition, cautioned also by the worsening state of the economy and strong western pressure. Even under the conditions of Jaruzelski's State of War security forces showed considerable restraint in comparison with military dictatorships in other parts of the world.

The tenor of communist rule in Poland, then, has generally reflected the awareness of its leaders of the weak foundations its structures of rule have in Polish society and of their low level of support among the Polish population. This does not mean that the position of the leadership has itself necessarily been an unstable one or that it is unable to call on additional power resources to maintain its position. Despite the impression of an unstable leadership which has been toppled by assertive workers on more than one occasion, Polish rulers have been able to call on the army and security forces to quash opposition and have done this on several major occasions, causing numerous fatalities in 1956, 1970 and 1981–2. Indeed, the security forces have had a relatively high political profile throughout the 1980s, and the murder of Father Popiełuszko in October 1984 provided only a recent example of their activity (Lewis, 1985b).

Elite instability and the fall of individual leaders has, rather, been brought about by conflicts within the leading group and the withdrawal of support at the highest levels of political power—although this kind of crisis has, of course, also had close links with developments in the broader society. The weak social base for communist rule in Poland has not, then, manifested itself primarily in leadership instability but rather through problems encountered in establishing the credibility of party leadership in general and in formulating conditions for the effective operation of the institutions of communist rule. The 'failure' of government proposals to gain a majority in the November 1987 referendum provided one more example of this important factor. Some of the major problems of political rule in communist Poland have arisen not because the parameters of rule have been Polish but because they have had to be presented as communist. But communist rule has clearly been sustainable by force and this could hardly be otherwise in view of Poland's location alongside the Soviet Union.

Despite the evident coercive underpinnings of communist systems and their essentially dictatorial (or, at best, centralist and highly qualified democratic) character it is not in fact through the use of force that they are run on an everyday basis. The main principle employed in the process of communist rule is that of party leadership and the authority, established on various grounds, of its leading cadres. The conditions of communist rule in Poland have been such, as already outlined, that models of party leadership and bases for the authority of its leading officials have been particularly difficult to develop. It is primarily these factors that have given rise to the specific dilemmas and challenges that have confronted Polish leaders. Particular problems can be associated with the different phases of communist rule in Poland. We shall first review these before turning to consider the persistent dilemmas that have confronted the leadership in the post-war period.

The Legacy of Weak Destalinization

One of the main consequences of the cautious approach taken by the leadership during the early stages of communist rule was a relatively controlled transition to a post-Stalin model of rule. By this means a national tragedy equivalent to or even worse than that experienced by Hungary in 1956 was avoided. This carried its own drawbacks, though, in bypassing the opportunity for a sharp break from the political practices of Stalinism and permitting the continuing existence of a firmly entrenched power apparatus and set of political and administrative officials. Although brutal, dogmatic and economically exploitative, Stalinist political policies were not applied in Poland with the same intensity as they were elsewhere in Eastern Europe and their effects were somewhat less severe.

Gomułka was never brought to trial for his 'right-wing deviation' and escaped the fate of discredited leaders like Rajk in Hungary and Slansky in Czechoslovakia who did not survive the Stalinist period. The collectivization policy stirred up much resentment in the countryside and had a disastrous affect on agricultural recovery, but its impact on the socio-economic structure of the peasantry was quite limited. By the end of 1955 only 189,000 families had been reorganized into collectives and the 'socialist transformation' of the Polish countryside was a slow-moving process even during the Stalin period (Sanders, 1958).

Its consequences for the urban population were nevertheless severe and in Poznań, which was the site of a major revolt in June 1956, bread was already in short supply in 1953 (Makowski, 1981). The rate of capital accumulation also rose dramatically, with dire consequences for the pool of resources available for consumption, housing and the welfare services, nearly reaching 40 per cent of national income in 1953 (Leslie, *et al.*, 1980). These initiatives had enormous implications for the structure and character of Polish society (see Chapter 2). The growth of education and the opportunities for bureaucratic expansion implied by the adoption of a programme of planned social change underwrote the creation of large numbers of white-collar jobs. In the small but crucial sphere of the party organization itself the number of political workers employed in the party apparatus rose from 5,478 to 12,650 between 1950 and 1953. Though many were in positions of influence and some power, the quality of these employees was low. As many as 40 per cent of those attending one provincial party school in 1951 had not completed their elementary schooling and some could barely read and write (Kozik, 1982).

But although far-reaching in their effects on the Polish economy, the distribution of its population and its employment structure, the care taken during the implementation of Stalinist policies and the attention paid to the condition of the working class meant that public dissatisfaction did not surface so directly as it did soon after Stalin's death in East Germany and Czechoslovakia, where demonstrations met resistance and violent repression in 1953. A major demonstration took place in June 1956 in Poznań, and fifty-three were admitted to have died before the opposition was crushed. But significant conflict within the elite was avoided after 1953 and policy changed gradually to meet the changing political conditions within the Soviet bloc—indeed, the Polish response to post-Stalin developments was characterized by extreme caution and hesitancy. Gomułka was only released from detention just prior to the Polish October. Such violent outbursts as occurred in Hungary in 1956 following extensive conflict within the ruling group between Stalinist conservatives and those committed to the New Course were also avoided, as was the bloody aftermath of the Soviet intervention.

The Poznań revolt was responsible for an acceleration of the pace of political change and it impressed the need for significant destalinization on the majority of the central leadership. Amidst spreading public debate and the progressive release of society from Stalinist controls, the return of Gomułka to the leadership was agreed by the ruling group and the necessity of the change as a *fait accompli* impressed on the Soviets. Despite the level of public activity, involving intellectuals and workers and, on the part of the peasantry, leading to the spontaneous dissolution of most of the collective farms, the major decision-making prerogatives were limited to the political elite and the central structural features of the political system remained intact.

Certain ambiguities remain in accounts of Gomułka's handling of the Polish political situation following his return to the leadership in October 1956. Brought back to power on a tide of popular opposition to the Stalin-sponsored dictatorship, to the suppression of Polish national independence and to the growing burden imposed by the overcentralized socialist economy, Gomułka stood up to Soviet military and security representaives and to a delegation headed by Khrushchev but was then soon directing most of his attention to the forces fuelled by Polish grievances and to the threat they were perceived to present to party leadership and the socialist regime in Poland. Some were suspicious of this rather sudden reorientation and raised doubts about the authenticity of the Polish break with the Stalinist tradition (Jedlicki, 1963; Sakwa, 1978).

Certainly, within a matter of weeks, a marked shift of emphasis occurred in Polish political life and debates within the party. Gomułka began to articulate a new approach and was soon directing most of his attention to the threat posed by 'party revisionists' and the reformers who had seen much hope in his return to power. Emphasis was placed on the need to defend the foundations of socialism against those who were pressing for the transition to the 'second stage' which would lead to the restoration of capitalism. Dogmatism (Stalinist authoritarianism) was indeed condemned, but viewed only as a minor infection in comparison with the 'fever' of revisionism (Gomułka, 1969).

The conspiratorial view of Gomułka's return to power in fact betrays an excessive cynicism about Polish developments after Stalin's death and an eagerness to interpret them less in their own terms than in the light of their consequences. It does, however, have the merit of directing attention to the strong elements of continuity between the pre-1956 situation and developments after that date. Unlike the dramatic *caesura* in Hungary in 1956, developments in Poland had to a far smaller extent the character of a sharply defined watershed. Many Poles, though certainly a minority, did have a strong vested interest in the survival of the system that had been established after 1945 and for others the intensity of the opposition provoked by the communist regime had not been sufficient to ensure its collapse. All were aware of the weighty military presence of the Soviet Union on Poland's border and few could forget the 'legacy of Yalta' (this is examined in more detail in Chapter 6).

The bulk of the political leadership, including Gomułka, were only too aware of the precariousness of their position and were reluctant to stray far from the limits laid down by the Kremlin (although they had certainly taken a calculated risk in standing up to the Khrushchev delegation which had arrived uninvited in Warsaw during the October Central Committee Plenum). The weakness of party authority that had restrained it from imposing the full rigours of Stalinism also held it back from making too sharp a break with the past and showed the narrow scope for change and political manoeuvre the leadership had open to it. Gomułka was reported to have held to the view that the Polish party was 'too weak to govern democratically' (Korybutowicz, 1983, p. 35). The capacity to contemplate only a limited spectrum of change landed the Polish leadership with some major problems.

While Stalinism in Poland proved to be relatively mild it was also durable and most of the gains made in October 1956 were soon lost. Officials who had acquired power during the period of Poland's cautious Stalinism generally retained it after October and played their part in the firmly entrenched power cliques that gradually came to exercise a stranglehold over Polish political life (Ascherson, 1981). While there was considerable change at local levels of the party organization much of this concerned junior staff and did not have the political consequences that might have been anticipated. The communist establishment that had consolidated its position in the early 1950s largely survived and its influence was certainly felt after 1956.

This soon became evident in public life. Press restrictions were reimposed in 1957 and the following years, although some areas of intellectual freedom were defended with greater success; the ferment in the party was swiftly brought under control, 'revisionists' expelled and unacceptable officials replaced; the influence of the newly established RR was rapidly curtailed (see Chapter 4) while the reinvigoration of the economy that followed the relaxation of central controls was of similarly short duration. The share of investment in national income began to increase again from 1958 and had a marked effect in slowing down the rise in levels of consumption (Mieczkowski, 1978, p. 264). The bulk of the party establishment remained intact and, although major personal changes occurred in the senior leadership with the reassertion of Gomułka's dominance, the costs of the leadership's inability to countenance more extensive change could be seen at other levels of the party-state bureaucracy.

The change of course in 1956 had relatively little impact on the composition of Central Committee membership, for example, an area where wider-ranging change might have been expected. Detailed study in fact showed a 'most interesting, and somewhat unexpected' stability between 1954 and 1959 (Pienkos, 1975, p. 37). More extensive change had to wait until the close of the Gomułka era, a change that foreshadowed the fall of Gomułka himself. A core of around 50 CC members managed to perpetuate their membership of the body from Congress to Congress between 1948 and 1968 and, even when a higher number of new members did come to join the CC in 1968, this was partly because the CC itself was considerably enlarged (see Table 5.1). Unlike most other Eastern European countries, which had significant levels of representation of specialist groups on their Central Committees, that in Poland was also more restricted and CC members were more often drawn from universities and institutes during the Gomułka period (Bielasiak, 1978). Decision-making authority seemed to remain highly

Table 5.1 Turnover amongst Central Committee Full Members (dated from successive congresses)

	1945–48	1948–54	1954–59	1959–64	1964–68	1968–71
No. of CC members originally elected	36	71	77	77	85	101
No. of new CC members at opening date	35	13	20	12	29	38
No. maintaining position as CC member	26	52	50	57	50	46

Source: Compiled from Pienkos (1975).

centralized and was not dispersed to the same extent as in other Eastern European countries. This gave less opportunity for the exercise of group influence in this way and restricted the scope of interest-group activity which some saw as the major sign of the communist countries' movement away from the totalitarian model (Skilling & Griffiths, 1971).

The weak integration of the central political leadership with the technical elite certainly played a part in Poland's poor economic performance in the 1960s. Average real wages rose by 20 per cent in Poland between 1960 and 1970, the slowest rate of growth in eastern Europe, where it ranged from 47 per cent and 43 per cent in Romania and Bulgaria to 27 per cent in Czechoslovakia (*Mały Rocznik Statystyczny*, 1981). This slow rate of growth was a significant cost imposed by the problems Poland's rulers encountered in changing the system. Unlike virtually all other Eastern European countries, Poland eschewed all reform initiatives and slid into stagnation. The precarious nature of party rule in Poland, reflected initially in the cautious approach taken during the Stalin period, thus also had its effect in the weakness of the destalinization process and had further consequences for the position of the regime.

Political Fragmentation and Problems of System Integration

The consolidation of the power apparatus in the early 1950s and its survival, largely unscathed, into the second Gomułka period reinforced elements of political continuity and further narrowed the range of political choices available to the senior leadership. During the purge of the revisionists there were reversals of some of the changes made in the party in the summer and early autumn of 1956 as its rulers considered their future and clashed over the appropriate way in which the necessary changes were to be managed. 'Corrections' within the newly elected local leaderships were already under way before the end of the year (Kozik, 1982). While this reflected the policy and political strategy adopted by Gomułka it also showed the strength of local political groups and provincial leaders. By the time of the Third Party Congress in 1959, according to a former minister and close associate of Gomułka (a 'revisionist' who did not last long in the ruling group), the central authorities had clearly lost ground and the balance of power had shifted decisively towards the executive apparatus and local party organizations (Bieńkowski, 1971b).

In his conception, the years following 1956 saw a 'feudalization' of the Polish political system, with central power becoming fragmented and at least partly subdivided and 'parcelled out' to the regions. Major beneficiaries of this process were the first secretaries of the twenty-two provincial party committees, representing the seventeen major provinces (*województwa*) and the five largest towns. Certainly by 1968, with the extensive political conflict and infighting that followed the reception of the outcome of the Arab–Israeli war in Poland, significant factions had developed within the PZPR and there were clear signs that major party officials were fighting to consolidate their position and extend their political influence. As Soviet leaders Khrushchev and Gorbachëv have also found, this tendency has not been limited to Poland and it reflects a deep-rooted structural problem in the operation of the communist system.

The Israeli victory had, it appeared, been enthusiastically received by some air force officers of Jewish origin, provoking disciplinary actions which promoted a growing mood of officially sponsored anti-Semitism. Between 1967 and 1969 341 Jewish officers were expelled from the army and the party (*Nowe Drogi*, February 1988). Jews and remaining 'revisionists' (party members of more liberal views) were criticized and, in many cases, removed from public office (there were only some 15 thousand Jews left in Poland by this stage in any case). This spelled the ultimate demise of reformism and the 'revisionist' tendency in the PZPR, a development that was to have important consequences and prompted the formation of the extra-party opposition in the 1970s (Michnik, 1976). Students demonstrated in March 1968 and were dispersed with considerable violence by the police. A public campaign of a generally anti-Semitic and anti-intellectual character was instituted which, while not being overtly directed against Gomułka, was designed to serve the interests of people like Mieczysław Moczar, Minister of the Interior and spokesman for nationalistically minded groups, and Edward Gierek, provincial secretary in Katowice, the leading industrial region.

Gomułka survived in office but had clearly suffered a further loss of power. His rule came to an end thirty-three months later, shortly before Christmas 1970, after striking workers in the northern ports were shot by military and security forces. He was swiftly succeeded by Gierek (who was supported by Moczar), who promised dramatic changes in political and economic life and the establishment of a different kind of communist rule. In recognition of the dispersal of power to the intermediate levels of the executive apparatus, though, one of Gierek's first moves was to shake up the provincial leadership of the party. Twelve of the twenty-two provincial leaders were changed during his first year in office (de Weydenthal, 1986).

Efforts to establish the more secure centralization of power followed in 1975, when the existing provinces were abolished and in their place forty-nine new administrative units set up. The power of the new provincial leaders was clearly more restricted than that of their predecessors and Gierek's move was successful in that he did not face any serious political challenge from that quarter in the following years. But in other respects the fragmentation of the political system persisted and in many respects worsened, qualifying central power and undermining attempts to put some order into Poland's economic processes, which had been badly affected by the country's high foreign debt in combination with international inflation and the post-1974 recession. The problems faced by Poland's rulers in concentrating political power and exercising it effectively were a persistent challenge and significant obstacle to the proper performance of a number of major economic and political tasks.

Central party authority was limited by factors other than those deriving from the power of local party leaders. At the beginning of the decade Gierek had publicized the slogan: 'the party leads and the government governs'. This was meant to provide some guidance in the complicated issue of the mutual responsibility of party and state bodies in what was in fact a unified party-state bureaucratic complex. It also had the advantage of placing executive responsibility firmly on the shoulders of the government organization. In fact, central party organs provided far more than the overall leadership and strategic direction. The Politburo soon became immersed in the finer details of the economic policy and its implementation and drifted away from the exercise of its function of general supervision and overall leadership (Gebethner, 1981).

At the same time the party leadership seemed to lose the capacity to control the government and, in particular, the behaviour and decisions of the Prime Minister, Piotr Jaroszewicz. In hearings before the Grabski Commission, set up in 1981 to pronounce on the responsibility of leading party-state officials for the crisis of the late 1970s, party leaders claimed an astonishing level of ignorance and incapacity with regard to governmental actions (Pomian, 1986). Gierek, for example (pp. 64–5), tried to move part of the blame for Poland's catastrophic level of indebtedness on to deputy prime minister Jagielski and to have found out himself only in 1978 that the viable limits had been exceeded. Much blame was placed on Jaroszewicz who, in the face of attempts to unseat him, was claimed to be virtually immovable. While much of this sounds like special pleading and an attempt to avoid unwelcome responsibility, there was probably at least some truth in these accounts.

Jaroszewicz had the reputation of being a Soviet confidant and guarantor of Soviet interests during the relatively experimental period of Gierek's 'new approach'. In the early 1950s he had been responsible for military aspects of economic planning and had worked closely with Soviet advisers (Checinski,

1983). Later he was based in Moscow as Poland's permanent representative to the executive committee of the CMEA. As such he was clearly in a strong personal position. He also appeared to disagree with the remedial economic measures taken in 1976 and was loath to release government information to workers in the party apparatus (Lewis, 1982).

In the light of such developments it becomes easier to understand how 'party leadership' was difficult to exercise in Gierek's Poland, particularly as general leadership rapidly developed into a more detailed form of supervision. The outcome was a dispersion of power at national level and further limitations on Gierek's decision-making capacity and the authority of the party. The novel solution adopted by Gierek to break out of communist Poland's political and economic impasse effectively generated its own restrictions and came into conflict with the conditions that were necessary for its success. This time the integration of the political system proved to be weaker on the horizontal plane and at national level. The power of the Polish communist leadership again showed itself to be limited and party authority insufficient to sustain effective rule or to maintain a viable form of administration within the country.

Control over Cadres

The low level of central party authority and weak integration of the political system made it difficult to maintain control over executive officials, a problem encountered in most communist systems and one which continues to command the attention of the military-party leadership in contemporary Poland. Further, the weakness of the destalinization process in Poland left much of the political establishment in place and increased its chances of survival. In the 1960s problems persisted concerning the poor educational background of many of the party cadres, reflecting weaknesses in the party organization that had become evident during the early stages of the consolidation of the communist regime.

While there was, of course, some turnover among officials there was also much continuity of office-holding. At the end of 1967, 37 per cent of party officials had been appointed at least eleven years earlier. The average party worker was becoming older: in 1967, 41 per cent of employees were forty or over compared with 23 per cent in 1963 (Cave, 1981). Lengthy office-holding in the party generally continued under Gierek (although he took care to introduce some new faces), this naturally being more pronounced at senior levels. In 1975, 59 per cent of provincial party leaders had begun their career in the apparatus over fifteen years earlier. Thirty per cent had started in 1954 or even earlier. Even in 1980, 24 per cent of provincial leaders had begun their career no later than 1954, while nearly three-quarters had received their first party appointment before 1965.

Table 5.2 Date of First Party Appointment of Provincial PZPR First Secretaries

	Number			Percent		
	1975	1980	1984	1975	1980	1984
Up to 10 years previously	7	7	20	16	16	41
11 to 20 years previously	24	13	21	55	29	43
21 to 30 years previously	12	18	5	27	41	10
Over 30 years previously	1	6	3	2	14	6
Total	44	44	49	100	100	100

Source: Compiled from Lewis (1986b, p. 381).

But at least under Gomułka, it seemed, this continuity in office and holding on to positions of official authority was not used to accumulate economic advantage or to establish a basis for excessive material privilege. It would, of course, be too much to expect that the political elite did not receive some material advantages from its position. But in Poland, claims sociologist Maria Hirszowicz (1986), the notion of a 'new class' based on political position found less support than elsewhere, though this was not a view shared by Kuron & Modzelewski (1968). If so, this was perhaps due to the ascetic lifestyle and discipline exerted in this area by Gomułka as PZPR First Secretary. It is a picture that certainly does not accord with the realities of life under Gierek in the 1970s.

One of the penalties for Gomułka's successor in seeking to maintain the regime by the operation of a relatively weakly integrated political system was the need to establish auxiliary means of assuring the compliance of his officials and perpetuating his own dominance within the elite. In contrast to the relatively puritanical Gomułka, Gierek was not averse to enjoying the privilege of office and was content to let those around him do likewise in order to enhance their personal commitment to the system. Not surprisingly, this attitude spread throughout the party-state bureaucracy and was given further impetus by the proliferation of official posts at provincial level: for example, the number of provincial party leaders rose from twenty-two to forty-nine (all of whom required executive housing and transportation facilities) when Gierek took measures to distance possible rivals from the political centre.

The official tone for this trend was set by the promulgation in 1972 of a decree on pensions, which established generous provision not only for a range of leading party and government officials but also for a number of relatives, dependents and grandchildren (Smolar, 1983). While these provisions were novel and outrageously generous, in that a restricted group legislated strictly for its own benefit, they were at least legal and passed by due process (they were finally annulled after the Ninth Congress in 1981). The material gains of privileged groups during the 1970s, however, went far beyond those legally permitted and involved diverse forms of corruption, embezzlement and improper personal enrichment. The process was facilitated both by the growing tendency towards bureaucracy and institutional proliferation (fuelled by the desire of others to get on the bandwagon) and by the enhanced availability of investment and other forms of public funding, augmented by large sums provided by foreign finance organizations.

The precise extent of such criminal abuse of office, let alone of legal, though morally suspect, forms of personal benefit, is difficult to establish and it spread throughout society permeating many public institutions. Records were collected by the Supreme Control Chamber, headed throughout the 1970s by M. Moczar (who probably hoped to use such evidence in furtherance of his undoubted political ambitions), and much came to light from this source as well as from others after the removal of Gierek in 1980 (*Zeszty Historyczne*, 1983). Abuses were recorded by the First Secretary himself, two CC secretaries, twenty-three provincial first secretaries, thirty-four other provincial secretaries, seven deputy prime ministers, eighteen ministers, and others. In addition to party punishments and expulsions, some were put on trial and sentenced. A few committed suicide. Personal abuse of public office had clearly been very extensive and, while the financial consequences must have been themselves of some significance, its social and political impact was of even greater importance and public mistrust of the communist leadership was compounded by contempt and profound distaste.

Party and government cadres, key officials appointed under the *nomenklatura* system, had clearly operated byeond public scrutiny and with inadequate regard for the effective operation of the economic system. To a certain extent they had also been acting in their own interest outside local and central control, though many of their transgressions had been tolerated and condoned by the higher authorities. The issue of institutional control continued to raise considerable problems for the national leadership and posed the question of how far the system, though in many respects a strongly centralized one, was in fact subject to central leadership and effective control. More than any other Eastern European country, Poland in the 1970s exemplified the dualism of political power in communist societies analysed by Urban (1985, p. 207), under which a strongly centralized system and apparently all-powerful leadership are 'counterparts to a state which in all fundamental respects is weak—or, more precisely, one which is composed of weak structures'.

The Gierek decade had seen the growth of the party apparatus (accompanying that of its mass membership) and the expansion of the government bureaucracy. Yet the same period saw probably one of the worst examples of communist maladministration and the virtual negation of any claim it had to authority and political leadership (Lewis, 1989). Even after the fall of Gierek, with the onset of overt economic crisis and the adoption of a considerably different political approach by the leadership headed by Stanislaw Kania, it was clear that major elements of the party-state bureaucracy were unsympathetic to the new strategy and, despite the critical situation in which the country and its leadership were now placed, were reluctant to change either their behaviour or the approach taken to Polish society, now finding an influential voice in the recently established Solidarity organization. Notions of 'control', checking and accountability were central to the activity and vision of Solidarity.

Kania's call at the Sixth Central Committee Plenum in early September 1980 for a new humility to be demonstrated by the authorities met with little practical response for the rest of that year. Moves to organize an Extraordinary Party Congress, already agreed at national level, were delayed and little concerted progress was made towards extending local democratic practices within existing organizations or establishing a working relationship with local Solidarity representatives. Greater changes in this respect began to take place in early 1981 under the pressure of local movements and protests organized against specific targets of popular dissatisfaction. Developments also gathered pace in the PZPR with the organization of a 'horizontal movement' linking local party activists against entrenched party conservatives (in conflict certainly with the conventional practice of democratic centralism and possibly with its theory as well).

Many established officials nevertheless continued to resist pressures for change and attempted to postpone the organization of a Party Congress, which would elect a new Central Committee and thus eliminate a major power base for much of the old guard. While the picture remains unclear it does seem certain that representatives of such forces organized the beatings at Bydgoszcz in March 1981 as a provocation to compromise the Kania-Jaruzelski leadership and part of a broader plan to facilitate Soviet intervention (Kukliński, 1987). But even when the Extraordinary Congress was held in July 1981 and a new leadership and Central Committee was elected much of the non-elected apparatus remained in place and continued, so it appears, to set the political agenda.

While there have been some suggestions that Jaruzelski's coup of December 1981 was directed against the old guard and its apparatus (Spielman, 1982–3), subsequent developments confirm rather that the State of War was designed to enhance central leadership control within the party, neutralize the political influence of Solidarity and implement major price rises, particularly for food production (see Kosta & Levcik, 1985, pp. 17 and 43). It was also not irrelevant that while Polish military expenditure had grown by an annual average of only 0.5 per cent between 1975 and 1980 it rose by 10 per cent in 1982, more than compensating for a 6.6 per cent decline in 1981. Growth again remained negative until 1985 (*SIPRI Yearbook*, 1987). Although the position of the party apparatus was changed and its influence limited by the appointment of military commissars, the conditions produced under the State of War were clearly more to its liking than those which had been prevalent during the Solidarity period.

Party Identity and the Polish Military

A further major problem has concerned the maintenance not just of the content but even of the form of party rule. The latter aspect came to the fore towards the end of 1981. The 'military coup' of 13 December 1981 was not mounted against the PZPR or the Polish government, but was rather a response to the persistent weakness of the party and the failure of its leadership during the crisis of 1980–1 to restore political and social order or reassert its mastery over the course of events. This is not to suggest that there were not important divisions within the party-state complex or even within the party organization itself. As we have demonstrated, important sections of the party apparatus had shown considerable autonomy for a lengthy period and had by no means always acted as a loyal executive force with no political will of its own. Reluctance to accept the reformist orientation of the Kania leadership had itself weakened the position of that leadership, encouraged talk of an imposed military solution to the political stalemate and, perhaps, played a major part in planning and bringing into being the State of War.

The precise origins and nature of the 'military coup' were complicated by the fact that the leader of Military Council of National Salvation (WRON), which took power on 13 December 1981, was General Jaruzelski who, as well as being Minister of Defence, had acted as Prime Minister since February 1981 and, since October, had been PZPR First Secretary in place of Kania. The personal position of the supreme leader himself was, therefore, in no way diminished by the announcement of the State of War. That of the government and the leading party bodies (Politburo, Central Committee and CC Secretariat) was, however, clearly affected by the emergence of a new decision-making and central executive body and party activities were virtually suspended for several weeks.

Nevertheless, the change in leading personnel was not total. Of the twenty military figures that made up the WRON three (Generals Kiszczak, Hupałowski, Piotrowski) had already been cabinet ministers responsible for, respectively, the Ministries of the Interior, Regional Administration, and Mining and Power. General Siwicki, Chief of the General Staff, was a Politburo member and three others (Generals Tuczapski, Molczyk and Janczyszyn) had seats on the CC. The degree to which the powers of the existing party and government leaderships were usurped also appeared to vary. While the influence of the reformers in the Politburo was clearly reduced there was probably little affect on the position of some others (notably CC secretaries Barcikowski and Olszowski, and General Milewski—who also held the position of Minister of Internal Affairs. Milewski disappeared from political life in the wake of the Popiełuszko affair.)

It is important, too, to identify the precise affiliation and background of the key military representatives. Particularly significant was the influence of the army's Main Political Administration (MPA), the organization responsible for political training and ideological awareness amongst the military. Jaruzelski had been made head of the MPA in 1960 at the age of thirty-six and held the post until 1965, for the last three years acting simultaneously as Deputy Minister of National Defence. Promoted to Minister of Defence in 1968, he held that post until 1983. General Baryła, in charge of the MPA from 1980, was also a member of the WRON and later appointed CC secretary in 1985, his position consolidated by inclusion in the Politburo as a full member after the Tenth Party Congress in 1986. General Honkisz, deputy head of the MPA, was transferred to take control of the CC Cadres Department in 1984, following the death in office of its existing military organizer.

Some of the key political posts during the State of War and the subsequent period, then, were held not by those coming from positions of direct military command but by men experienced in operating the ideological and educational apparatus that exercised political supervision over the armed forces. While clearly being part of the communist military establishment and being staffed by officers with extensive military experience, the MPA also had very close links with the central party organization and the CC apparatus. The precise character of those links and, particularly, the degree to which the MPA acts autonomously of central party authorities is a matter of some uncertainty. Some have claimed that it operates essentially as a Central Committee Department and others that no CC secretarial control is exerted at all (Checinski, 1982; Gerner, 1985). Others express the more likely view that the MPA is subject to some form of dual party-military subordination, or that control has been exercised directly by the First Secretary (Malcher, 1984; Davies, 1986, Weydenthal, 1986).

What is clear is that the army's MPA acts very much as the political wing of the military establishment and has very close links with the central party authorities but probably has, nevertheless, some measure of autonomy from the apparatus based on the CC. Soviet experience may be relevant here and there has, indeed, been some suggestion of a recent growth in the autonomy and political influence of the MPA in relation to the apparatus of the Communist Party of the Soviet Union (Simes, 1981–2). It is, further, likely that the Polish MPA has some direct links with the Soviet military authorities and their political establishment, but the precise nature of relations here is even more difficult to establish. But it is clear that the MPA plays a crucial role in what is most appropriately seen as the party-military 'dual elite' (Perlmutter & Leogrande, 1982).

Awareness of the relations between the military, the MPA and the party leadership helps us further with an understanding of the nature of the State of War. It was clearly not a coup 'against the party'—and could not really be one as the head of the WRON that proclaimed the State of War was at the same time the leader of the PZPR. Indeed, while there is evidently a difference between the operational military forces and the military's political apparatus represented by the MPA, it is also doubtful whether there was any such thing as a unified 'party' in real terms at the end of 1981. While the public divisions that had emerged at the beginning of the year between moderate and hardline central leaders, local horizontal movements and apparatus conservatives, were no longer in evidence after the Ninth Congress, there were certainly major internal differences that contributed in a fundamental way to the political weakness of its leadership and its growing loss of public support.

Neither did the WRON, or the party and government leadership acting under military jurisdiction during the State of War, take action that was markedly at odds with the preferences and policies of most of the party establishment, at least in the early stage. Some 12,000 members were expelled from the party in the two months following 13 December and the names of many others 'removed from party lists', bringing about a drop in party membership of 129,000 by the end of February 1982. Three hundred and forty-nine secretaries of town or district committees were removed, 307 from plant committees, and 2,091 leaders of primary party organizations were dismissed (*Życie Partii*, 3 March 1982).

The entire party organization in Toruń University, one of the major bases of the horizontal movement, was disbanded. The party organization of the Katowice steelworks, in former years the largest in the country, was also dissolved and reconstructed under strict supervision. But no departures occurred from the top leadership, at Politburo and CC secretary level (although General Kiszczak, Minister of Interior, did join the Politburo), and only three CC members were 'recalled' from it (including a leading 'horizontal' activist from Torun) at the first plenary meeting held under the State of War in February 1982.

The State of War did not, therefore, initially affect the composition of the senior party leadership although it certainly restricted decision-making to a narrow group and must surely have had a major impact on discussion and the kinds of question that could be raised in central policy-making bodies. The *Instrukcja* (executive instructions issued by the Politburo) that determined the conditions under which party life was to be conducted during the State of War not only eliminated the rights and freedoms that had become established during 1980–1 but also restricted all manner of rank-and-file activities provided for in the Party Statute, recentralized decision-making processes and concentrated power in the hands of the executive organs, major committees and key individuals.

All this was quite acceptable to much of the party apparatus and the remaining 'hard core' of the party members. Some leading officials, though, particularly those at provincial level, harboured doubts about the effect of the State of War on the party and its implications for the party's powers of recovery and political leadership. Developments under the State of War were, obviously, far less acceptable to the mass of the population, much of the working class and members of the now suspended Solidarity union, about a million of whom were or had been also party members. Party membership declined sharply in 1982, by some 364,000, partly as a result of expulsions but mostly due to resignations, failure to maintain contact with the party organization and a general reluctance to contemplate applying for party membership. Party numbers continued to fall and did not stabilise until mid-1985, since when they have only just begun to show any signs of recovery.

The position of the party in Polish society and its capacity to exercise political leadership of the kind conventionally found in Marxist regimes was, therefore, clearly affected by the introduction of the State of War. More conservative sections of the party and its apparatus clearly welcomed the reassertion of centralized control and reimposition of stronger discipline over the membership, not least the expulsion of Solidarity activists and drawing of a firm demarcation line between the two organizations. But this occurred at the cost both of the size and the status of the party, as the traditional powers of the party (many of which had in any case become seriously attenuated by the end of 1981) were taken over by military- and Politburo-appointed plenipotentiaries, security officials and even government representatives. The suspension of the State of War at the end of 1982 and its lifting in July 1983 did not really affect this situation and the position of the party in the Polish political system has continued to remain a relatively marginal one for a ruling communist party.

Ideology and the Weakness of Official Political Commitment

The four problems of party organization and authority discussed so far have reflected deep-rooted problems of party life that have also been associated with particular phases of Polish development. There have also been persistent problems in Polish politics that have confronted successive party leaders with specific dilemmas. A further aspect of the weak foundation the PZPR has managed to secure for itself in Polish society, and itself a contributory factor to that weakness, has been the lack of commitment to Marxist-Leninist ideology not just among the population as a whole but also among party cadres and the elite itself. The causes of this weak commitment are not difficult to identify: Poland remains a deeply Catholic nation and sustains a strong Church organization; historically it has maintained strong intellectual and cultural links with Western Europe rather than with countries to the East; pre-war communist organizations gathered little popular support and were far outweighed in terms of political influence by democratic socialist and peasant-orientated parties; an influential private peasant farm section has remained in existence. Some have expressed the view that communist efforts in the sphere of resocialization might themselves have been counterproductive 'in the sense of having created strong liberal propensities in countries such as Poland and Hungary where those orientations were relatively weak in the prerevolutionary era' (Almond, 1983).

The consequences of the social and economic policies officially adopted and implemented under party leadership (thus according to the principles of Marxism–Leninism) have also failed to provide any basis for the acceptance of communist ideology. While the policies of rapid industrialization adopted in the late 1940s made some sense in the less developed Balkan countries, they were less suited to the economies of the more advanced countries of the Eastern European northern tier and caused all manner of imbalances in production and shortages in the provision of retail goods. For a number of reasons this economic failure was more pronounced in Poland than elsewhere and produced, as we have seen, the slowest rate of wage growth in Eastern Europe throughout the 1960s and provided the conditions for a steadily worsening crisis of drastic proportions in the 1970s. Neither the principles of communist ideology nor its results, therefore, were such as to produce anything more than the most grudging acceptance by the Polish population.

Nevertheless, the conditions pertaining in Eastern Europe after World War II have necessitated both some form of communist party rule and public obeisance to the principles of Marxist–Leninist ideology. The leading role of a Soviet-sponsored political elite and the dominant role of the party have therefore been accepted on more pragmatic grounds. Accordingly, successive leaders of the PZPR have placed considerable importance on *raison d'état* and geopolitical reasons for the dominant role of the party in post-war Poland, giving these an important place in the 'operative ideology' (Taras, 1984) of the PZPR. Briefly, they have argued that, in the absence of a dominant native party, Poland would have to suffer direct Soviet rule. This was further supported by the lingering German threat to the integrity of the post-war Polish state, as the post-war Polish borders (which incorporated significant portions of what had been pre-war Germany) were not recognized by the Federal Republic until 1970.

Gierek also placed considerable emphasis on *raison d'état* as a major element of PZPR ideology although, particularly in view of growing awareness of the domestic conditions of Poland's persistently poor performance in economic and political terms, it carried less and less conviction. During the 1970s PZPR ideology became increasingly *ad hoc*, combining efforts to demonstrate the native Polish credentials of the party with claims to economic and technical expertise and somewhat muddled attempts to establish the Polish system's status as a variant of 'developed socialism' (Woodall, 1982). This amalgam became badly unstuck as economic crisis deepened towards the end of the decade (Walicki, 1985, p. 170). This was later a cause of specific Soviet criticism (Kolankiewicz, 1984).

Under Kania (1980–1) conflicts within the party and the contradictions in PZPR ideology became increasingly evident. *Raison d'état* became reduced to the threat of Soviet invasion, hardly a viable basis on which to establish the leading role of the Polish party. Tensions became particularly acute after the Extraordinary Ninth Congress (July 1981) and, just before his resignation as CC First Secretary in October, Kania expressed his awareness of the party's ideological bankruptcy. The party, he indicated, could not survive with an ideology based just on negative argument—it had to develop positive ideological commitment: 'the concept of *raison d'état*, although so vital to our political thought ... can only signify inevitability, while we are really concerned with the great positive opportunity for a socialist Poland in a socialist community' (*Nowe Drogi*, November 1981). His resignation was followed by the election of the prime example of Polish military authority, in the person of General Jaruzelski, to the leadership of the PZPR.

The failure of the PZPR to generate a political ideology with convincing positive components has been closely associated with long-standing intellectual resistance to party rule and this has been one of the major reasons for the relatively liberal tone of Polish public life for much of the post-war period. It has been no coincidence that Soviet literati and intellectuals have often seen Poland as some kind of bridge to the West in this respect. These conditions have, however, created further problems for successive party leaderships and produced a permanent challenge to their claimed leading role and political authority. It has presented them with a fundamental dilemma and recurrent political problem: the low level of commitment to the official values of the regime has encouraged the leadership to be tentative in the ideological sphere in order not to antagonize the population and to incorporate a broader range of social groups. On the other hand, tendencies to avoid dogmatism (by no means constant or a general phenomenon) and to soft-pedal on the ideological front have led to a further qualification of party identity and persistent ambivalence in policy areas.

A number of sociological studies and surveys, particularly those conducted under the less restricted conditions of 1980–1, have shown the resistance encountered in this area. In terms of trust in the party, for example, a well-publicized survey conducted in 1981 showed that only 32 per cent of the population as a whole had any trust in the PZPR as an institution, compared with 94 per cent expressing trust in the Church, 91 per cent in Solidarity and 89 per cent in the army (see Table 5.3). A survey of young people in 1986 showed a very similar ranking in terms of institutions like PZPR and the Church, although in comparison with the latter the Army and Sejm now played a considerably smaller role. But it has also been clear that the Polish

Table 5.3 Trust in Institutions, 1981 and 1986 (percentage expressing trust)

Institution	Population (May 1981)	Solidarity (October 1981)	Young people (1986)
Catholic Church	94	94	58
Solidarity	91	95	14*
Army	89	69	24
Sejm	82	50	25
RP	73	29	n.a.
NIK	69	35	n.a.
Government	69	21	12
Procuracy	60	24	n.a.
Courts	59	28	14
Branch Unions	56	21	n.a.
SD	53	28	2
National Unity Front	50	19	n.a.
ZSL	46	22	3
Militia	42	22	7
PZPR	32	7	6

* Underground Solidarity.
Source: Mason, 1985, p. 118, *Tygodnik Polski* 20 March 1988.

population has, in general, accepted the prevailing balance of power in Eastern Europe and the formal leadership of the PZPR in the political system. General lack of ideological commitment has conditioned not so much the position and role of the party itself as the caution the political leadership has had to exercise in dealing with institutions like the Church and its representatives and, more recently, the Solidarity trade union. But the issue only partly concerns the ideological convictions of the public at large and the regard in which Marxism–Leninism is held.

The problems posed by the lack of ideological commitment have been severe in terms of their effects within the party and in relation to the political elite and party apparatus. While some party activists have proclaimed themselves to be 'communists' (despite the fact that the word does not figure in the name of the PZPR) and have presented themselves as 'true believers', all the signs are that they are in a minority within the party itself and that the majority of party members share many of the ideas and values which form the mainstream of Polish social culture. The continuing adherence of many PZPR members to religious values, their attendance at religious services and desire to continue with customs like baptism for their children (in distinction to secular name-giving ceremonies) have long provided the leadership with serious problems. Developments in post-war Poland have led to the strengthening of the Church's role (note Table 5.3). A recent study has shown the growing involvement of the intelligentsia in this process—3 per cent of them were non-believers but nevertheless still attended Church (*Przegląd Tygodniowy*, 22 February 1987).

The post-Gomułka leadership tended to be more liberal in this respect and permissive in terms of party member's 'private' behaviour, although active clericism and promotion of the interests of the Church has always been condemned. This has been one of the most obvious signs of the weakness of ideological commitment in Poland and, as Taras (1984, p. 245) writes, 'On this question serious doubts arise as to how Marxist-Leninist Polish rulers really were . . . The necessity of compromising continually with the church demonstrated how desperately rulers sought to gain legitimacy'. But the continuing strength of the Polish religious tradition has been only one aspect of the PZPR's internal ideological problem.

Careerism, opportunism and corruption have been long-standing problems in communist states and persistent threats to the efficiency and status of the party-state bureaucracy. In Poland in the 1970s such institutional defects took on unprecedented proportions (and have subsequently been the focus of much attention in Gorbachëv's Russia, probably partly in the light of their consequences for Polish political stability, see Teague 1988). Such features demonstrated the relatively unprincipled character of many of those occupying positions of authority and the minimal ideological motivation of party-state officials in the post-Gomułka period. They also served to weaken party authority and demonstrate its ideological contradictions to the public at large.

But opportunitism and relations of material self-interest have also been related to the weakness of ideological commitment in other ways. They may also be seen as ways of integrating the elite and motivating its members in the absence of elements of strong ideological conviction (Staniszkis, 1982–3; Lewis, 1984). It is important in this connection to note not just the *content* of party ideology but also its social and political *functions*—an area where ideological weakness has major specific consequences. In most communist states, and particularly in the Soviet Union, the 'weak structures' that characterize their political systems are sustained and their internal authority relations enhanced by the imposition of a 'double bind' on office-holders which is made possible by conditions which ensure the dominance of an exclusive ideology (Urban, 1985).

Within this conception Marxist-Leninist ideology contains a variety of truths that are evident so long as they are not questioned: Leninist norms of democracy within the party, for example, are valid so long as they are not put into practice, the rationality of the central planning system is self-evident so long as its failures and contradictions are not identified. The existence of contradictions in the symbolic sphere is not significant so as they are not confronted. Once they are, the social functions of ideology may be critically weakened even though serious efforts to sustain ideological argument are maintained. Behaviour and communication within the terms of the dominant ideology thus strengthen relations between those willing and able to enter into its framework. Adherence to its symbolic structure and conformity with its norms clearly bring rewards to the elite member or obedient official—but the whole operation obviously depends on group adherence and conformity, a certain level of acquiescence on the part of the population at large and the capacity of the system to avoid anything more than minor crisis situations.

Awareness of these political functions of party ideology helps to explain why seemingly abstruse ideological conflicts or historical reappraisals of perhaps more practical significance have had a major political impact and provoked serious crises. The Polish writer Kazimierz Brandys (1984, p. 231) has thus described the reception in 1956 of Khrushchev's 'secret speech' detailing Stalin's crimes by party leaders who were then holidaying in an elite sanitorium. They were clearly shaken not by the crimes disclosed but by the fact disclosure; they were upset by the evident jolt to the system. Until then the ideological fabrications had served their purpose; Khrushchev's revelations, however, showed that the political machine was not working according to its former principles: 'They doubted whether the system's mechanism was still functioning. As long as it continued, any crime could be justified dialectically.' The system was able to persist, but those habituated to it had the capacity for change. In similar ways, the persistent weakness of the party ideology in Poland has had significant practical consequences largely unrelated to formal ideological content.

In more stable and solidly established communist sytems, like that of the Soviet Union, the mechanisms of ideological integration appear to have operated relatively smoothly and ensured extensive continuity (probably excessively so, in the view of Gorbachëv and his entourage). This has been largely due to the exclusive character of party ideology, the lack of any coherent opposition to it for much of the Soviet period, and the absence of social conditions that could have generated such opposition or sustained alternative cultural frameworks and competing ideologies. In short, this conceptualization of political power (Urban, 1985, p. 225) takes 'as a necessary condition for its validity the prevention of metacommunication (i.e. public discourse in the full sense of the term)'. This is precisely the condition that Polish society, with its strong sense of cultural continuity and highly developed informal social structures, has been unable to meet. The party ideology has thus been presented with strong competition, preventing any significant level of acceptance of the ideology among the population and weakening ideological commitment within the party and its leading cadres.

This has caused persistent problems throughout the post-war period, not least within the party apparatus and among its activists. The problem clearly became critical in 1980 and worsened with the evolution of Solidarity as a force of general opposition. The challenge proved too much for many within the party organization and Kania, just prior to his resignation, indicated the extent to which the party had declined as a political force: 'Lack of confidence . . . is paralysing the party from within. We must break our way out of this position . . . No one can have faith in a party that will not believe in itself' (*Nowe Drogi*, November 1981). The installation of a form of military rule bypassed this problem rather than solving it, and some reaffirmation of Marxist-Leninist ideology within Poland and among party members was clearly necessary if a viable form of normalization was to be achieved.

The problems surrounding the issue of ideology remained severe during the Jaruzelski leadership. Central party organs were quick to condemn all manifestations of fractionalism, 'anarcho-syndicalist influences' and 'opportunist-revisionist tendencies' within the PZPR, the latter clearly references to Solidarity sympathies among party members. Within the elite, though, there were many with a strong awareness of the essential political irrelevance under Polish conditions of pursuing ideological purity too rigorously; the party's authority, emphasized Wadja (in *Nowe Drogi*, July/ August 1982), 'depends less on the ideas it promulgates than on the degree to which they are realized'. Jaruzelski clearly did not favour the ideological purists, who represented a hardline alternative to the party-military centrist views he represented, and in consequence postponed a meeting of the Central Committee that had been called to discuss ideological matters in May 1983. The emphasis on ideological slogans was generally seen as counterproductive and greater importance was assigned to halting the decline in the number of party members and restoring the party's relations with the working class.

But neither was the soft-pedalling of the ideological approach notably successful in strengthening the position of the party organization or winning its leadership any greater popular support. The half-hearted revival of the Polish economy and the ambiguities present in the protracted process of economic reform failed to bring the benefits that Jaruzelski's pragmatic approach had sought. After the Tenth Congress (June–July 1986) more insistent calls for ideological vigilance were again heard and doubts were cast on the capacity of the PZPR to recover its position. Familiar criticisms of the influence of 'clerical ideology' within the party were expressed and tendencies to exaggerate the specific characteristics of a Polish road to socialism were attacked (*Nowe Drogi*, May 1987). Emphasis was now placed on the link between ideology and economic development and reform rather than their mutual distinctiveness (*Życie Partii*, 9 September 1987). While issues of economic reform were clearly to the fore in 1987 there were also signs that a reassertion of Marxist-Leninist ideology was also being contemplated.

The *Pays Réel*

As we have already established in the preceding discussion of the conditions and nature of communist rule in Poland, the problems experienced by the party in maintaining its authority and the difficulties it has encountered in promulgating Marxist-Leninist ideology, Polish society has erected formidable obstacles to the establishment and consolidation of a Marxist regime within its borders. In no other Eastern European country have competing political and social forces shown quite such strength, nor have they coalesced in quite such a way as they did in Poland to produce the situation in which Solidarity was able to emerge in 1980 and maintain an autonomous, if by no means comfortable, existence for nearly sixteenth months.

The contrast between the public, formal sphere of party-dominated government and state organs and diverse social organizations, on the one hand, and the private informal sphere of traditional and spontaneous social groups and voluntary associations, on the other, is often referred to as the difference between the *pays legal* and *pays réel*. It is a difference which Szczepański (1970, p. 50) suggests foreign observers are 'particularly inclined to underline'. The distinction points to the excessive formality and artificiality that has pervaded much of Poland's official party-dominated life and the vigour and resilience of its national community and society. It is this contrast that lies at the root of Poland's political instability, that has produced some of the major dilemmas that have faced the regime and most of the challenges it has had to face.

The *pays réel* in this sense constitutes an alternative society, distinct from and in frequent conflict with the institutions and practices of official life, a competitor with the formal society of communist Poland and a force to which the latter has often had to accommodate itself. It has confronted Polish leaders with another of the major dilemmas, in that while it has clearly been necessary to take account of social forms and inclinations in order to develop any viable basis for party authority, the evident minority status of communist forces in social terms has threatened in this process the swamping and loss of the party's Marxist-Leninist identity. The preservation by the party organization and its leadership of its purity, however, would leave these groups isolated and largely lacking in social influence.

One of the major and longest-established elements in the Polish *pays réel* is the Catholic Church and its strong roots in the Polish national community. It is doubtful as to whether the role of the Church in Poland has ever been as critical for the spiritual as well as physical survival of the nation as it is today. The multidimensional crisis outlined above and in what follows has placed an enormous burden of responsibility upon the Church, its hierarchy, priests and laity and brought them into situations demanding new responses which in turn require internal changes to practices rooted in tradition stretching back through a millennium.

Since the one-sided abolition of the Church-State concordat signed in 1925 and abrogated in September 1945 the communist state has sought to confine the Church to the realm of 'private' activity, whilst the Church for its part has found itself increasingly called upon to become more public in its perceived role as defender of Polish national identity in the face of the alien and imposed Marxist-Leninist Soviet model of socialism. Despite claims by successive post-Stalinist leaders that the Polish Church was privileged by comparison to other countries of real socialism, which was an indicator of regime good-will, the Church presents its freedom to function as the litmus for the broader lack of autonomy in society. Not wishing to be confined to the 25,000 catechetical points of instruction, the Church has been drawn into the so-called 'wars of the crosses' which is more than simply an argument as to whether crucifixes can be displayed in schools and hospitals. Given that even by the regime's own estimates at most only 7.2 per cent of the population declared themselves as non-believers (*Przegląd Tygodniowy*, 22 February 1987) while the Church calculates that 95 per cent of Poles are baptised members, it is argued that the dominant world-view, socio-political and economic structures, etc., ought to reflect this fact. The Church believes that because it is an independent national and international body (hence the importance of the Rome connection), the forty years of communist rule have been primarily about finding a place for the Church in the socialist scheme of things (*Przegląd Katolicki*, 24 May 1987).

For its part the regime has sought to incorporate the Church through the creation of secular political bodies such as the organization 'Pax' (and indeed the formation of the state-dominated Polish Catholic Church), at the same time seeking recognition and legitimation of its rule in Poland from the Vatican. Both Pope John XXIII and Paul VI are viewed with favour as having brought the Polish regime out of the cold during the 1960s and 1970s. Various joint committees, rights to give opinions on legislation affecting such matters as education as well as periodic high-level meetings between Jaruzelski and Primate Glemp point to a working relationship, not rooted however in formal ties. In particular the regime since martial law has sought to obtain support from the Church for its policies of national reconciliation, be they elections, referendum, amnesties or the setting up of various councils aimed at bringing oppositional intellectuals into active dialogue and cooperation with the party.

The formation of a post-war state composed almost exclusively of ethnic Poles, in contrast to the more variegated composition of the pre-war Republic (let alone its pre-nineteenth-century ancestors), obviously influenced the development of this situation. Accelerated economic development on Soviet lines and 'socialist industrialization' did little to change it. In 1982, Poland contained 34.8 million Catholics, 94.6 per cent of the total population (*Polityka*, 3 January 1987). But, of course, it was not just a numerical preponderance that gave the Church its strength.

Cardinal Wyszyński, head of the Polish Church since 1948, was involved in increasing conflicts with the party-state leadership and was interned from September 1953 until Gomułka's return to the leadership in 1956. The reinstated communist leader and Wyszyński perceived a greater commonality between the interests of Church and state authorities, and the immediate post-October period saw a marked improvement in their relations. This, however, did not last, and conflicts developed over the taxation of Church assets, censorship and the state of religious education in schools (Staron, 1969, p. 591). At the same time, the growing scepticism of the Polish population about the record, capability and truthfulness of the Gomułka leadership led them to pay greater attention to the Church authorities.

Particularly important, though, were the political events of 1968, the demise of the party revisionism and the general disillusion of Marxist and non-party socialist forces with the prospect of change within established political institutions. In addition to traditionalists and right-wing forces, these groups now also began to look on the Church more positively (Cviic,

1983, p. 99). Gierek, paying due attention to the need to consolidate his leadership, attempted to strengthen relations with the Church and establish some kind of working partnership between what he perceived as the two leading Polish institutions. Developments during the 1970s and the growing emphasis placed by the Church after 1970 on human rights and the defence of the Polish workers (Nowak, 1982, p. 11), however, prevented the further strengthening of this partnership.

The first source of conflict concerned the new Constitution (see Chapter 3). This was a threat the Church felt it could not maintain a distance from; the issue was, in the view of the Episcopate, 'not only of a government nature but also moral and social' (Raina, 1978, p. 224). The second was the treatment in 1976 of the strikers and demonstrators in Ursus and, particularly, Radom. This prompted the formation of a small group committed to their defence whose objective was reflected in the title they took: the Committee for Workers' Defence, (KOR). Following the success of their activities the group reformed itself as the Committee for Social Self-Defence (KSS), its members henceforth acting under the title KSS-KOR. One of the signatories of the initial KOR appeal in September 1976 was the Catholic priest, Jan Zieja, and the Church clearly lent its support to the new enterprise, the Plenary Conference of the Episcopate launching an equivalent appeal to the state authorities in the defence of victimized workers (Lipski, 1985, pp. 51–5).

The two major currents of Poland's *pays réel* thus forged a closer relationship and developed increasingly shared conceptions of how both sets of values reflecting Polish traditions and reformist political objectives might be extended and pursued in ways that avoided the bloody confrontations of 1956 and 1970. The approach was summed up in Adam Michnik's (1976) expression 'the new evolutionism', in association with which he argued for the 'unceasing struggle for reforms, in favour of evolution which will extend civil liberties and guarantee a respect for human rights'. The political role of the Church in Poland, already stronger than others in Eastern European countries, continued to grow and was reflected in Polish political preferences.

Clearly the whole idea of party preferences in free elections in Poland must be extremely hypothetical; the survey evidence we can examine was gathered by the Audience and Public Opinion Research Department of Radio Free Europe, itself funded by the US government and having a direct interest in a particular direction of political change in Poland. The same doubts, though, could be raised about the results gathered in several Eastern European countries both in 1971–2 and in 1979–80, and they do appear to show some significant differences and changes. They suggest (Table 5.4) a consistently high preference in Poland for a Christian Democratic or Peasant

Table 5.4 Party Preferences in Hypothetical Free Elections (per cent)

	Poland	Hungary	Czechoslovakia
1971–72			
Communist Party	4	10	7
Democratic Socialist	36	36	41
Christian Democratic or Peasant Party	43	39	31
1979–80			
Communist Party	6	7	3
Democratic Socialist	32	43	44
CD/Peasant Party	50	36	36

Source: Radio Free Europe Audience and Public Opinion Research Department, 1973 and 1981).

Party option (the latter also implying strong religious allegiance) and a growth in the tendency throughout the 1970s, compared with a decline in this preference in Hungary and an equivalent rise (though at a lower level) in Czechoslovakia. The Democratic Socialist choice was less popular in Poland at the end of the 1970s and the overall left-wing inclination (Democratic Socialist plus communist party) was at a lower level throughout the period.

The growth of the emphasis on human and civil rights bore some practical fruit soon afterwards, with the first steps being taken towards the setting up of free trade unions, and received a great boost with the election of a Polish pope in 1978 and, particularly, with Pope John Paul II's visit to Poland the following year. Further human rights and political groups were established and became active. These included groups like ROPCiO and the KPN. Just one year later the process accelerated dramatically with the summer strikes of 1980 and the establishment of the Solidarity union. For over a year Poland's 'underground' or 'alternative society' achieved virtual dominance in the public arena and drove the official processes and institutions of the communist *pays legal* into apparent retreat.

Jaruzelski's coup of December 1981 drastically changed this situation. The party-state authorities, largely in the form of the security organs, the military and its commissars, reasserted their control over the public arena and drove much of the *pays réel* and its independent forces off the streets and out of sight, many leading figures forming part of the 5,000-strong population of the newly established internment camps. Solidarity was forced underground and reduced to mounting a series of public demonstrations whose effectiveness was becoming increasingly open to doubt by the autumn of 1982, when the independent union was officially abolished.

The legal status of the Church, of course, remained unchanged although Cardinal Glemp, Primate of Poland following Wyszyński's death in May 1981, exercised considerable caution in the attempt to maintain constructive relations with the political leadership. During the State of War, and under the conditions of continuing repression after it was formally lifted, the Church assumed a higher-profile social role and took on even greater significance both as a symbol of Polish social independence and as a physical area of autonomy and relative freedom from the actions of security agents (Szajkowski, 1983, p. 194). Yet this autonomy was itself circumscribed, as the harassment of several priests and, particularly, the death of Father Popiełuszko demonstrated.

Nevertheless, Poland's *pays réel* was far from being subdued and the post-1981 political leadership succeeded only in partially restricting its public expression rather than weakening its social base. The party-state authorities had little success in gaining any measure of popularity or the confidence of the mass of the population and were faced with ruling a relatively sullen and mistrustful citizenry. Many of them remained attached to the ideas expressed by the Solidarity movement in 1980 and 1981 and continued to support its underground organization. 'The Independent Self-Governing Trade Union still exists, not only as a symbol, but also as a real, independent organization of working people', claimed the Helsinki Committee in Poland. 'In hundreds of work-places in Poland people pay their union dues, distribute and read the Union press, a great number of factories have their own factory newspapers, and Secret Factory Commissions protect people from acts of repression' (*Uncensored Poland*, August 1986).

The cautious and relatively light-handed policy adopted by the Jaruzelski leadership (interspersed by not infrequent violent actions by the police and security organs) was by no means unproductive, though. In a further amnesty during September 1986 virtually all political prisoners (225 in all) were released and moves were made within days to set up a Provisional Council of Solidarity, while nevertheless preserving its underground leadership (the TKK). By taking this initiative the Jaruzelski leadership at least caused a 'great deal of confusion and misunderstanding among members of Solidarity and sympathisers' (joint statement by Wałęsa and TKK, *Uncensored Poland*, October 1986). It was admitted in the underground press that by their tactical moves 'the authorities have had the political initiative, which is amazing, considering the deepening crisis' (*Uncensored Poland* May 1987).

Poland's *pays réel* has therefore remained strong without posing a direct threat to the political stability of the post-1981 regime. Measures like the 1986 amnesty did not reflect a major change in the regime's approach. Nevertheless, the authorities took care to show considerable sensitivity in their handling of relations with the Church. Immediately before the Pope's visit to his home country the government spokesman took evident pride in announcing that 90 per cent of adult Poles evaluated Church–State relations positively, compared with 73 per cent in 1986. This was the highest positive evaluation obtained in surveys since 1978 (*Rzeczpospolita*, 1 June 1987). Further evidence of the leadership's desire to establish firmer relations with independent social forces came with the unexpected convocation of a Central Committee meeting in October 1987 and the decision to hold a referendum over further reform proposals. But the result of the referendum, with government proposals failing to get the approval of more than 50 per cent of those eligible to vote, did little to improve the relations of the regime with Polish society.

The Continuing Crisis of Party Leadership

One of the primary characteristics of Marxist-Leninist regimes is the claim by a monopolistic communist party to exercise a leading role and its capacity to exercise some reasonably effective form of political rule. This dimension has, as we have shown, been a source of major problems throughout the communist period and is a condition of communist rule that has been only partially met in Poland since the end of the Gierek period. Although military rule (the 'State of War') was suspended at the end of 1982 and lifted in mid-1983, the regime has retained the services of a number of important military figures (not least the CC First Secretary himself) and has not seen the restoration of conventional party rule.

The steady decline in the number of PZPR members, which began slowly after the strikes of August 1980 and accelerated in 1981, continued until mid-1985 and membership levels recovered only to a very limited extent after that date. The changes in party membership since 1980 are shown in Table 5.5. The two years after the low-point of mid-1985 saw an increase of only 21,000, a small fraction of those lost each year between 1980 and 1984.

A major cause of this situation and an important factor in the continuing crisis of party leadership was the experience of the State of War initiated on 13 December 1981 and which remained in full force throughout 1982. While, of course, this measure found some level of social support it was

Table 5.5 PZPR Membership 1980–7

Date	Thousands
Mid-1980	3,150
1980	3,092
Mid-1981	2,869
1981	2,691
1982	2,327
1983	2.186
1984	2,117
Mid-1985	2,112
1985	2,115
Mid-1986	2,126
1986	2,129
Mid-1987	2,133
1987	2,149*

* Totals end of year unless otherwise stated.
Source: *Życie Partii*, 3 June 1987 and 3 March 1988; Lewis (1989).

profoundly unpopular amongst the great majority of Polish citizens. Surveys carried out in 1982 showed that at least nine out of ten Poles in most groups differentiated by level of education thought that the party had been compromised by this action. The proportion expressing this view did not fall below 85 per cent in any of the groups identified (*Krytyka*, 16).

The problem, as already noted (Chapter 2), was particularly pronounced in relation to younger age groups and the working class. The proportion of PZPR membership officially made up by workers fell 6 per cent between the end of 1980 and the end of 1982. The decline was particularly evident in industrial centres like the Lenin shipyard in Gdańsk, where a party membership of 3,300 in August 1980 fell by 36 per cent over the next two years. If categories like pensioners and the retired were excluded from the total the rate of decline was even steeper, some 55 per cent. Party officials began querying publicly whether the party could be described as representing the working class when the external signs of that representation were so weak (*Życie Partii*, 24 November 1982). Others maintained that the true level of working-class membership in the party was as low as 14 per cent and that by 1983 the level of party membership had in fact fallen below 2 million

(*Krytyka*, 16). Popular reaction against the measures taken to restore communist order after the Solidarity period had a critical affect on the level of party membership and the organization's claim to exercise political leadership.

Party affiliation was, moreover, not only a status lacking in attractiveness but also a socially divisive factor identified as a source of social antagonism by nearly a third of those questioned in 1987 (Table 5.6). With the formal lifting of the State of War in 1983, then, the leadership was faced with a major challenge in terms of the restoration of normal processes of political rule and the return to some conventional state of party leadership.

Table 5.6 The Sources of Social Antagonism in Poland (percentage mentioning factor)

Pay, earnings	75.6
Property, material possessions	60.5
Power, official position	42.2
Political opinions	41.8
Membership of PZPR	32.6
Division between manual and white-collar work	29.4
Urban/rural residence	27.3
Difference between older and younger generation	23.2
Education	18.4
Faith and religious practice	17.5
Social origin	15.5

Source: *Polityka*, 11 July 1987.

Renewed attempts to improve the party's image were made from the beginning of 1984 with the holding of a National Conference of Congress Delegates, that is, the delegates who had been elected to the Ninth (Extraordinary) Congress of July 1981. Of the 1,962 members elected to the Ninth Congress sixteen had died by the time of the 1984 Conference, nineteen had been subject to some form of party discipline and were therefore disqualified from attending, while forty-eight were no longer party members. The 1984 Conference eventually saw the reassembly of 1,835 delegates. Its proceedings were largely non-controversial and aroused little public interest, but it did give Jaruzelski an opportunity to express a policy of social conciliation. It was not, he said, sufficient 'to decree the leading role of the party', and he admitted that while 'socialism cannot be built without a Marxist-Leninist party, it is not communists who can build it by themselves'. Some months later the practice of holding CC meetings outside Warsaw, in major industrial centres, was begun and workers who were not even party members were invited to attend them. Rather appropriately, the first of such meetings was held in June 1984 in the Grand Theatre of the city of Łódź.

All this had relatively little impact on the public and the popular view of the PZPR did not change. In 1985 people were asked which institutions served Polish society well and were most congruent with its interests. Only 16.6 per cent mentioned the party in their response and more frequent nominations were the Church, the Sejm, the army and the government (*Polityka*, 10 August 1985). Nevertheless, the continuing decline in PZPR membership was halted around the middle of 1985. The change was hardly spectacular, though. Sixty-three thousand names were removed from party lists for various reasons that year and 64,000 were added (*Polityka*, 1 February 1986).

The relative lack of success of this policy of conciliation provided some encouragement for advocates of a harder political line and there were again calls for a greater emphasis on ideological matters. These may have received some Soviet support when Gorbachëv became Soviet leader, the new General Secretary being reported to be quite concerned about the scale of the Church's social role in Poland. Neither calls for more ideological offensiveness or for social conciliation have had much effect and party authority in Poland has remained weak and its social influence still very limited. Dissatisfaction with this state of affairs has not been absent from the higher party organs themselves, and one member of the CC complained at the Sixth Plenum in late 1987 that party leadership had degenerated to a process of muddling through; today's party, he said, 'as a whole is not capable of tackling the tasks that face it' (*Polityka*, 5 December 1987).

Normalization and Current Policies

The continuing problems surrounding party leadership have caused considerable difficulties in the process of normalizing Poland's political life under military auspices. The effort has not been facilitated, either, by the depth of Poland's economic crisis and the extent of economic dislocation or by the international economic climate which has created great problems for many states, capitalist and communist alike. The economic dimensions of the

Polish crisis have given a special character to the Polish normalization of the 1980s (Valenta, 1984, p. 145). The political and economic problems involved here are intimately connected. The capacity to secure effective economic recovery is a crucial factor in the leadership's attempt to restore its credibility, but public confidence—or the lack of it—in the good faith and competence of the authorities is also a major element in the ability of the authorities to develop and implement appropriate policies.

The indications are that this complex of problems provided the Jaruzelski leadership with increasing difficulties following some success in securing economic stabilization in the first half of the 1980s. Popular expectations of economic improvement fell markedly between 1985 and 1987 (Table 5.7). Further, in November 1987, 35 per cent of those questioned did not regard the economic reforms and solutions proposed by the leadership as likely to be effective. The continuing obstacles to Polish economic recovery clearly had a major effect on the political situation of the leadership, while their failure to enhance their political stock and social authority made the economic task correspondingly more difficult.

Table 5.7 Expectations of the Economic Situation

	Percentage anticipating	
	Improvement	Deterioration
December 1985	42.4	16.4
August 1987	24.9	31.6
November 1987	22.6	45.6

Source: *Polityka*, 5 December 1987.

To some extent this problem is not a new one. The formulation of coherent policies and their consistent implementation have, particularly in the economic sphere (see Chapter 4), been persistent areas of weakness in Polish national life since the official break with Stalinism in 1956. Conflicts over priorities and policy choices take place, of course, in all political systems and may involve, in communist states, the need to balance the demands of industrial investment and long-term economic growth with the objectives of raising the population's standard of living and reducing social class inequalities (Mason, 1983). In the 1980s the choice has become tougher, and one of the desired objectives may be rather the maintenance of or return to former living standards, which may not even be met. In the contemporary Polish context it is the return to the living standards of 1978 that is presented as a goal. Differing emphasis has been placed on these objectives at different times over the years and attempts to pursue all three objectives equally have certainly come to grief.

This was attempted between 1953 and 1956, but could not be sustained for a longer period of time. An attempt to combine these policy objectives was also made during the 1970s, leading on this occasion to economic bankruptcy and a major crisis. Under Jaruzelski's leadership, particularly after the political challenge of Solidarity had been faced and the process of political consolidation advanced under the State of War, the emphasis has increasingly been laid on the pursuit of long-term economic recovery and growth. The aim of increasing or even restoring living standards to the levels of the late 1970s has had to be shelved, and by 1986 national income had barely returned to the level at which it stood ten years earlier.

The pursuit of social equality has also been subordinated to the policy of economic growth, and the need for incentives and higher levels of remuneration for key groups and sectors has increasingly become a component of socialist economic strategy. Contemporary state policies have also had the effect of extending hidden areas of social inequality (Chapter 2). One result has been repeated price increases and a rise in the number of people living below the poverty line (Chapter 2). The strongly market-orientated philosophy of the New Right has found some fervent supporters in Eastern Europe, in Poland as elsewhere. This has prompted a reappraisal of social and welfare policies (Chapter 2). The question of whether the Polish Marxist regime should feel itself obliged to maintain a welfare state has even been raised within the party's ruling bodies. Jaruzelski remarked in 1983 on the emergence of 'extreme, controversial voices concerning the extension of the social and welfare functions of the state' (*XIV Plenum*, p. 54).

Wage differentials during the first stage of the economic reform appeared already to have moved to the disadvantage of some previously less privileged groups (education, health and social welfare), while the real income of Polish employees had in general fallen in the early 1980s (Table 5.8). In 1985 the average real income gained from employment in the socialized economy stood at 81 per cent of the 1980 level (*Mały Rocznik Statystyczny*, 1986). Thus even relatively privileged groups (industrial workers as a whole, technologists) had only in rare cases improved on their 1980 position in real terms. Workers in the extraction industries, in which miners held pride of place, had maintained their relative advantage but, again, saw little improvement in real terms. But one of the peculiarities of Polish political life, certainly in

Table 5.8 Average Monthly Earnings in the Socialized Economy

	1980	1985	1986	First half 1987
Overall average	(6,040 zł. = 100)	(20,005 zł. = 100)	(24,095 zł. = 100)	(27,639 zł. = 100)
Industrial average	108	113	114	114
Extraction industry	174	203	204	183
Construction	112	111	112	110
Manufacturing	100	100	101	103
Forestry	84	90	87	87
Retail trade	82	82	84	85
Science, technology	105	108	121	121
Administration, justice	95	99	100	107
Education	81	83	79	81
Health and welfare	79	77	76	81

Source: Calculated from figures presented in *Polityka* (19 September 1987).

contrast to a country like Hungary, has been less the problems associated with formulating policies and programmes of reform than the obstacles apparently encountered in implementing them.

The surge of new thinking that occurred in 1956 brought forward a diversity of new economic ideas—but no real programme of economic reform was ever enacted and the *ad hoc* solutions applied to the problems of the economy were clearly associated with its poor performance throughout the 1960s (Chapter 4). A sequence of semi-implemented reform proposals introduced considerable instability into the economy, which 'not only involved high economic costs but also undermined confidence in reforms as a possible cure for Poland's economic ills' (Zielinski, 1978, p. 3). The experience of the long-drawn out first phase of the 1980s version of economic reform (Chapter 4), accompanied by even more severe dislocation, has only compounded and extended this problem. The failure of government proposals to secure the required majority in the 1987 referendum was a further reflection of this.

The discussion in the preceding sections has highlighted the relevant factors: the existence of areas of significant social autonomy has restricted the leadership's capacity to take policy initiatives (or, more probably, has impressed on it the conviction that this is likely to be the case), and the weakness of ideological commitment has limited the vision of the leadership and reduced its motivation to draw up and implement coherent economic plans. It should not be forgotten, for example, that the price rises that sparked off the 1970 demonstrations were presented as part of the preparations for a subsequent programme of economic reform. Gierek, on the other hand, took over the leadership with a strong commitment to structural reform as a means of stimulating economic growth. As he discovered that broadly comparable results could be achieved, at least in the short term, by the injection of sizeable foreign credits, the commitment to reform rapidly dissipated and little was heard of it after 1974 (Chapter 4).

The vicious circle of economic decline and political collapse has placed the current leadership in a situation from which it has shown few signs of being able to extricate itself. The process of delegitimation, in combination with grave economic problems, has confronted it with two interdependent crises, the resolution of each of which is imperilled by the other. Thus, 'the government cannot regain a minimum of credibility without tangibly improving the economic situation, while, on the other hand, national energy cannot be mobilized to overcome the economic crisis if the government . . . is deeply distrusted and the entire system is seen as one in which it does not pay to work' (Walicki, 1985, p. 169). Subsequent discussion of the second stage of reform and the continuing problems of leadership credibility serve to underline this relationship (Chapter 4).

The attempt to defuse potential opposition and construct a broader social consensus has formed a major part of the policy pursued by the Jaruzelski leadership, which in theoretical terms received some elaboration in terms of a 'coalition method of exercising power' and the drive to forge cooperative relations with political forces outside the immediate ambit of the PZPR. It was, as we have seen (Chapter 3), by no means uncontroversial and came under criticism for, among other things, appearing to confuse the idea of the leading role of the party and to neglect the dictatorship of the proletariat, promoting a dubious conception of what a Polish model of socialism might involve. Such disagreements reflected not only the recurring conflicts within the party about the way in which ideological issues should be treated but also the continuing tension within the Polish leadership between the need to exercise a guiding role through the party and the problems of doing so in the face of a politically alienated and mistrustful population. As it stands, the only forces capable of overcoming the institutional obstacles to change are rooted in society. They however, have not and probably cannot be harnessed for such objectives as they are not provided with and are unable themselves to form their own, authentic and credible means of action.

Recent discussion of the perennial problems of reform has pointed to more structural aspects, identifying two dimensions: the problem of introducing society to new solutions and the resistance of institutions and structures to changes that might threaten their continued existence. But the focus on external obstacles to effective policy formulation and implementation which are often strongly emphasized may well, it was suggested, be misleading. Reference to conditions outside the scope of direct leadership control and the anticipation of future difficulties have sometimes been a pretext for not contemplating serious change at all, and served as an excuse for leadership passivity and a continuing tendency to muddle through (*Polityka*, 4 July 1987). The beginning of the second phase of the economic reform programme, however, was accompanied by the announcement of what promised to be an unusually radical overhaul of the central administrative apparatus (Chapter 3) and a further attempt to gain effective control over the price mechanism. Whether the second phase of the reform policy, with greater emphasis on structural reform and changes in the central institutions of government, achieves more success than earlier programmes remains to be seen.

6 Contemporary Poland: Bridge or Bastion?

Throughout the making of modern Poland and in the evolution of its more recent policies, relations with neighbours and competing powers have been of determinant importance. While the unique character of the regime in place throughout the 1980s has perhaps masked these relations in the political sphere, the way in which Poland's persistent economic crisis has driven it towards closer links with the Soviet economy shows this to be a continuing fact. Accompanying this strong awareness of the historical dimension to social life, many Poles have a sharp perception of the international determinants of their national existence.

The Legacy of Yalta

For much of the post-war period, the nature of Poland's relations with the Soviet Union has been the dominant aspect of this situation and for most the central reference point in this situation has been the agreement reached between the Great Powers in February 1945 at Yalta in the Crimea. But 'Yalta', in Poland as elsewhere, has meant different things to different people. It may even be claimed, as establishment publicist Ryszard Wojna has done (*Rzeczpospolita*, 13–14 June 1987), that agreement on common reference points and a shared historical memory may serve not as a basis for social unity and a form of social mortar but, in a case like Poland, as a focus for conflict and a factor promoting disunity. Discussion and competing claims surrounding the issue of Yalta have certainly recurred at times of conflict and political disagreement, although many of the conflicting views are due also to the ambiguous character and roots of the Yalta agreement itself as well as to conflicting political interests and differences in interpretation. 'Yalta' has, in different ways, been a major reference point both for those who see contemporary Poland as a bastion of socialism and for those who prefer to view Poland as a bridge to the Western nations (Hiscocks, 1963).

For those opposed to the Soviet role in Eastern Europe and the extension of the Stalinist dictatorship that Yalta appeared to prepare the way for, the agreement represents a cynical division of post-war Europe into spheres of influence, the unilateral redrawing of state frontiers (involving the ceding of

40 per cent of the territory of pre-war Poland to the Soviet Union), the virtual abandonment of the war-time government in exile in favour of an amended communist grouping (notably with the addition of Stanisław Mikołajczyk, the exiles' prime minister), and the delivering of Eastern Europe into an unwelcome Soviet embrace. From this perspective Yalta has symbolized the external limits placed on autonomous national and social development in Eastern Europe since 1945. It has been a barrier to the development of Eastern Europe and a symbol of negative continuity throughout the post-war period.

This was the view often expressed in Solidarity circles during 1981, sometimes accompanied by demands for its annulment or 'renegotiation'—at least to the extent that countries, like Poland, whose fate was critically affected by the agreement should have some say in its outcome. The tendency has been strengthened by Western political currents which have reflected dissatisfaction with the consequences of the Yalta agreement and became more prominent in the early 1980s as President Reagan's drive against the Soviets' 'evil empire' gathered pace and the fortieth anniversary of the original agreement approached. A more sophisticated variant of this point of view was the call by the politically influential academic of Polish origin, Zbigniew Brzezinski, for the rejection of the 'historical legacy' of Yalta rather than of the agreement itself (*Foreign Affairs*, 1984/85).

The view of the Polish political establishment has been different and has consistently emphasized the role of Yalta in securing an agreement for a balance of forces in Europe that avoided military conflict and produced political stability for four decades (*Nowe Drogi*, June 1983; *Polityka*, 26 January 1985). It has been presented as a major element in arguments concerning Poland's *raison d'état*, which has been an important part of the PUWP's claim to political authority. Several months into military rule, as Jaruzelski's regime continued to be met by numerous demonstrations of popular resistance, the party's theoretical monthly devoted forty-eight pages to reprints from the stenographic reports from the three meetings of the war-time great powers, a fact that showed considerably more than just a historical interest in the international politics of that period (*Nowe Drogi*, July/August 1982).

Great-Power Influence on Post-War Poland

Both interpretations of Yalta have their strengths as well as weaknesses. American leaders as well as the Soviet/Polish authorities have denied that Yalta reflected a division of Europe into spheres of influence, although the cases of both are rather shaky. There had been a few signs before World War

II that the Soviet Union accepted Poland's right to independent statehood, and the 'fourth partition' of the country in September 1939 between Nazi Germany and the Soviet Union was described by Soviet Foreign Secretary Molotov as securing the disappearance of the 'monstrous bastard of Versailles'.

It took forty-eight years, and the accession of Gorbachëv to the Soviet leadership, for this statement to be officially repudiated and rejected as being 'contrary to historical truth and inadmissible in relation to the Polish nation' (BBC SWB SU/8664/A2/1). Stalin reportedly made it clear in December 1941 that the western border of the Soviet Union was for their side 'the main question in the war', and requested the addition of a 'small protocol' to the original Anglo-Soviet treaty of alliance which would already have secured British agreement to the Soviet acquisition of Eastern Poland in 1939 (Coutouvidis & Reynolds, 1986, p. 92; Nogee & Donaldson, 1981, p. 44).

At that stage Soviet requests were rejected, but by the time of the Tehran meeting in December 1943 the Soviet position had strengthened. The tide had turned against the German army in the East and Stalin was extremely impatient for Anglo-American forces to open up a second front in Europe. In this context it was in fact Churchill who suggested that the victorious powers should receive a reasonable measure of territorial and strategic satisfaction for their efforts, and that the Soviet Union might well agree to the westward movement of the Polish state and the acquisition by the Soviet Union of Poland's pre-1939 eastern territories. There appeared to be no American resistance to this plan, although Roosevelt refrained from publicly endorsing it in order to avoid domestic Polish opposition during his 1944 election campaign. In this way, already before the end of 1943, the 'concession at Teheran of Russia's "security needs" by way of the cession of Polish territory sealed the fate of Poland and made moot the issue of Polish self-determination' (Nogee & Donaldson, 1981, p. 48).

The principle of Great Power spheres of influence was therefore already becoming established in practice well before Yalta. The Polish government in exile, at that time the generally recognized legal representative of a state whose integrity had been infringed both by Germany and (less unambiguously) by Soviet Russia, was naturally not inclined to enter into any agreement that would allow others to take its territory. This view, of which (of course) all Great Powers were well aware, was overridden by the understanding reached at Tehran. The intransigence of the government in exile, however, has generally been overplayed by the more influential political actors involved—particularly those representing or associated with Soviet interests.

While naturally unwilling to cede territory over which they still had legal jurisdiction, the government in exile also realized the pressures to which their powerful allies were subject and were aware of the political realities of the situation. Before the Tehran conference, then, the British were informally told that the Polish government in exile would countenance a different post-war territorial settlement and that, indeed, it might welcome the imposition of an ultimate British-US solution rather different from that it publicly insisted on if that were necessary to secure the later survival of an independent Polish state (Coutouvidis & Reynolds, 1986, p. 96).

A second factor often overlooked in the use of Yalta as a general symbol is that, while endorsing the westward shift of the Polish state and the Soviet acquisition of formerly Polish territory—and continuing the line they had laid down earlier, the Western powers did build into the agreements reached at both Yalta and Potsdam a commitment to the immediate holding of 'free and unfettered elections' in Poland (*Nowe Drogi*, July–August 1982, pp. 183, 208). This clearly indicates a point of weakness in Soviet/Polish claims about the nature and consequences of the Yalta agreement and makes official Polish statements to the effect that its decisions 'have created the basis for the rebirth of Poland as strong, free, independent and democratic' (*Polityka*, 26 January 1985) tenable in only a very limited sense.

It may be concluded, then, that the current positions of both the United States and the Soviet Union and their apologists carry a fair amount of hypocrisy in terms of their interpretation of Yalta. It was clearly a formula in which the conflicting interests of the major parties were accommodated—and which inevitably had to come into opposition with those of the mass of the Polish population. While representatives of all the Great Powers agreed that the post-war regimes of Eastern Europe should be both democratic and friendly towards the Soviet Union there was never a formal attempt to define what those terms should mean.

Regardless of whether democratic regimes were likely to be friendly to the Soviet Union (and certainly in the case of Poland severe doubts were in order), it was not difficult to understand that the Soviet Union would not accept what it interpreted as a bourgeois democracy—and this is surely what Churchill and Roosevelt must have had in mind. Stalin would accept as democratic only countries in which significant internal transformations had already occurred and this, as in a more academic guise Brzezinski (1967, p. 32) has pointed out, would necessarily put Eastern European relations on a quite different footing.

These ambiguities make of Yalta a flawed symbol—although contemporary Polish conflicts over its interpretation only echo those of the years preceding its formulation. But they also reflect conflicts within the society over Poland's place in Europe in a more general sense. In contrast to the conception of Poland implied by post-Yalta developments in Eastern Europe, as part of a Soviet empire and a bastion of socialism like its fraternal protector, many Poles have looked to the West and continued to identify themselves with the values of liberal or pluralist, rather than socialist democracy. Less than a bastion of socialism they have seen themselves as a bridge between East and West.

Poland in the Socialist Camp

In practice this dual tendency has given Poland a special place in the Soviet bloc and led it to develop a characteristic approach to international affairs. This has manifested itself in several ways. As the largest and most populous country in the Soviet bloc, member of the CMEA and the Warsaw Treaty Organization, and key segment of the Soviets' defensive *glacis*, Poland has been for forty years a 'bastion of socialism' and clearly will be one for the foreseeable future. This status is both maintained by and reflected in the monolithic party-state system and the care taken to ensure at least the appearance of the 'leading role' of the Workers' Party. It is also associated with some form of central direction of the economy and its insulation from direct engagement with the major processes of international capitalism.

The key-stone of Poland's socialist status, though, is formed by bilateral treaties with the Soviet Union and the integration of its military forces within the Warsaw Treaty Organization. With its standard military forces calculated at something over 300,000 Poland has, after the Soviet Union, the largest army in Eastern Europe (this is roughly the same size as the British army, but considerably smaller than those of France or West Germany). Integration with the socialist camp was originally based on bilateral Soviet-Polish military agreements and given more substance by the placing of Soviet military representatives in positions of direct command over Polish forces. This practice ceased in 1956, although the WTO (founded in 1955) has always been under firm Soviet control and its forces subject to Soviet military command.

Nevertheless, Soviet-East European military relations have not remained unchanged and the mode of military integration still fluctuates. Until 1961, for example, the 'Warsaw Pact as such lacked political and especially military substance', and it was only in the 1960s that the East European forces began to play a greater role in Soviet military planning within a conception of 'coalition warfare' (Ross Johnson, 1984, p. 261). While this idea of tight coordination became somewhat diluted in the light of East European instability and political uncertainty, not the least of which has been the enhanced political role of the military in Poland, there is no question that the close Soviet control of the armed forces of Poland and its immediate neighbours remains a major strategic and political priority of the Soviet authorities. A further channel of Soviet military influence is provided by the 40–50,000 Soviet personnel stationed in Poland under an agreement reached in 1956 with the Polish leadership. Unlike the Soviet military presence before 1956 the role of these forces has been restricted to their agreed duties as they do not appear themselves to have exerted a political influence.

From the viewpoint of economic relations and the integration of Poland in the sphere of Soviet economic dominance, the role of Soviet interests and the influence of the Soviet model has clearly been of paramount importance. In terms of costs and benefits, though, economic relations between Poland and the Soviet Union have clearly changed over time and have been the source of some disagreement. Some observers now see Eastern Europe as a clear economic liability to the Soviet Union (Bunce, 1985). Others see the issue in less clear-cut terms and suggest that the Soviet liability, if there is one, is of very small scale and note that the Soviet subsidy to Poland in particular is smaller than that to other Eastern European states—larger only than Romania's, an even less intimate ally of the Soviet Union (Marer, 1984).

What is clear, though, is that Poland is clearly situated within the Soviet sphere of superpower influence and that the relation between Poland and the Soviet Union is comparable, say, to that of Mexico with the United States. Parallels between the processes of incorporation of Poland and Mexico within the respective spheres of interest may also be drawn, although 'here Poland has lagged behind Mexico' (Hughes, 1986). Both Poland and Mexico ran into deep economic crisis towards the end of the seventies, and it may be argued that the Soviet mode of integration provides for somewhat less traumatic means of coping with crisis than does the American (Mexican standards of living, for example, were fully halved between 1982 and 1987).

Poland and the West

In some ways Poland has maintained closer relations with the West than most of its neighbours and has attempted to open up perspectives that range beyond the Soviet bloc and its immediate allies. It has always engaged in closer economic relations with the West than the other European communist states. Throughout the 1950s and 1960s Polish trade with the West stood at around 30 per cent of total turnover, compared with between 10 and 20 per cent in the other Eastern countries (Kanet, 1981, pp. 375, 395). Another important mode of expression of this tendency has been the taking of initiatives designed to reduce East–West tension and further European disarmament.

One example was the Rapacki plan, launched in 1957 and named after the Polish Foreign Minister of the time. It proposed banning nuclear weapons from the Central European states of Poland, Czechoslovakia and the two Germanies. In view of NATO fears concerning their side's relative weakness in terms of conventional weapons it met with little success at the time. A more recent initiative in this area has been the Jaruzelski plan, announced in 1987. Taking account of the fate of its predecessor, the plan proposed the progressive elimination of tactical and battlefield nuclear weapons from Central Europe but also associated this with possible reductions in conventional weapons, a form of linkage claimed to be innovatory in this area (*Polityka*, 6 June 1987). The plan did not receive much publicity outside Poland and was overshadowed by the bolder Gorbachëv–Reagan initiatives which overtook it. The Western reception of it was described 'in euphemistic terms as mixed' (*Polityka*, 9 April 1988). There were, nevertheless, attempts to relaunch the plan under the new conditions created by the 1987 US–Soviet intermediate nuclear force agreement (*Życie Partii*, 23 March 1988).

Rapacki could claim greater eventual success with a proposal in 1964 for an all-European security conference, which led later to the Helsinki conference and agreement of 1975. Clearly, the receptiveness of the Western powers in this case and the changed outlook of the Soviet Union, with a recent commitment to *détente*, both played a large part in the progress of the latter proposal. But in the immediate post-1956 period the likelihood of real openings to the West having some chance of success were also reduced by Gomułka's close identification, particularly following 1957, with the interests and policies of the Soviet leadership and his desires for greater integration within the European socialist world, notably in the area of economic integration (Leslie *et al.*, 1980, pp. 381–2, 393). This inclination, particularly in the latter aspect, may well have been strengthened by his disappointment at the low level of American economic aid granted after 1956 and the meagre appreciation this seemed to imply of the stand taken for independence during the Polish October (Dziewanowski, 1977, pp. 187–8). But it also appears that Gomułka's political outlook was dominated by an extremely strong awareness of Poland's geopolitical position and by a virtual obsession with his country's potential and historical weakness. From this point of view, it has been argued, the post-war division of Europe—in short, Yalta—was 'from the Polish point of view, ideal' (Bethell, 1970, p. 239). Poland's greatest threat would be, as it had been in the past, a strong Germany combined with a strong Russia. A divided Germany, particularly one where a Sovietized East could be seen as a buffer against a potentially threatening capitalist West, was a very positive benefit. This situation did change to some extent, though, with the agreement reached by Gomułka with the Federal Republic on Poland's western borders a matter of weeks before his removal from office in December 1970.

The virtual coincidence of these two events means that it is impossible to tell whether the final accord on Poland's borders would have modified Gomułka's appreciation of the consequences of the Yalta agreement and his very close association with the position of the Soviet leadership. Given his age at this time and in view of Poland's domestic situation, probably not. But it is nevertheless instructive that, although the Gierek leadership took the important decision to extend the purchase of foreign licences and to use them as a major component of an accelerated economic growth strategy in mid-1971, it was not until after the ratification of Gomułka's agreement by the Polish and West German parliaments in May 1972 that he began his associated diplomatic offensive towards the West (Leslie *et al*., 1980, p. 428).

Once he began, though, Gierek led Poland to a higher level of East–West exchanges and communication, particularly in terms of politics and economics but also in cultural and scientific matters, and more practical aspects like tourism and international travel. This opening up also had an internal dimension and concerted measures were taken to establish better relations with the Church on a stable basis, a process which led to Gierek's audience with Pope Paul in 1977. A further significant development was the election of Cardinal Wojtyła to the Papacy; this could hardly be attributed directly to the Gierek leadership but was nevertheless formally welcomed by them and accommodated to their policy of internal and external *détente*. Apart from matters of domestic policy, this shift towards the formation of more stable and favourable relations with the West was facilitated by the development of *détente*—and the onset of global economic recession, which prompted Western economic powers to seek new markets for investment as well as producer and consumer goods. By 1975 the proportion of Polish trade turnover conducted with the West was nearing one half of the total (although by this stage countries like Romania were following the same pattern).

But there is little evidence that this turn towards the West reflected any fundamental rejection of Eastern links. Care was certainly taken to emphasize the strength and importance of political ties with the Soviet Union, and

Poland was a full participant in measures taken to strengthen integration within the CMEA framework. Whether the Gierek period represented a genuine turn away from his predecessor's attachment to the Soviet association and, indeed, the principles of Yalta must remain open to some question. What can be said is that Gierek was a strong proponent of both the bridge and the bastion conception of Poland's international role, but nevertheless neglected the fact that both bridge and bastion require adequate foundations–and this his regime failed to provide in terms of domestic stability.

The collapse of the Gierek regime in any case led to the emergence of grave doubts in Western, and particularly financial, circles about the advisability of further close association with the Eastern countries and the viability of forging economic links as a form of bridge-building between the capitalist and socialist systems. The experience of the latter Gierek years and the eruption of the Solidarity union placed an equally significant question-mark over the role of Poland as a reliable member of the Eastern bloc and a bastion of socialism. The period of direct military rule accompanied, on the Western side, by an attenuation of political relations and the application of economic sanctions meant a further weakening of official Polish links with those countries. Regardless of the degree of Soviet involvement in the decision-making process leading up to General Jaruzelski's coup of December 1981 (and, in view of the involvement of critical security and military groups, this cannot have been inconsiderable), the process of political normalization and the catastrophic economic consequences of Gierek's *affaire* with international capitalism necessarily meant a reorientation of the Polish system towards closer links with the Soviet Union. This has not been a simple or uncontentious process.

The Politics of Re-integration

In October 1987, *Trybuna Ludu* carried a long article commenting on Poland's trade relations with the world in general and with the Soviet Union in particular. A particular paragraph could not fail to catch the attention of the reader;

Certain voices seek to impute that under Moscow's diktat, Poland is limiting its economic relations with the West. Further they claim that Moscow imposes a trading sphere of specialization on Poland within the framework of the CMEA and thus seeks to tie Poland to itself through control over raw mateials, cooperation agreements between enterprises, joint ventures. . . . with the aim of making Poland politically dependent upon the USSR. [*Trybuna Ludu*, 19 October 1987]

Whilst the debate over 'who subsidizes whom' within the Soviet bloc continues unabated (Poznanski, 1988) there has undoubtedly been a clear initiative launched by the Jaruzelski and post-Brezhnev Soviet leadership to put Polish-Soviet relations on a new footing. If normalization in post-Solidarity Poland has been about pre-empting the re-emergence of similar, system-redefining social and political movements in the future, then an important element in any such strategy must be the whole question of how to ensure Poland's continued active and productive participation within the Soviet bloc without the spectre of anti-Sovietism re-emerging. Polish ministers on frequent occasions have re-iterated that *perestroika* and *glasnost* have their comparators in reform and renewal in Poland (*Czerwony Sztandar*, 3 March 1988). More than this, Polish-Soviet relations have been raised to a qualitatively new plane as exemplified in the new economic, political and cultural ties between the two countries which have the ultimate aim of bringing the populations of the two countries closer together (*Rzeczpospolita*, 12–13 March 1988). Old forms of co-operation such as the Polish- Soviet Friendship Society have been given new content with revised statutes and more consequential execution of their stated tasks. This 'new wine in old bottles' may have distracted those who were not prepared to acknowledge the 'revolution without shots' which was being enacted in the Kremlin and which could not help but have some fall-out in the sphere of bilateral and multilateral relations between the Soviet Union and its bloc partners.

The centrality of the Polish-Soviet axis is heightened, however, by the dawning realization of the extent to which Soviet domestic policy is a response to the early warning which the Solidarity phenomenon gave to the system of 'real socialism' (Kolankiewicz, 1983; Teague, 1988). This is not the place to examine the symbiosis between developments in both the countries since 1982, but suffice to note that matters relating to inner party democracy, local government reform, electoral rule changes, censorship, self-management and trade-unionism, even the 'informal organizations' running loose in the Soviet political terrain, were all presaged by changes in Poland. Even in the realm of economic reform, Poland with its tri-sectoral (private, cooperative and state) economy and an industrial structure akin to that of the Soviet Union, make it a prime candidate for experimentation, as the Soviet leadership navigates the uncharted waters of restructuring which involve the introduction or highlighting of certain non-socialist features. A recent example is the recognition by the Union of Soviet Kolkhozniks (collective farmers) as it moves into the *zveno* (autonomous work-team) system of disaggregating large farms into smaller group-managed units, that the Polish ZSL or peasant party is a legitimate opposite number, given that the latter seeks to represent Poland's individual peasant farmers (*Trybuna Ludu*, 20 February 1987; *Financial Times*, 22 March 1988).

Dependence in Crisis

During the 1980–1 period, over and above the 'will they or won't they' debate as to the Soviet Union's intentions *vis-à-vis* Solidarity, a powerful body of moderate opinion was calling for the 'societalization' of relations with Poland's powerful Eastern neighbour by removing them from the sole prerogative of the party-state. A 'people to people' solution was envisaged which would remove some of the distrust apparent in bilateral relations and not make the latter the object of manipulation (*Kultura*, 17 May 1981). Trade relations, the limits to internal reform as well as the ultimate authorship of Poland's 1970s profligacy, often the subject of speculation and conscious distortion, would be more easily managed in a spirit of openness and direct contact (*Gazeta Robotnicza*, 24 October 1981). Whereas the 'revelations' published by the defector Colonel Kukliński seemed to undermine those who had argued that the martial law option was a purely domestic decision (*Kultura*, April 1987), by then the Soviet model of broad-ranging cooperation was well in place.

During 1981, as Poland's economy reeled under the burdens of Western debt-servicing, disruptions of production due primarily to materials shortages and poor distribution (and to a much lesser extent to the strike activity prevalent at the time), plans were being made to exploit the spare capacity in Polish industry. Some of the stranded foreign investment projects, not least the controversial Katowice steel works, were also discussed, whilst the whole question of the longer-term re-structuring of Polish industry dove-tailed into the broader question of where Poland was to go from there. Western financial support was still an option, but the imposition of sanctions after martial law, coupled with the subsequent nascent reform debate in the post-Brezhnev Soviet Union, naturally shifted the focus of attention to the Soviet Union. The latter built on the atmosphere engendered by the cuts in Western credits (e.g., chickens dying because of a lack of US feed) and presented itself as the reliable partner. Re-orientation of the Polish economy away from the West was presented as deflecting 'interference' in Poland's internal affairs, fostering agricultural and ultimately industrial self-sufficiency and allowing Poland to complete the beneficial investments of the Gierek era. The Soviet Union, which had steadfastly refused to take on the role of the debtor of last resort during the 1981 crisis, now launched a major rescue operation. In early 1982 a large group of deputy ministers visited 113 large Polish enterprises and were reported to be 'pleasantly surprised by the potential' of Polish industry (*Życie Gospodarcze*, 13 June 1982). It was agreed that the Soviet partners would supply the necessary raw materials to keep factories running and the Polish side would be paid by a proportion of the product being left behind. Given that imports from the West during 1981–2 had dropped by 25 per cent, a certain fatalism in accepting what was already apparent as a longer-term solution was not surprising. The coordination and alignment of the 1983–4 economic plans of the two countries, culminated in the agreement over plan coordination up to 1990 and then the much-publicized 'Year 2000' Agreeement. Signed by Chernenko and Jaruzelski in May 1984, 'The Long-Term Programme for the development of economic, scientific and technical cooperation between the USSR and Poland' was seen by some as removing key sectors of the Polish economy from under domestic control, and did in fact provide a blanket agreement for all subsequent cooperation (*Pravda*, 6 May 1984). Evidently most of these agreements were couched in terms of broader CMEA policy, which also sought to become independent of the West and duly cut its imports by 43.5 per cent in the first quarter of 1982.

Whether through luck or forethought, the focus of Soviet cooperation policy was to be the industrial enterprise, that most political of institutions. Long before Gorbachëv was to enunciate his reform programme granting greater independence to enterprises in their dealings with trading partners (*Ekonomicheskaya Gazeta*, no. 4, January 1987), cooperation agreements between Polish and Soviet enterprises had grown from fifty pairs in 1983 to well over two hundred at the present time. In due course, not only was there to be an exchange of production materials, but also of party secretaries, groups of employees, holiday facilities, childrens' camps, cultural exchanges, almost the whole gamut of activities located at the level of the socialist enterprise. At the same time Poland along with its other CMEA partners undertook, at Soviet behest, to participate in the construction of major industrial and extraction projects in the Soviet Union, such as the Jamburg gas pipe-line. Joint ventures were also envisaged, one of which, the Miraculum cosmetics and allied products enterprise in Cracow is already in operation. Propaganda stimulus to all these efforts at cooperation was to be provided by the revamped Polish-Soviet Friendship society (TPPR) with its 6 million strong Soviet opposite number. Directors of cooperating enterprises met under the auspices of the said TPPR, as did groups of peasants (*Dziennik Ludowy*, 29 December 1986). This latter was presumably deemed necessary as the agreements included the three-fold growth in export of fresh vegetables and flowers to the Soviet Union.

Although commentators were aware that the direction of the agreements seemed to reproduce the energy and material-intensive structure of Polish industry, it was felt that Poland had no option but to cooperate given its dependence upon Soviet fuel and raw materials supply (*Trybuna Ludu*, 16 April 1985). Furthermore Poland's only chance at bridging the R & D gap which separated it from the West was to hitch its star to that of the stronger partner, and in due course both could provide the products that would find clients in Western markets and thus in the long term contribute to the diminution of the Polish hard currency debt, which by 1988 stood at $39.2 billion. That Poland had almost achieved current account balance in terms of its trade with the Soviet Union by that same year indicates what the cooperation priorities were.

That this was to be part of a broader-based policy of re-establishing Polish-Soviet relations on a firm footing was made evident by the signing of the so-called 'Agreement on Ideology, Culture and Science' by Jaruzelski and Gorbachëv on 21 April 1987. This agreement was intended to foster direct cultural contacts, and deal with the so-called 'blank spots' in the history of Polish-Soviet relations, e.g. Katyn and the 1939–41 Soviet occupation of the Eastern Territories, the immediate post-war period and other thorny issues. It also spawned a whole series of further agreements dealing with higher education, tourism, the recognition of the considerable *émigré* population residing in the Soviet Union and their cultural rights as 'Polonia', as well as generally making the Polish-Soviet border more permeable and therefore less physically and socially divisive. The growth in tourism brought with it all the problems characteristic of Poles travelling abroad and in the first few months of its existence the new Polish consulate in Lwów (Soviet Ukraine) dealt with 6,000 Poles charged with various misdemeanours (*Gazeta Robotnicza*, 16 October 1987).

The fostering of cross-border cooperation and trade, e.g. selling goods in short supply in the respective border areas or the use of Soviet collective farm machinery in assisting the Polish harvest, was mixed in with joint party meetings from these areas (*Trybuna Ludu*, 10 June 1987).

Elsewhere the Polish trade unions in the form of the OPZZ signed an agreement with the All-Union Council of Soviet Trade Unions on deepening ties and cooperation, with factory level contacts, health, sport and tourism as well as housing, that most pressing of Polish problems (*Trybuna Ludu*,

24 February 1987). Keeping in tune with the high level of public relations so characteristic of the *glasnost* era, a 'Telemost' or television bridge was organized between two studio audiences in the respective capitals, while the latter in their own right signed a cooperation accord again exchanging party, youth, union and other organizations (*Życie Warszawy*, 6 August 1987).

Although many of these projects are still very much on paper only they demonstrate a sense of new purpose aimed at not allowing this most crucial of areas to go by default. 'The new cannot be dealt with in the old ways', is the common sentiment to all these agreements, and why should Western observers assume that this is simply more of the same when elsewhere the Gorbachëv initiatives, despite opposition (as is all too apparent in the area of bilateral relations), appear to be backed with a significant sense of purpose.

Despite the obvious scope and detail of the proposed Polish–Soviet relations, which were given considerable publicity in the press of both countries, it is only recently that concern has surfaced in opposition sources to the possibility that Poland will be subsidizing Gorbachëv's reforms, by providing the goods and services required to act as incentives for the profit and productivity-oriented Soviet work-force. The provision of hotel accommodation, urban renovation, and similar services being constructed for the Soviet Union when they are in such obvious short supply in Poland is a case in point (PWA, 27 January 1988). At a more general level there is concern that despite the rhetoric of independence associated as might be expected with these plans, the sense is that most forms of cooperation are guided from above. The stated desire of creating 'planned conditions for autonomous competition' seems to convince nobody (*Trybuna Ludu*, 7 January 1987). Likewise the argument that the CMEA countries are only doing what the EEC nations have been doing for years and thus reaching a higher level of integration (intra- rather than inter-branch integration) is difficult to sustain in the absence of short-term introduction of more than bilateral and highly artificial convertibility of currencies.

There can be little doubt that the nature and eventual success of Polish economic and political reform is inextricably tied to the fate of Gorbachëv's domestic efforts. Although emerging with its own internal logic since martial law, Jaruzelski's 'legitimation through reform' strategy is now locked into the broader train of events in the Soviet Union. Here the supposed good relations between Jaruzelski and Gorbachëv are in part a result of the fact that little the Soviet Union does internally can appear as new and therefore threatening to the Polish leadership. However the further the Soviet Union progresses along its path of reform, so Jaruzelski's room for manœuvre against his internal opponents, both in terms of Solidarity as well as the hard-liners, is increased.

The Politics of Reciprocal Engagement

Mention was made above of the background of Western sanctions against which the Soviet policies of re-integration were initiated. During this period, 1981–7, the United States also embarked upon its own course, firstly into sanctions and suspension of trade privileges, and then after 1983, the lifting of these sanctions and the re-establishment of diplomatic if not full economic ties.

In response to martial law and the subsequent banning of Solidarity the United States suspended fishing rights, restricted high-technology exports to Poland, refrained from granting new credits for food, withheld support for Poland's admission into the IMF and refused to negotiate debt rescheduling. In October 1982 with the passage of the Trade Union Law abolishing Solidarity and the other unions, the United States suspended MFN status to the Poles.

With the June 1983 amnesty and the July visit of John Paul II to Poland, the United States agreed to discuss debt rescheduling. According to the Polish government the 1981–3 restrictions apart from being an unwarranted interference in Polish internal affairs cost the country $10.5 billion of lost trade (*Polityka Stanów Zjed*, 1984, p. 131). US estimates of the likely consequences differed considerably. Be that as it may, the Reagan administration set out three conditions which had to be fulfilled prior to the United States abandoning its policy of 'disengagement', i.e. lifting of martial law, release of political prisoners and the instigation of a dialogue between government and society. To underline the break in relations, neither country nominated an ambassador until 1988.

It has to be admitted that the Polish government fulfilled the conditions, at least on the surface, much more adroitly than many might have thought possible, with the rapid suspension of martial law in December 1982, its lifting in July 1983, the fourth and most telling amnesty in September of 1986, and the deployment of councils, consultations, elections and the November 1987 referendum, all aimed at stimulating a 'dialogue' with society.

Poland's accession to the IMF and reinstatement of MFN status were just some of the signs of external approval for actions taken in what has come to be called the 'step-by-step' approach to Polish–US normalization of relations (Hardt & Boone, 1987). The United States has made small contributions to the economic plight of Poland as far as bilateral relations are concerned, chiefly in supporting much needed water projects, science and technology exchanges and fostering the activities of such foundations as the Ford and Rockefeller Brothers initiatives in agriculture. Patently, the US policy makers are waiting on the outcome of 'socialist pluralism', the growth in workers' rights which could mean trade-union pluralism as well as the translation into practice of the myriad details of the 'second stage of economic reform' with a particular eye to the growth of the private sector, as well as export-led growth. However the United States is also aware of the constraints on Poland as it enters into the qualitatively new set of dependencies with the Soviet Union and other CMEA partners, not to mention the internal sources of opposition to reform (Hardt & Boone, 1987). Visitations by the IMF as well as by the US deputy Secretary of State John Whitehead (January 1988) were reciprocated by a variety of Polish representatives, with the latter chiefly reiterating how crucial the reinstatement of normal finance and credit realities were to the success of Polish reform. The United States for its part, before making any move in this direction demands proof of societal support for the reform and for the regime.

Nevertheless it would be difficult to deny that Jaruzelski has come a long way out of the political isolation his regime faced in December 1981. Relations with London (a visit by Margaret Thatcher in 1988) and with Japan, West Germany and the Vatican are in varying stages of improvement. Relations with the Third World are better on the political level than on the economic, with the realization that Third World markets are falling to the newly industrializing countries of the Pacific rim rather than being the natural focus for the lower quality goods from the CMEA.

There are 13 million persons of Polish origin living outside of Poland. Of these the vast majority are to be found in the United States (8.4 million). While they are not as well organized as other ethnic minorities they have brought such politicians as George Bush and Edward Kennedy, not to mention the much maligned President Carter, to the airport at Okęcie. That 1.2 million are now admitted as living in the Soviet Union, with the full status of Polonia, may not carry the same electoral weight in that country but with the likely increase in the importance of the ethnic question in Gorbachëv's policy platform, it provides for political possibilities far beyond mere numbers.

The Polish regime likes to claim that its foreign policy is non-contentious and bipartisan. Changes in the passport law allowing for the unhindered return of *émigrés* and the *de facto* recognition of the Polish *gastarbieter*, whilst they do not erase the non-provision of a passport for Wałęsa, do intimate of a generally more relaxed foreign stance. When fundamental questions about what constitutes a socialist country are up for discussion, when the concept of

'Mitteleuropa' or the *rapprochement* between the two Germanies is on the lips of publicist and politician alike, then the sheer size, political significance and recent history of Poland make it a key variable in any future superpower equation.

Poland in the Gorbachëv Era

While Poland's foreign policy has been developed and pursued with persistence, subtlety and a certain measure of success since the *impasse* of the early 1980s, the resolution of many of Poland's major problems remains a distant prospect. The possibility of their resolution depends in large measure on factors far beyond the control of Poland's native rulers. Of these the most important, particularly in the light of the unfortunate consequences of Poland's engagement with the world economy during the 1970s, remains the prospect of further change in the Soviet Union and the perspectives opened up by Gorbachëv's perspectives of *perestroika* and accelerated development. In 1988 this process is still at an early stage and its prospects of success are uncertain. Moreover, while Gorbachëv's agenda for change on a national and international scale is a broad one and certain issues have clearly taken precedence (economic recovery in the Soviet Union, superpower relations), other matters have not received decisive attention and the form of the 'new thinking' here remains less definite.

One of the areas where this appears to be the case is that of Poland and Eastern European relations in general. Earlier disagreement over the origins of the Polish crisis seem to have subsided, but traditional hard-line views of intra-bloc relations appeared to retain great influence in the higher reaches of the Soviet party bureaucracy in the post-XXVII CPSU Congress (1986) period and the state of policy formation remained fluid (Dawisha & Valdez, 1987). The new CPSU programme adopted at that Congress was, as Dawisha (1988) has pointed out, more circumspect in its references to the parameters of reform in Eastern Europe than some of the statements of Gorbachëv himself. Former reappraisals of the past by Soviet leaders have been followed by political turmoil in Eastern Europe (Poland and Hungary in 1956) and even relatively limited notions of economic reform have formed part of a process that came to involve serious political repercussions in that area (the Kosygin reforms of the 1960s and the Czechoslovak events of 1968). It is understandable, therefore, that the Gorbachëv leadership has adopted a highly cautious approach in this respect.

In the case of the more reform-oriented countries like Poland (and only

Hungary can be treated as a member of the same category here) that caution must be redoubled, because the contemporary Polish political and economic predicament persists despite concerted, and repeated, espousal of reform programmes that, certainly by Soviet standards, have been radical and probably further-ranging than anything envisaged by Gorbachëv. Precisely how far reform would have to be taken to resolve the Polish dilemma remains an unknown and a prospect probably quite unacceptable to much of the Soviet establishment, and possibly Gorbachëv himself. This must be the case if, for example, the logic and spirit of the 'Moscow Spring' under Polish conditions were understood to encompass the formation of an independent trade union led by Lech Wałęsa (Gati, 1987).

Yet if the Gorbachëv initiative does take root in the Soviet Union it will surely effect a profound transformation in Soviet relations with Poland and the Eastern European countries. The growing integration of the Polish and Soviet economies during the 1980s and the strengthening of ties in other fields can only make the relationship a more intimate one. Whatever the form that eventual domestic and international change in the two countries does take, there can be little doubt that the path of development taken by the Soviet Union's largest ally will have a profound impact not just in the Soviet bloc but also in European affairs more generally.

Bibliography

Abbreviations of Polish publishers used in the bibliography: IFiS PAN, Instytut Filozofii i Socjologii, Polska Akademia Nauk; IPPM-L, Instytut Podstawowych Problemów Marksizmu-Leninizmu; IS UW, Instytut Socjologii, Uniwersytet Warszawski; KiW, Książka i Wiedza; PWE, Państwowe Wydawnictwo Ekonomiczne; PWN, Państwowe Wydawnictwo Naukowe.

Abramsky, Chimen, Jachimczyk, Maciej, & Polonsky, Anthony (eds) 1986. *The Jews of Poland*. New York, Basil Blackwell.

Albright, Madeline K. 1983. *Poland: The Role of the Press in Political Change*. New York, Praeger.

Almond, G. A. 1983. Communism and political culture theory. *Comparative Politics*, vol. 15, no. 2, pp. 127–38.

Andorka, Rudolf, & Zagorski, Krzysztof, 1980. *Socio-Occupational Mobility in Hungary and Poland: Comparative analysis of surveys 1972–1973*. Warsaw, Polish Academy of Sciences.

Andrews, Nicholas, G. 1985. *Poland, 1980–81: Solidarity Versus the Party*. Washington DC, National Defense University Press.

Andrzejewski, A. 1977. *Sytuacja Mieszkaniowa w Polsce w latach 1918–1974*. Warsaw, PWN.

Ascherson, Neal, 1981. *The Polish August: The Self-Limiting Revolution*. Harmondsworth, Penguin Books.

Aslund, Anders, 1985. *Private Enterprise in Eastern Europe: The Non-agricultural Private Sector in Poland and the GDR 1945–83*. New York, St Martin's Press.

Aspaturian, Vernon V. 1984. Eastern Europe in a world perspective. In T. Rakowska-Harmstone (ed.), *Eastern Europe in the Sixties*. Bloomington, Indiana University Press.

Bakuniak, G., & Nowak, K. 1987. The creation of a collective identity in a social movement: the case of 'Solidarność' in Poland. *Theory and Society*, vol. 16, pp. 401–29.

Baryka, C. 1982. Polish communists, 1937–44. *Survey*, vol. 26, no. 4, pp. 127–55.

Bauman, Z. 1974. Officialdom and class: bases of inequality in socialist society. In F. Parkin (ed.), *The Social Analysis of Class Structure*. London, Tavistock.

Beksiak, J. 1972. *Społeczeństwo Gospodarujące*. Warsaw, PWN.

Beskid, L. 1984. *Warunki Życia i Potrzeby Społeczeństwa Polskiego 1982*. Warsaw, IFiS PAN.

Bethell, N. 1970. *Gomułka: His Poland, His Communism*. Harmondsworth, Penguin Books.

Bielasiak, J. 1978. Lateral and vertical elite differentiation in European communist states. *Studies in Comparative Communism*, vol. 11, no. 1–2, pp. 121–41.
Bieńkowski, W. 1971a. *Socjologia Klęski*. Paris, Instytut Literacki.
— 1971b. *Drogi Wyjścia*. Paris, Instytut Literacki.
Blazyca, George, 1985. The Polish economy under martial law: a dissenting view. *Soviet Studies*, vol. 37, no. 3.
— 1987. The new round of economic reform in Eastern Europe. *National Westminster Bank Quarterly Review*, November.
Błażejczyk, M. 1985. *Samorząd Załogi Przedsiębiorstwa*. Warsaw, Instytut Wydawniczy Związków Zawodowych.
Blit, L. 1971. *The Origins of Polish Socialism: The History and Ideas of the First Socialist Party, 1878–1886*. Cambridge, Cambridge University Press.
Brada, J., & Montias, J. M. 1985. Industrial policy in Eastern Europe. In Congress of the United States, 1985.
Brandys, K. 1984. *A Warsaw Diary, 1978–81*. London, Chatto and Windus.
Bromke, A. 1967. *Poland's Politics: Idealism vs. Realism*. Cambridge, Mass., Harvard University Press.
Brumberg, A. (ed.) 1983. *Poland: Genesis of a Revolution*. New York, Vintage Books.
Brzezinski, Z. K. 1967. *The Soviet Bloc: Unity and Conflict*. Cambridge, Mass., Harvard University Press.
— 1984–5. The future of Yalta. *Foreign Affairs*, vol. 63, no. 1, pp. 279–302.
Bunce, V. 1985. The empire strikes back: the transformation of the Eastern bloc from a Soviet asset to a Soviet liability. *International Organization*, vol. 39, no. 1, pp. 1–46.
Cave, J. 1981. Local officials of the Polish United Workers' Party, 1956–75. *Soviet Studies*, vol. 33, no. 1, pp. 125–41.
Chałasiński, J. 1946. *Społeczna Genealogia Inteligencji Polskiej*. Łódź.
Checinski, M. 1982. *Poland: Communism, Nationalism, Anti-Semitism*. New York, Karz-Kohl.
— 1983. Poland's military burden. *Problems of Communism*, vol. 32, no. 3, pp. 31–44.
Ciechocińska, M. 1965. *Położenie Klasy Robotniczej w Polsce 1929–39*. Warsaw, KiW.
Congress of United States 1985–6. *Eastern European Economies: Slow Growth in the 1980's*, Vol. 1, Selected Papers. Joint Economic Committee, US Congress, Washington DC.
Coutouvidis, J., & Reynolds, J., 1986. *Poland, 1939–47*. Leicester, Leicester University Press.
Cviic, C. 1983. The Church. In Brumberg (ed.), 1983, pp. 92–108.
Czarzasty, M., Gilejko, L., & Nowacki, G., 1987. *Robotnicy, Reforma, Rzeczywistość*. Warsaw, Akademia Nauk Społecznych.
Czepulis-Rastenis, R. 1973. *'Klassa Umysłowa' Inteligencja Krolewstwa Polskiego 1832–62*. Warsaw, KiW.
Davies, N. 1982. *God's Playground: A History of Poland* (2 vols). Oxford, Oxford University Press.

— 1984. *Heart of Europe: A Short History of Poland*. Oxford, Oxford University Press.
Dawisha, K. 1988. *Eastern Europe, Gorbachev and Reform*. Cambridge, Cambridge University Press.
— & Valdez, J., 1987. Socialist internationalism in eastern Europe. *Problems of Communism*, vol. 36, no. 2, pp. 1–14.
Dobrowolska, D. 1984. *Wartość Pracy Dla Jednostki w Środowisku Przemysłowym*. Wrocław, Ossolineum.
Dobrzyńska, M., & Wallis, A., 1971. *Inteligencja Polska XIX i XX Wieku*. Wrocław, Ossolineum.
Drewnowski, J. (ed.) 1982. *Crisis in the Eastern European Economy: The Spread of the Polish Disease*. New York, St Martin's Press.
Dziewanowski, M. K. 1977. *Poland in the 20th Century*. New York, Columbia University Press.
Experience and Future (Doświadczenie i Przyszłość) 1981. *Poland Today. The State of the Republic*. White Plains, NY, M. E. Sharpe.
Fallenbuchl, Z. M. 1986. The economic crisis in Poland and prospects for recovery. In Congress of the United States, 1985–6.
Feher, F., Heller, A., & Markus, G. 1983. *Dictatorship Over Needs: An Analysis of Soviet Societies*. Oxford, Basil Blackwell.
Fikus, D. 1984. *Foksal 81*. London, Aneks.
Garton-Ash, Timothy, 1985. *The Polish Revolution: Solidarity*, 2nd edn. New York, Vintage Books.
Gati, C. 1987. Gorbachev and Eastern Europe. *Foreign Affairs*, vol. 65, no. 5, pp. 958–75.
Gebethner, S. 1981. Political and institutional change in the management of the socialist economy: the Polish case. In Borstein, M., Gitelman, Z., and Zimmerman, W. (eds), *East-West Relations and the Future of Eastern Europe*. London, Allen & Unwin, pp. 252–82.
Gerner, K. 1985. *The Soviet Union and Eastern Europe in the Post-War Era*. Aldershot, Gower.
Gomulka, S. 1986. *Growth, Innovation and Reform in Eastern Europe*. Madison, University of Wisconsin Press.
— & Rostowski, J., 1984. The reformed Polish economic system, 1982–83. *Soviet Studies*, vol. 36, no. 3.
Gomułka, W. 1969. *O Naszej Partii*. Warsaw, KiW.
Graham, L. S., & Ciechocińska, M. K. (eds) 1987. *The Polish Dilemma: Views From Within*. Boulder, Colorado, Westview Press.
Hahn, W. G. 1987. *Democracy in a Communist Party: Poland's Experience Since 1980*. New York, Columbia University Press.
Hann, C. M. 1985. *A Village Without Solidarity: Polish Peasants in Years of Crisis*. New Haven, Yale University Press.
Hardt, J., & Boone, J. F. 1987. *Poland's Renewal and US Options: A Policy Reconnaisance. Update*. Report for the Sub-Committee on Europe and the Middle East. Committee on Foreign Affairs, US House of Representatives. Washington DC.

Hass, L. 1973. Układ sił i zasięg oddziaływania ruchu zawodowego wśród klasy robotniczej w latach drugiej rzeczypospolitej. In S. Kalabiński (ed.), *Polska Klasa Robotnicza, Vol. IV*, Warsaw, PWN.

Hirszowicz, M. 1986. *Coercion and Control in Communist Society*. Brighton, Wheatsheaf.

— & Morawski, W. 1967. *Z Badań Nad Społecznym Uczestnictwem W Organizacji Przemysłowej*. Warsaw, KiW.

Hiscocks, R. 1963. *Poland: Bridge for the Abyss?* London, Oxford University Press.

Holzer, J. 1983. *Solidarność 1980–81. Geneza i Historia*. Warsaw, Krąg.

Hryniewicz, J. 1985. Ruchliwość społeczna w polsce w latach 1945–58. *Przegląd Socjologiczny*, vol. 35, Lodz, Ossolineum.

Hughes, J. L. 1986. The politics of dependence in Poland and Mexico. In J. Triska (ed.), *Dominant Powers and Subordinate States*, Durham, Duke University Press, pp. 342–69.

Hutchings, R. L. 1983. *Soviet-East European Relations: Consolidation and Conflict*. Madison, University of Wisconsin Press.

Jarosz, M. 1984. *Nierówności Społeczne*. Warsaw, KiW.

Jasiewicz, K. 1986. *Polacy '84 Z półtorarocznej perspektywy. Raport wstępny z badania 'opinie polakow-jesien '85'*. Warsaw, Uniwersytet Warszawski.

Jedlicki, W. 1963. *Klub Krzywego Koła*. Paris, Instytut Literacki.

Jerschina, J. 1983. System wartości młodych robotników i inteligentów w procesie przemian. *Kultura i Społeczeństwo*, vol. 27, no. 2.

Johnson, A. Ross, 1984. The Warsaw Pact: Soviet military policy in Eastern Europe. In S. Terry (ed.), *Soviet Policy in Eastern Europe*, New Haven, Conn., Yale University Press.

— & Kliszewski, B. 1983. *The Polish Military After Martial Law: Report of a Rand Conference, October 14, 1982*. N-2001-AF, Santa Monica, Calif., Rand.

— & — 1987. *United States Policy Towards Poland: A Conference Report*. R-3545-FF, Santa Monica, Calif., Rand.

Kalabiński, S. 1974. *Ruch Zawodowy w Polsce. Zarys Dziejów. Vol. 1–3*. Warsaw, Instytut Wydawniczy CRZZ.

Kalinski, J., & Landau, Z. 1978. *Gospodarka Polski Ludowej. 1945–55*. Warsaw, KiW.

Kamiński, B. 1985. The dying command economy: Solidarity and the Polish crisis. *Journal of Contemporary Studies*, vol. 8, no. 1, pp. 5–35.

Kanet, R. E. 1981. Poland, the socialist community and east-west relations. In Kanet & Simon, 1981, pp.371–401.

— & Simon, M. D. (eds), 1981. *Background to Crisis: Policy and Politics in Gierek's Poland*. Boulder, Colorado, Westview Press.

Karczewski, J. 1982. Linia programowa i zasady organizacji związków zawodowych w PRL w latach 1945–80. In W. M. Goralski, *Spór o Związki Zawodowe, Vol. 2*. Warsaw, Instytut Wydawniczy Zwiazkow Zawodowych.

Kolankiewicz, G. 1980. The new 'awkward-class': the peasant-worker in Poland. *Sociologia Ruralis*, vol. 20, no. 1–2.

— 1981a. Bureaucratised political participation and its consequence in Poland. *Politics*, vol. 1, no. 1, pp. 35–40.

— 1981b. Renewal, reform or retreat: the Polish Communist Party after the Extraordinary Ninth Congress. *The World Today*, vol. 37, no. 10, pp. 369–75.

— 1982. Employee self-management and socialist trade unionism. In Woodall (ed.) 1982.

— 1984. The Polish question: Andropov's answer. In L. Schapiro & J. Godson, *The Soviet Worker: From Lenin to Andropov* (revised edition), London, Macmillan.

— 1987. Polish trade unions 'normalized'. *Problems of Communism*, vol. 36, November–December, pp. 57–68.

— 1988. Poland and the politics of permissible pluralism. *Eastern European Politics and Societies*, vol. 2, no. 1.

— 1989. The horizontal movement: The PZPR and internal reform. In L. Polakiewicz & N. Davies (eds), *Solidarity, Martial-Law and the Aftermath*, forthcoming.

Kolarska-Bobińska, L. 1985. Interesy społeczne i postawy egalitarne a zmiana ładu gospodarczego. *Studia Socjologiczne*, no. 2.

Koralewicz, J. 1987. *Autorytaryzm, Lęk, Konformizm*. Warsaw, Ossolineum.

Korbonski, A. 1982. The Polish Army. In J. Adelman (ed.), *Communist Armies in Politics*, Boulder, Colorado, Westview Press, pp. 103–27.

Korybutowicz, Z. 1983. *Grudzień 1970*. Paris, Instytut Literacki.

Kosta, J., & Levcik, F. 1985. *Economic Crisis in the East European CMEA Countries*. Cologne, Crisis in Soviet-Type Systems Research Project.

Kozik, Z. 1982. *PZPR w latach 1954–57*. Warsaw, PWN.

Kukliński, R. J. 1987. Wojna z narodem widziana od środka. *Kultura*, no. 475, pp. 3–57.

Kulpińska, J. 1985. Hypoteza o nowej klasie robotniczej. In J. Kulpińska (ed.), *Społeczeństwo i Socjologia*, Warsaw, Ossolineum.

Kuratowska, Z. 1988. Złużba zdrowia-kto winien? *Krytyka*, no. 23–4.

Kuron, J., & Modzelewski, K. 1968. *An Open Letter to the Party*. London, International Socialism.

Labedz, L. 1984. *Poland Under Jaruzelski*. New York, Scribner's.

Landau, Z. 1985. Głowne tendencje rozwoju gospodarczego Polski Ludowej. In A. Müller (ed.), *U Zródeł Polskiego Kryzysu*, Warsaw, PWN.

— & Tomaszewski, J. 1971. *Robotnicy Przemysłowi w Polsce 1918–39*. Warsaw, KiW.

— & — 1985. *The Polish Economy in the Twentieth Century*. London, Croom Helm.

Łapińska-Tyszka, K. 1984. *Czynniki Żróznicowania Standardu Materialnego Rodziń Chłopskich*. Warsaw, Ossolineum.

Leslie, R. F., *et al*. 1980. *The History of Poland Since 1863*. Cambridge, Cambridge University Press.

Lewis, P. G. 1973. The peasantry. In Lane, D. S., & Kolankiewicz, G. (eds), *Social Groups in Polish Society*, London, Macmillan.

— 1982. Political consequences of the changes in party-state structures under

Gierek. In Jean Woodall (ed.), *Policy and Politics in Contemporary Poland. Reform, Failure and Crisis*, London, Frances Pinter, pp. 76–98.

Lewis, P. G. (ed.) 1984. *Eastern Europe: Legitimation and Political Crisis*. London, Croom Helm.

— 1985a. Institutionalization of the Party-state regime in Poland. In B. Misztal (ed.), *Poland After Solidarity*, New Brunswick, Transaction Books.

— 1985b. Turbulent priest: Political implications of the Popiełuszko affair. *Politics*, vol. 5, no. 2, pp. 33–9.

— 1986a. The tenth congress of the Polish United Workers' Party. *Journal of Communist Studies*, vol. 2, no. 1, pp. 432–5.

— 1986b. The Polish party apparatus: changes in provincial first secretaries, 1975–84. *Soviet Studies*, vol. 38, no.3, pp. 369–86.

— forthcoming 1989. *Political Authority and Party Secretaries, 1975–86*. Cambridge, Cambridge University Press.

Lindenberg, G. 1986. *Zmiana Społeczna a Świadomość Polityczna Studentów Warszawy 1979–83*. Warsaw, IS UW.

Lipski, J. J. 1985. *KOR: A History of the Workers' Defense Committee in Poland*. Berkeley, University of California Press.

Lovenduski, J., & Woodall, J. 1987. *Politics and Society in Eastern Europe*. London, Macmillan.

Makowski, E. (ed.) 1981. *Wydarźenia Czerwcowe w Poznaniu 1956*. Poznań, Wydawnictwo UAM.

Malanowski, J. 1981. *Polscy Robotnicy*. Warsaw, KiW.

Malcher, G. C. 1984. *Poland's Politicized Army: Communists in Uniform*. New York, Praeger.

Marer, P. 1984. The political economy of Soviet relations with Eastern Europe. In S. Terry (ed.), *Soviet Policy*, pp. 155–88.

— & Poznanski, K. Z. 1986. Costs of domination, benefits of subordination. In J. F. Triska, *Dominant Powers and Subordinate States: The United States in Latin America and the Soviet Union in Eastern Europe*, Durham, Duke University Press, pp. 371–99.

— & Siwinski, W. (eds) 1987. *Creditworthiness and Reform in Poland: Western and Polish Perspectives*. Bloomington, Indiana University Press.

Marody, M. 1987. Sens zbiorowy a stabilność i zmiana ładu społecznego. In Marody & Sułek (eds) 1987.

— & A. Sułek (eds) 1987. *Rzeczywistość Polska i Sposoby Radzenia Sobie z Nią*. Warsaw, IS UW.

— *et al*. 1981. *Polacy '80*. Warsaw, IS UW.

Mason, D. S. 1983. Policy dilemmas and political unrest in Poland. *Journal of Politics*, vol. 45, no. 2, pp. 397–421.

— 1985. *Public Opinion and Political Change in Poland, 1980–82*. Cambridge, Cambridge University Press.

— 1987. Poland's new trade unions. *Soviet Studies*, vol. 39, no. 3, pp. 489–508.

Mastny, V. 1979. *Russia's Road to the Cold War*. New York, Columbia University Press.

Mazurkiewicz, E. 1979. *Ewolucja Polityki Rolnej w Polsce Ludowej*. Warsaw, IPPM-L, KC PZPR.

Michnik, A. 1976. The new evolutionism. *Survey*, vol. 22, no. 3–4, pp. 267–77.

Mieczkowski, B. 1978. The relationship between changes in consumption and politics in Poland. *Soviet Politics*, vol. 30, no. 2, pp. 262–9.

Miller, R. F. (ed.) 1984. *Poland in the Eighties*. Occasional Paper 18, Dept. of Political Science, Canberra, Australian National University.

Mokrzycki, E. *et al*. (eds), *O Społeczeństwie i Teorii Społecznej*. Warsaw, PWN.

Monkiewicz, J. 1983. *Licencje: Mity i Rzeczywistość*. Warsaw, Instytut Wydawniczy Związków Zawodowych.

Monticone, R. 1986. *The Catholic Church in Poland, 1945–85: Forty Years of Church–State Relations*. Boulder, Colorado, East European Monographs, 1986.

Morawski, W. 1980. Society and the strategy of imposed industrialization. *Polish Sociological Bulletin*, no. 4.

— (ed.) 1983. *Demokracja i Gospodarka*. Warsaw, IS UW.

— 1985. Ideologia uprzemysłowienia w Polsce w Latach 1949–56. In Kulpińska, 1985, pp. 45–71.

— (ed.) 1986. *Gospodarka i Społeczeństwo*. Warsaw, IS UW.

Müller, A. (ed.) 1985. *U Zródeł Polskiego Kryzysu*. Warsaw, PWN.

Narojek, W. 1980. *Społeczeństwo Otwartej Rekrutacji*. Warsaw, PWN.

Naumiuk, J. 1985. *Na Początku Trudnej Drogi*. Łódź, Wydawnictwo Łodzkie.

Nogee, J. L., & Donaldson, R. H. 1981. *Soviet Foreign Policy since World War II*. New York, Pergamon.

Nowak, J. 1982. The Church in Poland. *Problems of Communism*, vol. 31, no. 1, pp. 1–16.

Olson, D. M., & Simon, M. D. 1982. The institutional development of a minimal parliament: the case of the Polish Sejm. In D. Nelson & S. White (eds), *Communist Legislatures in a Comparative Perspective*, London, Macmillan.

Panków, W. 1987. U zródeł konfliktu przemysłowego w powojennej polsce. In Marody & Sułek, 1987.

Perlmutter, A., & Leogrande, W. M. 1982. The party in uniform: toward a theory of civil-military relations in communist political systems. *American Political Science Review*, vol. 76, no. 4, pp. 778–89.

Pienkos, D. 1975. Party elites and society: the shape of the Polish Communist Party Central Committee since 1945. *Polish Review*, vol. 20, no. 4, pp. 27–42.

Pohoski, M. 1983. Ruchliwość społeczna a nierówności społeczne. *Kultura i Społeczeństwo*, vol. 27, no. 4.

Polacy '84 1986. *Raport z Badań Polacy '84: Dynamika konfliktu i konsensusu*. Warsaw, IS UW.

Pomian, G. 1986. *Polska 'Solidarności'*. Paris, Instytut Literacki.

Pounds, N. J. 1964. *Poland Between East and West*. Princeton, NJ, Van Nostrand.

Poznanski, K. Z. 1988. Opportunity cost in Soviet trade with Eastern Europe: discussion of methodology and new evidence. *Soviet Studies*, vol. 40, no. 2.

PZPR 1978. *Statut*. Warsaw, KiW.

— 1983. *XIV Plenum KC PZPR, Podstawowe dokumenty i materiały*. Warsaw, KiW.

— 1984. *Krajowa Konferencja Delegatów PZPR, podstawowe dokumenty i materiały*. Warsaw, KiW.

(RFE) Radio Free Europe, Audience and Public Opinion Research Department Reports (1973–81). Munich.

Raina, P. 1978. *Political Opposition in Poland*. London, Poets and Printers Press.

Rajkiewicz, A. 1959. Przyczynek do zagadnienia zmian w strukturze klasy robotniczej w Polsce Ludowej. *Nowe Drogi*, vol. 13, no. 11.

Raport: Polska 5 Lat po Sierpniu 1986. London, Aneks.

Ratyński, W. 1970. Zmiany strukturalne i położenie ekonomiczne klasy robotniczej w Polsce w latach 1929–35. In S. Kalabiński (ed.), *Polska Klasa Robotnicza. Vol. 1*, Warsaw, PWN.

Reiquam, S., & Lorenz, C. 1987. *The Legacy of Solidarity*, Perspectives Series. Washington, DC, The Woodrow Wilson International Centre for Scholars.

Rocznik Polityczny i Gospodarczy 1984 1985. Warsaw, PWE.

Rocznik Statystyczny 1986. Warsaw, GUS.

— *1987*. Warsaw, GUS.

Rothschild, J. 1974. *East-Central Europe Between the Two World Wars*. Seattle, University of Washington Press.

Rychard, A. 1987. *Władza i Interesy w Gospodarce Polskiej u Progu Lat 80*. Warsaw, IS UW.

Rydygier, W. 1985. Pułapka zadtużenia. In Müller (ed.), 1985.

Sakwa, G. 1978. The Polish October. *Polish Review*, vol. 23, no. 3, pp. 62–78.

— & Crouch, M. 1978. Sejm elections in communist Poland: an overview and a reappraisal. *British Journal of Political Science*, vol. 8, no. 4, pp. 403–24.

Sanders, I. T. (ed.) 1958. *Collectivization of Agriculture in Eastern Europe*. Lexington, University of Kentucky Press.

Sanford, G. 1986. *Military Rule in Poland*. London, Croom Helm.

Secomski, K. 1985. Przesłanki demograficzne w polityce społecznej. In Kulpińska, 1985, pp. 139–53.

Siemieńska, R. 1986. Wartości, aspiracje i oczekiwania społeczeństwa polskiego a perspektywy zaspokajania potrzeb. In J. J. Wiatr, *Zaspokajanie Potrzeb w Warunkach Kryzysu*, Warsaw, IS UW, pp. 516–61.

Simes, D. K. 1981–2. The military and militarism in Soviet society. *International Security*, vol. 6, no. 3, pp. 123–43.

SIPRI Yearbook (annually). Stockholm International Peace Research Institute, Oxford University Press.

Sisyphus: Sociological Studies 1982. *Crisis and Conflicts: The Case of Poland 1980–81*. Warsaw, PWN.

Skilling, H. G., & Griffith, F. 1971. *Interest Groups in Soviet Politics*. Princeton, NJ, Princeton University Press.

Słabek, H. 1972. *Dzieje Polskiej Reformy Rolnej 1944-48*. Warsaw, Wiedza Powszechna.

Smolar, A. 1983. The rich and powerful. In Brumberg (ed.) 1983, pp. 42–53.

— 1987. Jews as a Polish problem. *Daedalus*, vol. 116, no. 2, pp. 31–73.

Spielman, R. 1982–83. Crisis in Poland. *Foreign Policy*, vol. 49, pp. 20–36.

Spiski, P. 1983. *Od Trzynastego do trzynastego*. London, Polonia.

Staniszkis, J. 1982–83. Martial law in Poland. *Telos*, vol. 54, pp. 87–100.

— 1983. 'Solidarność' jako związek zawodowy i ruch społeczny. In Morawski (ed.) 1983, pp. 331–71.

— 1987. *The Dynamics of Dependency*. Occasional Paper No. 10, The Wilson Centre, Washington DC.

Staron, S. 1969. State-Church Relations in Poland. *World Politics*, vol. 21, no. 4, pp. 575–601.

Szajkowski, B. 1983. *Next to God ... Poland: Politics and Religion in Contemporary Poland*. London, Frances Pinter.

Szczepański, J. 1970. *Polish Society*. New York, Random House.

— 1973. *Raport o Stanie Oswiaty w PRL*. Warsaw, PWN.

Szelenyi, I. 1979. Social inequalities in state socialist redistributive economies. *International Journal of Comparative Sociology*, vol. 19, no. 1–2.

— 1986–87. The prospects and limits of the East European new class project: an auto-critical reflection on the intellectuals on the road to class power. *Politics and Society*, vol. 15, no. 2, pp. 103–44.

Szurek, J. C. 1987. Family farms in Polish agricultural policy, 1945–1985. *Eastern European Politics and Societies*, vol. 1, no. 2.

Talmon, J. L. 1961. *The Origins of Totalitarian Democracy*. London, Mercury Books.

Taras, R. 1984. *Ideology in a Socialist State: Poland 1956-83*. Cambridge, Cambridge University Press.

Teague, E. 1988. *Solidarity and the Soviet Worker*. London, Croom Helm.

Terry, S. 1981. The Sejm as symbol: recent Polish attitudes towards political participation. In Kanet & Simon, 1981, pp. 27–64.

Terry, S. M. (ed.) 1984. *Soviet Policy in Eastern Europe*. New Haven, Conn., Yale University Press.

Thomas, W. L., & Znaniecki, F. 1958. *The Polish Peasant in Europe and America*. Chicago, University of Chicago Press.

Tomaszewski, Z. 1974. *Przeobrażenia Ustrojowe w Rolnictwie Polski Ludowej*. Warsaw, Ludowa Społdzielnia Wydawnicza.

Torańska, T. 1985. *Oni*. London, Aneks.

Turlejska, M. 1987. Kommuniści wobec społeczenstwa polskiego. Ciągłość i zmiana techniki władzy. In Marody & Sułek (eds), 1987, pp. 37–64.

Tymieicka, A. 1981. Ruch zawodowy w latach 1934–39. In S. Kalabiński (ed.), *Ruch Zawodowy w Polsce. Zarys Dziejow: Vol. 2 1929-44*. Warsaw, Instytut Wydawniczy Zwiazkow Zawodowych.

Urban, M. E. 1985. Conceptualizing political power in the USSR. *Studies in Comparative Communism*, vol. 18, no. 4, pp. 207–26.

Valenta, J. 1984. Revolutionary change, Soviet intervention and 'normalization' in East-Central Europe. *Comparative Politics*, vol. 16, no. 2, pp. 127–51.

Walicki, A. 1985. The paradoxes of Jaruzelski's Poland. *Archives Européens de Socjologie*, vol. 26, pp. 167–92.

Wasilewski, J. 1981. *Kariery Społeczno-Zawodowe Dyrektorów*. Warsaw, Ossolineum.

Weber, M. 1978. *Economy and Society*, 2 vols. Berkeley and Los Angeles, University of California Press.

Wedel, J. 1986. *The Private Poland: An Anthropologist's Look at Everyday Life*. New York, Facts on File.

Wesołowski, W. 1982. O Typach Stosunków Politycznych i Artykulacji Interesów. Unpublished manuscript.

— & Mach, B. 1986. *Systemowe Funkcje Ruchliwości Społecznej w Polsce*. Warsaw, IFiS PAN.

de Weydenthal, J. B. 1986. *The Communists of Poland* (revised edition). Stanford, Hoover Institution Press.

Wiatr. J. J. 1967. The hegemonic party system in Poland. In J. J. Wiatr (ed.), *Studies in Polish Political System*, Wrocław, Ossolineum.

— 1979. Awans narodu, społeczeństwa, jednostki. In *Pięc Esejów o Polsce Współczesnej*, Warsaw, PWN.

— (ed.) 1983. *Władza Lokalna u Progu Kryzysu*. Warsaw, IS UW.

— (ed.) 1987. *Władza Lokalna w Warunkach Kryzysu*. Warsaw, IS UW.

Widerszpil, S. 1979. *Refleksje Nad Rozwojen Współczesnego Spoleczeństwa Polskiego*. Warsaw, Instytut Wydawniczy CRZZ.

Wnuk-Lipiński, E. (ed.) 1987. *Nierówności i Upośledzenie w Świadomości Społecznej*. Warsaw, IFiS PAN.

— 1988. Spectrum polskie. *Więż*, no. 1.

— & Kolosi, T. (eds) 1984. *Nierówności Społeczne w Polsce i na Węgrzech*. Wrocław, Ossolineum.

Wojcik, P. 1984. *Położenie Klasy Robotniczej w Polsce*. Five volumes entitled: Warunki pracy i poziom zdrowotności robotników (1984); Kwestia mieszkaniowa (1984); Warunki bytu robotników (1984); Problemy patologii i przestępczości (1985); Zagrożenie ekologiczne (1985). Warsaw Vol. 1, IPPM-L; Vols 2–5, Akademia Nauk Społecznych, KC PZPR.

Woodall, J. (ed.) 1982. *Policy and Politics in Contemporary Poland*. London, Frances Pinter.

Woś, A. 1981. *Społeczno-Ekonomiczna Przebudowa Wsi i Rolnictwa w Polsce*. Warsaw, IPPM-L.

Zaborowski, W. 1983. *Obrazy Struktury Klasowej w Świadomości Mieszkańców Warszawy*. Warsaw, IFiS PAN.

Żarnowska, A. 1974. *Klasa Rabotnicza Królewstaw Polskiego 1870–1914*. Warsaw, PWN.

Żarnowski, J. 1973. *Społeczenstwo Drugiej Rzeczpospolitej: 1918–39*. Warsaw, PWN.

Zielinski, J. G. 1976. On system re-modelling in Poland: a pragmatic approach. *Soviet Studies*, vol. 30, no. 1, pp. 3–37.
Znaniecki, F. 1952. *Cultural Sciences: Their Origin and Development*. Urbana, University of Illinois Press.

Newspapers and Periodicals

Most of the up-to-date empirical material was gleaned from the following daily newspapers and periodicals both official and unofficial.

BBC British Broadcasting Corporation: Summary of World Broadcasts
Biuletyn CBOS
Czerwony Sztandar
Dziennik Ustaw
Ekonomika i Organizacja Pracy
Gazeta Pomorska
Głos Wybrzeża
Gospodarka Planowa
Kierunki
Krytyka
Kurier Polski
Odrodzenie
Perspektywy
Polityka
Praca i Zabezpieczenie Społeczne
Prawo i Życie
Przegląd Katolicki
Przegląd Tygodniowy
Przegląd Ustawodawstwa Gospodarczego
Przegląd Wiadomości Agencynych
Rada Narodowa-Gospodarka- Administracja
Radar
RFE (Radio Free Europe), *Przegląd Prasy Obiegu Niezaleznego*
RFE, *Polish Press Summary*
Rzeczpospolita
Słowo Powszechne
Sztandar Młodych
Trybuna Ludu
Trybuna Opolska
Tygodnik Demokratyczny
Tygodnik Mazowsze

Tygodnik Polski
Tygodnik Powszechny
Uncensored Poland News Bulletin, Information Centre for Polish Affairs, UK
Zeszty Historyczne (Instytut Literacki, Paris)
Związkowiec
Życie Gospodarcze
Życie Partii

Index